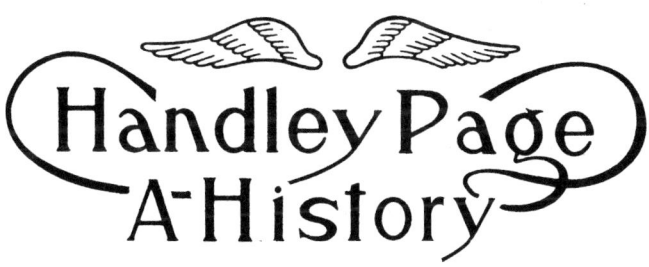

When you have read the book you can take the test and try to identify all the Handley Page aircraft in this picture! Handley Page frequently used the front cover of *Flight* magazine for advertising. These hybrid flying machines appeared on the issue of 26 December 1968, the last time that *Flight International* (as it had then become) had an advertisement on the front. The following week it changed to an editorial front cover.

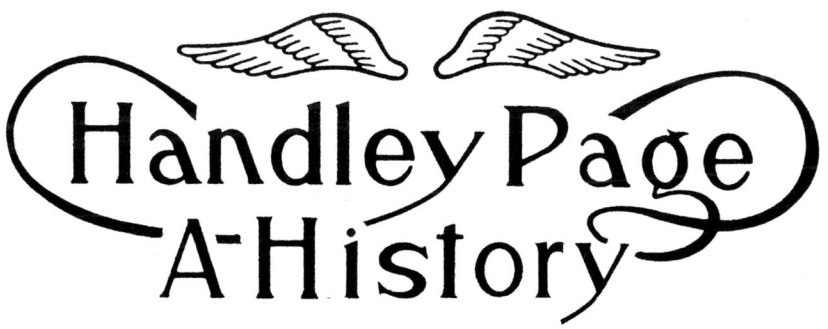

Alan Dowsett

TEMPUS

Handley Page Association

The Handley Page Association was formed in 1979 and provides members with a regular newsletter, plus the opportunities to attend Handley Page-related lectures and film shows and visits to places of interest. There is also a large collection of archive material. For further details write with SAE to the Hon. Membership Secretary, 77 Bowershott, Letchworth, Herts. SG6 2EU, UK.

First published 2003

PUBLISHED IN THE UNITED KINGDOM BY:
Tempus Publishing Ltd
The Mill, Brimscombe Port
Stroud, Gloucestershire GL5 2QG

PUBLISHED IN THE UNITED STATES OF AMERICA BY:
Tempus Publishing Inc.
2 Cumberland Street
Charleston, SC 29401

© Alan Dowsett, 2003

The right of Alan Dowsett to be identified as the Author of this work has been asserted in accordance with the Copyrights, Designs and Patents Act 1988.

All rights reserved. No part of this book may be reprinted or reproduced or utilised in any form or by any electronic, mechanical or other means, now known or hereafter invented, including photocopying and recording, or in any information storage or retrieval system, without the permission in writing from the Publishers.

British Library Cataloguing in Publication Data.
A catalogue record for this book is available from the British Library.

ISBN 0 7524 2782 2

Typesetting and origination by Tempus Publishing.
Printed in Great Britain by Midway Colour Print, Wiltshire.

Contents

Acknowledgements   6

1. Handley Page – An Overview   7
2. How It All Began   23
3. Big Bombers   37
4. The Handley Page Slot – Aeronautical Panacea   49
5. The Dawn of Civil Aviation   62
6. Military Aircraft Between the Wars   79
7. The Second World War – More Big Bombers   94
8. The Post-War Transports   111
9. The Victor   124
10. Handley Page (Reading) Ltd   146
11. Research and Some 'Paper Projects'   158
12. The 1960s – A Turbulent Decade   170

Appendix A.
    Table of Handley Page Aircraft Designs   188

Appendix B.
    Sir Frederick Handley Page – Honours and Achievements   192

Acknowledgements

The author wishes to thank Harry Fraser-Mitchell of the Handley Page Association and formerly Chief Aerodynamicist of Handley Page Ltd for his valuable help in compiling this book. This is both for information supplied and for access to the large photographic archive which includes recent donations and also dates back to the early days of the Handley Page Public Relations Department.

Thanks also to the following for their contributions, both big and small, without which this book would be much the poorer. In alphabetical order:

John Allam, Ron Asplin, BAE SYSTEMS, Victor Bingham, Chaz Bowyer, Bryan Bowen, Noel Brailsford, Roger Brooks, Geoff Burling, Ralph Burridge, Terry Chapman, Ray Cherry, Dereck Couzens, Peter Cronbach, Gerry Cullen, Dave Fitzjohn, Flight International, Gerald Gracey-Cox, Handley Page Association newsletter, Ian McMillin, Adrian Meredith Photography, Ministry of Defence Crown Copyright Section, Karen Monk, Ralph Pointer, Don Pratt, Gordon Roxburgh, Science Museum, Mary Varnill, Mike Wilson.

If anyone has been left off the list please accept this as an acknowledgement, with my apologies.

Finally, thanks to my wife Barbara who has put up with my neglect of the house and garden during the preparation of this book.

Chapter 1

Handley Page – An Overview

Small Beginnings

This is the story of Handley Page Ltd, the first company in the world to be constituted exclusively for the design and manufacture of aeroplanes. From humble beginnings in 1908 it was incorporated as a limited liability company on 17 June 1909, with a factory located near Barking, to the east of London. The end came on 27 February 1970, when a short-lived American rescue bid lost the support of its financial backers and Handley Page, by then based at Radlett, ceased to exist.

Much had happened in those intervening sixty years, in both peace and war, with many triumphs and a few tribulations. This book can only skim the surface, but it is hoped that readers will gain an appreciation of the achievements that will ensure the name Handley Page lives on in the annals of aeronautical endeavour.

The business began in 1908 at small premises in Woolwich with the manufacture of propellers for aeroplanes and airships. Frederick Handley Page's first aircraft design was a fairly simple man-carrying glider. It was built in 1909 after a move across the River Thames to Creekmouth, near Barking. This site had large areas of open space from where his early flying experiments were conducted.

There is no record of the glider making any successful flights. It would not have been helped by the distinct lack of glider launching facilities at the Barking flying ground. This seemed to comprise a level, albeit bumpy field separated from the Thames by dykes.

A notable feature of the glider was its curved, gently swept back wings, a shape originating from Handley Page's association with José Weiss. This crescent-type wing planform was proposed by Weiss as a way of providing inherent stability in an aircraft. These were the days when the science of aircraft controllability was in its infancy, so the more naturally stable an aircraft could be made, the better its chances of sustained flight.

Weiss had constructed a powered crescent-winged monoplane with pusher propellers. He agreed with Handley Page to exhibit at the 1909 Aero and Motor Boat Show at Olympia, using the Weiss monoplane as a centrepiece. Subsequent attempts to fly this aircraft were not successful.

There followed a series of Handley Page designed powered monoplanes which also employed the crescent wing planform. The first, known as the Type A, did not fly successfully, even when fitted with progressively more powerful engines which resulted in its re-designation as the Type C. Other types of aircraft were also being built to order at this time, including a biplane for Robert Fenwick which was given the Handley Page designation Type B.

Handley Page's first successful design, the Type E *Yellow Peril*. This is in its original form with wing warping control and a rectangular fin. The 'crescent' wing shape can be clearly seen.

More crescent-winged monoplanes followed. The Type D might have been successful had it not been badly damaged in a crash whilst being flown by Fenwick in July 1911.

First Success

The next monoplane, the Type E, went on to become Handley Page's first truly successful aeroplane. It was popularly known as the Yellow Peril because of the colour of its wings and tail, or alternatively as the E/50 because of its 50hp Gnome rotary engine. It was a two-seat design and was taken into the air for the first time by Edward Petre on 26 April 1912, not from Barking but from a large playing field a few miles to the north at Fairlop. Handley Page had rented a part of this field which now provided a long smooth take-off run, a big improvement on the facilities available at Barking. Within a few weeks it had made its first cross-country flight to Barking, only to suffer damage in a landing accident. Petre was not injured and the damage was repairable.

By July both designer and pilot had sufficient confidence to fly the Type E to Brooklands on a journey which followed the Thames for much of the way. A Handley Page product was now to be seen at this famous centre of early British aviation. It also appeared on the Handley Page stand at the Olympia Aero Show in February 1913.

By the end of 1913 the Yellow Peril had carried several hundred passengers and visited many parts of the country, much of the time in the hands of Handley Page's staff pilot Ronald Whitehouse. By now the company had its mind on other aircraft and the *Yellow Peril* was converted to a single seater and made available to the Beatty

Frederick Handley Page in 1913 sporting a short-lived moustache. In his own handwriting on the back of the original print he states 'Myself and a background (unknown to me) at Hendon, before I shaved the moustache off before the war'.

School of Flying at Hendon, where it remained until the outbreak of the First World War in 1914.

The last of the monoplanes to employ the crescent wing was the Type F. This was a side by side two-seater built for the 1912 Military Aeroplane Trials which were held near Stonehenge. These trials were in fact a competition between a number of designs for a two-seat observation aeroplane for the British Army. The Type F arrived late for the trials and the situation was further aggravated when the wings were damaged in a landing accident. The aircraft was effectively out of the competition and was taken back to Handley Page's newly acquired North London premises in Cricklewood Lane for repair. It subsequently flew well but frequent problems with the 70hp Gnome engine finally resulted in tragedy when the engine failed soon after getting airborne from Hendon. The pilot, Lt Wilfrid Parke, and his passenger Arkell Hardwick were killed when the aircraft entered a spin and crashed.

The crescent wing, as inspired by Weiss, was to see one more application in Handley Page's early designs. Not this time on a monoplane but on the Type G biplane. It was a two-seater with a fuselage and upper wing based on those of the Yellow Peril and a lower wing derived from the Type F. Ailerons were fitted to the upper wings and it was powered by a 100hp Anzani engine. This aircraft, also known as the G/100, made its first flight from Hendon in November 1913 with Ronald Whitehouse at the controls. After its test flying and a few modifications it was delivered in April 1914 to Rowland Ding, the first customer for a Handley Page aeroplane. He made numerous flights around the country giving displays at fairs and other public gatherings. Several hundred people were given their first air experience in this aircraft. Ding continued to use it up to the start of the First World War when the aircraft was requisitioned for service use.

O/100 bomber number 3116, one of the first to be delivered to the squadrons in France. The picture was taken at the Kingsbury works, near Cricklewood, in November 1916 and came from the personal album of chief designer George Volkert, who was a keen photographer. The long engine nacelles of the O/100 contain fuel tanks at the rear.

The Type G was undoubtedly a very successful aircraft. Had the war not intervened, more designs using that configuration would have been produced, including a contender for the Daily Mail's £10,000 prize for the first non-stop transatlantic flight!

Big Bombers

After war broke out in August 1914 Handley Page and his chief designer, George Volkert, were invited by Capt. Murray Sueter of the Admiralty Air Department to a meeting where a naval requirement for a large patrol bomber was to be discussed. The outcome was an order for a small quantity of a twin-engined design with a wing span of 100ft. Because of its size there was also a requirement that the wings could be folded to enable the aircraft to fit in existing hangars. Such an ambitious design was a bold step for a company that had thus far produced only a handful of relatively small single-engined aircraft.

What emerged in December 1915 was the Handley Page O/100, which was to be the start of the company's long association with large aircraft. It was powered by two Rolls-Royce Eagle engines and development proceeded relatively smoothly such that by September 1916 production examples were being delivered to the Royal Naval Air Service training unit based at Manston in Kent. From here they would proceed to the squadrons in France. The first offensive operation took place in March 1917.

Forty-six O/100s were produced before production switched to the definitive model, the O/400, of which several hundred were to be built. This was externally very similar but had several modifications, for example the moving of the fuel tanks from the rear of the engine nacelles to the fuselage.

The offensive load of these big bombers comprised sixteen 112lb bombs stowed vertically within the fuselage, or alternatively one 1,650lb bomb carried externally.

The pilot and observer sat side by side in an open cockpit, while Lewis guns for defence were located in an open cockpit in the extreme nose and in a mid-fuselage position.

With Handley Page now well established in the big time of aircraft design and manufacture, there was even bigger to come in the shape of the V/1500, or 'Super-Handley' as it became known. It was powered by four Rolls-Royce Eagle engines and had a wing span of 126ft. It first flew in May 1918. Sadly, the prototype crashed in June killing all on board except for the occupant of the tail gunner's cockpit. Subsequent machines set about making a reputation for the aircraft, not only because of its sheer size but also in performance. One carried forty passengers over London in November 1918, and another made a flight of eleven and a half hours in May 1919, having taken off at a weight of over eleven tons.

Although it had great potential as a weapon of war, the V/1500 did not see any action in Europe. It came very close because three aircraft were being prepared at Bircham Newton, Norfolk, for a raid on Berlin at the very time the Armistice was being signed in November 1918. One V/1500 was shipped to Newfoundland after the war for an attempt at the first non-stop Atlantic crossing. However, problems with the radiators caused a delay and before replacements could be fitted the Vickers Vimy took the prize and the Handley Page attempt was abandoned, the aircraft embarking on a tour of the USA instead.

The HP39 Gugnunc was well equipped with trailing edge flaps and leading edge slats. Completed in 1929 for the Guggenheim Safe Aircraft Competition in the USA it could demonstrate spectacular low speed flying qualities, thanks mainly to its 'Handley Page slots'. Here test pilot Maj. James Cordes performs a 'party trick' tail dragging manoeuvre.

Slotted Wings

Having already shown they were an innovative company with their development of large aircraft, Handley Page were to make another very significant contribution to the progress of aviation in the years following the First World War. This was the development of the slotted wing which was instrumental in improving safety in the air by making aircraft more controllable at low airspeeds. It achieved this by having a narrow slat along the leading edge of the wing which could be opened at low speeds to form a slot through which air could pass to the wing upper surface. During manoeuvring or decelerating flight the slot had the effect of delaying the break-up of the flow above the wing to a lower speed than would have occurred without the slot, thereby delaying the stall. This was a subject close to the heart of Frederick Handley Page following the death of two close colleagues in the Type F monoplane. This had crashed due to a stall following engine failure.

In 1928 the Air Ministry ordered that 'Handley Page slots', as they became universally known, should be fitted to all British service aircraft. It resulted in a significant reduction in spinning accidents which had occurred because of inadvertent stalls.

The Handley Page patent on the slotted wing provided a welcome source of income during the relatively lean years of the 1920s and early 1930s. The slot principle was also applied to trailing edge flaps, enabling larger flap deflection angles to be used. Wing leading edge devices on modern aircraft can be traced back to the Handley Page research in the early 1920s, and slotted flaps are still in widespread use.

The Dawn of Mass Air Travel

Although Handley Page would continue to be associated with big bombers, in the immediate aftermath of the First World War their attention, together with many aircraft manufacturers, turned to the potential civilian market. With an established bomber design having the benefit of a capacious fuselage, Handley Page were in a

Four W.10 airliners were delivered to Imperial Airways for their cross-channel route. This is the first example, G-EBMM, taking off from Cricklewood in February 1926 in the hands of Hubert Broad.

Handley Page's classic airliner of the 1930s, the HP42. This is G-AAUE *Hadrian* somewhere 'on the Empire route'. The flagpole was lowered into the cockpit before take-off.

good position to exploit any market for passenger carrying. It was not the V/1500, which would have been difficult and expensive to operate in the commercial world, but the O/400 which was to pioneer the civil air routes. There were also a number of surplus examples available at a bargain price, a point not missed by the financially astute Frederick Handley Page.

The O/400 in its bomber form did not have the ideal interior for passenger carrying and needed some modifications to rectify this. The fuselage fuel tanks were moved back to the rear of the engine nacelles, as on the O/100, and the internal diagonal bracing wires were replaced by struts in a 'V' arrangement, making access to the seats much easier, if not perfect. Square windows were provided at intervals along the sides of the cabin. The pilots, however, still had to sit in the open.

In June 1919 Handley Page Transport Ltd was formed to operate the converted bombers. The first service from Handley Page's own Cricklewood aerodrome to Paris was flown on 2 September 1919 by an O/400 with the civilian registration G-EAAE and named *Vulture*. Later that month a thrice-weekly service to Brussels was inaugurated.

The limitations of the O/400 were such that it was not long before a new design was in the air. This was the W.8 which was specifically designed as an airliner. It had a shorter wing span than the O/400 and an unobstructed passenger cabin. There followed the three-engined W.9a and the twin-engined W.10, all of a basically similar layout. When air transport services were nationalised in 1924, Handley Page Transport had to merge with other airlines to form Imperial Airways. This airline operated until the outbreak of the Second World War in 1939 with a variety of aircraft, notable among which was a prestigious Handley Page airliner, the HP42.

Luxury Air Travel

The HP42 took to the air for the first time in November 1930 and eight were to be built for Imperial Airways. It was a large biplane with an upper wing spanning 130ft and was powered by four Bristol Jupiter engines. It may have been slow, having a cruising speed of 100mph, but offered passengers unprecedented comfort in cabins reminiscent of the Pullman class railway carriages. From their well-upholstered seats they had an excellent view from the soundproofed cabin situated beneath the wings and enjoyed a full catering service. The pilots also had the benefit of an enclosed cockpit. Passenger capacity was between eighteen and thirty-eight, depending on the type of operation.

The HP42s were the mainstay of Imperial Airways from 1931 until the war started in 1939. Not one passenger had been harmed during those eight years, although one of the aircraft, *Hengist*, had been destroyed in a hangar fire at Karachi in 1937.

After the war had started most of the surviving HP42s were impressed into RAF service as transports, but none survived beyond 1941 for various reasons such as being blown over in gales or by forced landings. The original HP42, *Hannibal*, went missing over the Gulf of Oman in 1940. The four passengers and four crew members on this wartime flight became the only fatalities suffered on the HP42 during its entire career. These aircraft, however, will always be remembered as the world's first real airliners, with the graceful appearance which epitomised air travel in the 1930s.

The Inter-War Military Aircraft

For Handley Page Ltd the military business of the 1920s and 1930s consisted of single-engined designs which did not go into production, and a number of twin-engined ones which did. There was much competition to produce single-engined aircraft for the RAF and Royal Navy but Handley Page were not fortunate enough to win any of the orders. However, some of the company's designs continued the development of the slotted wing.

The HP21 or Type S was a small single-seat monoplane shipboard fighter built to an order from the United States Navy. Powered by a Bentley rotary engine it made its first flight in 1923 and had full span leading edge slats. No production order was placed. There were several biplane designs built in the 1920s to specifications for bombers and torpedo carriers. These included the Hanley (the first aircraft to be designed from the outset with slotted wings) followed by the Hendon, Handcross, Harrow and Hare. There was also the HP39 Gugnunc which was built for a safe aircraft competition in the USA in 1929 and which later gave some wonderful demonstrations of slow flying with the aid of its slotted wings and full-span trailing edge flaps.

Handley Page's main contribution to the military aviation scene in the period between the First and Second World Wars was a series of twin-engined bombers, beginning in 1923 with the Hyderabad. It was originally known as the W.8d and as this designation suggests it was very similar in layout to the W.8 airliner. It had Napier Lion engines and was followed in production by the Hinaidi with two Bristol Jupiter radial engines. The Hinaidi in its Mk.II form also saw the all-wood construction of the Hyderabad replaced by a fabric covered metal tubular structure. These biplane bombers equipped several RAF squadrons and were popular with their crews.

The RAF's final biplane bomber was the Handley Page Heyford which first flew in June 1930 from the company's new aerodrome at Radlett. It did not have a conventional biplane layout in that the fuselage was attached to only the upper wing because this was shown to reduce drag. Another novel feature was its retractable rotating 'dustbin' gun turret beneath the fuselage. One hundred and twenty-five Heyfords were built.

The Harrow of 1935 was a twin-engined monoplane designed as a bomber-transport. It had an all-metal high mounted wing, a fabric covered metal tube fuselage and a fixed undercarriage. Power came from two Bristol Pegasus radial engines. It did not see war service as a bomber but many were switched to the transport role to continue service for most of the Second World War. One hundred were built.

Bombers of the Second World War

Handley Page aircraft formed a significant part of RAF Bomber Command from 1939 to 1945. At the start of the war there were no heavy bombers in service with the RAF. There were several twin-engined medium bombers, including the Handley Page Hampden. This was a novel design having a narrow but deep forward fuselage, with the tail unit carried on a rear fuselage that was little more than a slender boom extending aft of the wing. It was also the first Handley Page aeroplane to feature a retractable undercarriage. Power was provided by two Bristol Pegasus radial engines.

Hampden medium bombers on Radlett aerodrome in 1938. Over 1,500 Hampdens were built and with the Wellington, Whitley and Blenheim they provided Bomber Command's main striking power in the early part of the Second World War until the four-engined 'heavies' arrived in strength from 1942.

Defensive armament initially consisted of swivelling single Vickers guns in the nose and the upper and lower mid-fuselage, at the point where the narrow tail boom commenced. The mid-fuselage ones were later modified to twin mountings but even so they still proved very inadequate and the aircraft were found to be terribly vulnerable on daylight raids in the early weeks of the war. Hampdens and the other medium bomber types in the Bomber Command inventory were thereafter switched mainly to night bombing. Later in the war Hampdens were adapted for mine laying and torpedo carrying.

The Hampden appeared at a time of rapid rearmament when the RAF required aircraft in quantity. This resulted in production also being organised at English Electric in Preston and at a Canadian factory. Another variant with two Napier Dagger engines, known as the Hereford, was put into production at Short Brothers in Belfast. The Daggers were not a success and many of the 150 Herefords produced were re-engined to Hampden standards. In all over 1,500 Hampdens were built.

Handley Page's main contribution to the war effort was the Halifax heavy bomber. Built to a 1936 specification for a large twin-engined bomber, the design was revised at an early stage to a four-engined version using Rolls-Royce Merlins. It made its first flight in October 1939. Defensive firepower came from power-operated turrets in the nose and tail, later augmented by a mid-upper gun turret.

More than 6,000 Halifaxes were to be produced, not only by Handley Page but also by English Electric, Fairey Aviation, Rootes Group and the London Aircraft Production Group. The latter comprised mainly coach and bus body builders. The Halifax accounted for about forty per cent of the RAF's heavy bomber force.

A significant development of the Halifax came with the Mk.III which was the first variant to be fitted with Bristol Hercules radial engines. The new engines together with aerodynamic improvements eliminated some of the performance and handling shortcomings of the early Halifaxes and transformed it into a really effective operational aircraft. The Mk.III was produced in greater numbers than any of the other marks.

Halifaxes performed well in other roles in addition to bombing, such as maritime patrol, meteorological reconnaissance, glider towing and parachute dropping, including special operations over occupied Europe to drop agents and supplies to the resistance forces. It was also developed as a heavy transport in its Mk.VIII form which had a large freight pannier fitted below the bomb bay. After the war civilian freight and passenger conversions helped to re-establish the British airline industry. Many of these aircraft were also to be pressed into service on the Berlin Airlift.

The Post-War Transports

As with the O/400 after the First World War, the civil conversions of the Halifax were no more than an interim solution to the needs of the re-emerging civil aviation business. Handley Page were working on new designs for civil and military transport aircraft before the end of the war. The first one to appear was the Hermes I civil transport. The wing was based on that of the Halifax, but with greater span. It had the

RT935, one of the last of 1,592 Halifaxes built by Handley Page (RT938 was the very last), made its first flight on 23 October 1946. It was an A.IX airborne forces version, complete with glider towing hook behind the tailwheel. Sub-contractors accounted for another 4,586 which made a grand total of 6,178 Halifaxes, including the prototypes, built between 1939 and 1946. This photo was taken at Portsmouth where the aircraft was being used for trials with the Airspeed Horsa glider. *(BAE SYSTEMS)*

Hastings C.2 WD334 of RAF Transport Command. The Hastings entered service in 1948, just in time to join in the Berlin Airlift. It provided the backbone of the RAF's long range transport needs until the Hercules came along in 1968. A few continued in the radar training role until 1977.

Hercules engines of its forebear, but had a new circular section fuselage with a single fin and rudder. Like the Halifax it was a 'tail-dragger' with two large single main wheels and a castoring tailwheel. The Hermes I crashed on its first flight in December 1945 killing both crew members.

After that disastrous start came the very successful Hastings military transport which was externally similar to the Hermes I. The total production run was 150 aircraft and it went on to serve the RAF in various roles for nearly thirty years.

Development of the Hermes airliner continued and culminated in the production of twenty-five Hermes IVs for BOAC. This was a considerable redesign of the Hastings concept, the main external differences being a longer fuselage and a tricycle undercarriage. The Hermes IV entered service in 1950 and the last one was retired by the independent airline Air Links in 1964.

Handley Page (Reading) Ltd

In 1948 Miles Aircraft Ltd at Reading were in financial trouble and Handley Page took over the ailing company to create Handley Page (Reading) Ltd. At this time Miles had been completing the development of the Marathon. This was a small feeder-liner powered by four de Havilland Gipsy Queen engines. Forty-two were built, including twenty-eight that were delivered to the RAF as navigation trainers.

The prototype Dart-Herald airliner G-AODE poses beside the famous control tower at Croydon aerodrome in 1958, about nineteen years after the last of the HP42s had departed. They would have set off on their European routes from this very spot. Croydon aerodrome finally closed for flying in 1959.

The Marathon was given the Handley Page designation HPR1. There was also a single example of a twin-engined Marathon II, or HPR5, but this was relegated to a test-bed role.

The first new design from the Reading team was the HPR2 two-seat military trainer. It was similar in appearance to the Percival Provost, but it was the latter which was chosen to equip the RAF training schools.

The Handley Page Reading company will be best remembered for the Herald airliner, which first flew in 1955. It was powered initially by four Alvis Leonides Major radial engines but was re-engined in 1958 with two Rolls-Royce Darts to become the Dart-Herald. Fifty of these fifty-seat airliners were produced, including the two prototypes. This total included eight that were originally built as military transports for the Royal Malaysian Air Force, but these were eventually sold off for airline use. Heralds gave good reliable service to numerous airlines until the last example was retired in 1999. Further developments of the Herald were proposed, including a rear loading military transport and a jet powered derivative, but for various reasons none of these were proceeded with.

The change to Dart engines came a little too late to give the Herald a significant advantage over its rivals in the 'DC-3 replacement' market, the Avro 748 and the Fokker Friendship. Had the Darts been fitted from the outset, three years earlier, then the sales figures would almost certainly have been better.

In the early 1960s the Reading operation, including Herald production, was gradually transferred to the main Handley Page plants at Cricklewood and Radlett and the Reading site became an industrial estate.

Victor

By the end of the Second World War two very significant developments in aviation technology had taken place. These were the jet engine and the swept wing. Together these enabled aircraft performance to increase dramatically. Handley Page were soon applying this new technology to a design for a high-speed long-range bomber. Initial studies were based upon a swept wing design with a very short fuselage and fins on each wing tip. This eventually evolved into the Victor, one of the trio of V-Bombers which were built to provide Britain's airborne nuclear deterrent during the Cold War. There were also designs for an airliner and a military transport based on the Victor, but they were not built.

The Victor's swept wing had a distinctive crescent planform in which the angle of sweep decreased in stages from root to tip. This was the second time that the term 'crescent wing' had been applied to Handley Page products, but it was quite unlike that of the early monoplanes where the sweep back increased towards the tip, and was for different aerodynamic reasons.

The Victor first flew in 1952 in the hands of Sqn Ldr Hedley Hazelden, widely known simply as 'Hazel.' Prior to this, a small crescent-winged experimental aircraft, the HP88, had been tested in 1951. It had only completed limited aerodynamic research when it was lost in an accident which killed the pilot.

The Victor prototype WB771 in its original silver paint scheme shows off its graceful lines in 1953. The sweep back of the wing decreases in two stages towards the tip, so the description crescent-winged came to be applied to the Victor's characteristic shape, just as it had been some forty years before with Frederick Handley Page's early designs. *(Crown Copyright/MOD)*

The Victor B.1 entered service as a bomber late in 1957, followed by the much more powerful B.2 which first flew in 1959. There was also the B(SR).2 strategic reconnaissance version, sometimes referred to as simply SR.2. Victors relinquished their bombing role in 1968, but their service life was far from over because they proved to be ideally suited to the air-to-air refuelling role, first with converted B.1s, followed later by the similarly converted B.2s. The Victor K.2 tanker played a vital role in the Falklands conflict of 1982 and also in the Gulf War of 1991. They were finally withdrawn from service in October 1993.

Decline and Fall

In the late 1950s and early 1960s there was much consolidation under way in the British aircraft industry. Most of the old independent firms came together to form two main groups, Hawker Siddeley Aviation and the British Aircraft Corporation. This was actively encouraged by the Government who let it be known that future military orders would only be placed with these large groups. Sir Frederick Handley Page (he had been knighted in 1942) had had an offer from Hawker Siddeley in 1962 which he rejected and, following his death in April of that year, the Board under the chairmanship of G.C.D. Russell continued on the independent course. This meant that no more military orders would be forthcoming despite the fact that the RAF would have preferred the proposed military Herald and also the military transport derivative of the Victor as a long range strategic transport. The competitors in the form of the Andover and the Belfast were ordered instead,.

Handley Page were therefore committed to 'going it alone' and put in place a number of commercial, non-aviation activities including the manufacture of radar scanners, brewery equipment, air cushion conveyor systems and oil-filled domestic radiators. This was in addition to the production of Heralds and the modification and refurbishment of Victors and Hastings. Handley Page were also involved in supersonic research and played a significant part in the Concorde development programme with the highly successful HP115 research aircraft investigating the low speed behaviour of narrow delta wings. This aircraft first flew in 1961. The company also kept up a long-term research programme into drag reduction using boundary layer control (see Chapter 11).

This aircraft work would inevitably run down and in 1965 a decision was made that the company would endeavour to continue doing what it had always been good at, namely designing and building aeroplanes. The new commercial aeroplane would have to be tailored to the resources of the company, given that no Government money could be counted on.

The aircraft, which made its first flight in 1967, was the HP137 Jetstream, a small twin turboprop commuter airliner or executive aircraft powered by two French Turboméca Astazou engines. It was destined to be the last Handley Page design to be built. With many advance orders and attractive design features, such as its generous headroom, it had much promise and could have been the saviour of the company. However, protracted development and modification increased the costs and meant late deliveries and a serious cash flow situation. The principal creditors refused to continue injecting cash and Handley Page went into receivership in August 1969.

There was a ray of hope when the American Cravens Corporation agreed to back the reconstituted Handley Page Aircraft Ltd, but this backing only lasted until the end of February 1970 when the company was finally wound up. Two things might

Jetstream G-ATXI, the second prototype of Handley Page's final product, takes to the air for the first time at Radlett on 8 March 1968. Chief test pilot John Allam was accompanied by Spud Murphy and Ray Funnell.

have saved Handley Page in the medium term. There had been considerable interest from the United States Air Force in a utility and casualty evacuation version of the Jetstream, to be designated C-10A, with a potential order of several hundred. This order was not placed. There was also a pending contract for conversion of the Victor B.2 bombers to K.2 tankers, for which Handley Page had prepared detailed proposals. Delays in the decision to proceed on this meant that the company collapsed before the contract was placed. There was much dismay among the former workforce when the contract was awarded to Hawker Siddeley within weeks of the company's closure.

The Jetstream went on to have a successful career. Certification of the Series 200 with uprated Astazou engines was achieved after the collapse of the company, mainly through the efforts of some ex-Handley Page people. As well as achieving further commercial sales, it also went into RAF service as the Jetstream T.1 for multi-engine training. By this time Scottish Aviation at Prestwick was much involved. These aircraft are still serving in 2003 ensuring that Handley Page's once proud boast can continue; since its formation in 1918 the RAF has never been without a Handley Page aeroplane. This will only cease to be true when the last Jetstream T.1 is retired.

In the late 1970s British Aerospace at Prestwick produced a re-engined version of the Jetstream with various other improvements and this sold in large numbers as the Jetstream 31. Many of these still give good service.

★ ★ ★ ★

The foregoing was just an introduction to the Handley Page story. The following chapters take a closer look at the man and the products of his company.

Chapter 2

How It All Began

Frederick Handley Page was born in Cheltenham on 15 November 1885 and was the second of four sons in a Plymouth Brethren family (there was also one daughter). His father, Frederick Joseph Page, ran a furniture and upholstery business and on Sundays he preached, assisted by his wife Ann Eliza (née Handley). Young Frederick came to use his middle name as though it were part of the surname, but it should never be seen hyphenated (a frequent mistake in aviation writings). His signature would read 'F. Handley Page.' Hereafter he will be variously referred to as Frederick Handley Page, Handley Page, HP or, after 1942 when he was knighted, as Sir Frederick.

He was educated at Cheltenham Grammar School where he received a broad education, including the classics. Because of his upbringing he had a detailed knowledge of the Scriptures, which he would regularly quote during the rest of his life, often to the joy of his friends and to the discomfiture of his adversaries. On completion of his basic education he moved to London, against his family's wishes, to study electrical engineering at Finsbury Technical College under Prof. Sylvanus P. Thompson. It was an interest in electrical traction systems that inspired him to enrol at the college, and it was here that he first became interested in the mechanics of flight. He discovered that there appeared to be some analogy between fluid motion and electromagnetic fields, a point that had been noticed by other eminent researchers of the day. He also tried some experiments with flapping wing models but these were not successful.

In 1906 Frederick Handley Page commenced his first full-time job at electrical machinery makers Johnson & Phillips Ltd in Charlton, east of London, where he was appointed chief designer. In May 1907 he delivered a lecture to the Institution of Electrical Engineers entitled The Present State of Direct Current Design as Influenced by Interpoles. Members of the international audience were impressed by his presentation and he received an offer of employment from the Westinghouse Electric Co. in the USA. He did not take up the offer. It has been said that he was so struck by the advanced age of many in the audience that he was convinced that the rate of progress for a young man in that industry would be very slow. Correspondence of the time also seems to indicate that he wanted too much money! However, his attention by then was becoming increasingly oriented towards the up and coming science of aeronautics.

In 1907 he joined the Aeronautical Society of Great Britain, forerunner of the Royal Aeronautical Society, which at that time was in need of some reform (HP himself would later be instrumental in bringing about some of those reforms). He left Johnson & Phillips in 1908, or to be more accurate he was dismissed due to an alleged misunderstanding over some aeronautical experiments he was conducting at work!

Stand number 30 at the Aero and Motor Boat Exhibition at Olympia in March 1909. Frederick Handley Page is wearing the top hat. The other seated gentleman is probably José Weiss, whose monoplane is exhibited on the stand. The model in the foreground shows the crescent wing developed by Weiss and used on HP's first designs.

However, it would have only been a question of time before he parted company with Johnson & Phillips for he lost no time in setting up his own business in rented premises in nearby Woolwich, close to the Town Hall at 36 William Street. Here he offered to build and test aeroplanes to any required design. One of his first commissions was to build a quadruplane for G.P. Deverall Saul, a fellow member of the Aeronautical Society. Saul was an enthusiastic inventor with fanciful ideas for flying machines but precious little practical aptitude. HP by now was very knowledgeable in engineering and had a natural understanding of anything mechanical. The Saul aeroplane was built but almost certainly never flew, having only 8hp available from the engine, but Handley Page had been paid to build it and that was the important thing!

In 1908 Handley Page began an acquaintance with José Weiss, a Swiss landscape artist who, when not engaged in painting, had experimented with model gliders whose wings had curved leading edges with increasing sweep back towards the tips. The wings were also turned up at the tips and had a camber, that is the curvature in cross-section, which decreased from root to tip. The inspiration had come from the study of eagles in the Alps, and also from the seed leaf of the zanonia plant, a tropical vine of the cucumber family. In planform the wing bore a resemblance to that of the swallow. It came to be referred to as the 'crescent wing'. Weiss had found that this wing design provided his models with an inherent lateral and longitudinal stability. He had a company called the Weiss Aeroplane & Launcher Syndicate and Handley Page decided to become a shareholder.

At a later meeting with Weiss in December 1908 HP saw a powered monoplane which Weiss had been building and the two agreed to share a stand at the 1909 Aero and Motor Boat Exhibition to be held at Olympia. The Weiss monoplane would form the centrepiece. A deal was also struck whereby HP would build a set of wings of sound design and construction for Weiss's next glider in return for the right to use Weiss's patent wing shape in his own future designs. He duly set about building a glider with just such a wing.

To further eke out an existence Handley Page took on bread and butter work by manufacturing propellers for airships and aeroplanes. He supplied two propellers, to the design of Weiss, for the Willows No.2 airship which in August 1910 flew from London to Cardiff. He had also taken on his first employee, Tucker, a pattern maker from Johnson & Phillips.

The small premises at Woolwich had no flying ground nearby so this prompted the first move of the business across to the north side of the Thames at Creekmouth, near Barking. There were some rudimentary sheds and a few acres of ground for experimental flying. The ground was far from perfect, being crossed by drainage ditches and there were grazing cows to contend with. There were also large mounds forming dykes along the riverside as a result of clay dumping during the construction of the London Underground.

Neither the Weiss monoplane nor HP's glider were to achieve flight. Quite how flying was attempted with the glider does not seem to have been recorded, but it certainly involved hauling it to the top of a dyke, possibly combined with a towing arrangement (a motor car tow had been used in an attempt to persuade Weiss's monoplane to leave the ground). The glider would probably never have been successful without modification, relying as it did almost entirely on a natural stability from its crescent wing. The pilot sat under the wing in a spruce frame which incorporated a tricycle undercarriage. The only control was a forward mounted elevator. There was no roll or yaw (rudder) control and so flight, if it occurred at all, would necessarily have been brief and uncontrolled!

A major milestone for Handley Page (and indeed for aviation) came on 17 June 1909 when he turned his business into a limited company. Handley Page Ltd was the first company to be registered in the United Kingdom for the construction of aeroplanes. It was destined to trade under the same name for over sixty years. In the words of the company registration document, it was set up 'to enter into an agreement with Handley Page and to carry on the business of manufacturers, letters to hire and repairers of and dealers in aeroplanes, hydroplanes, airships, balloons, aeronautical apparatus and machines, automobiles, motor cars etc'. This was surely a remarkably foresighted and elastic definition of a new business venture.

Frederick Handley Page was now turning his attention to powered flight and there emerged from the Barking sheds the first in a series of Weiss-inspired monoplanes. This was the **Type A *Bluebird*** and it was exhibited in an incomplete form at the Olympia Aero Show in March 1910. Power came from a 20hp Advance vee-four engine. It made its first tentative hop into the air in May 1910, with HP at the controls. There was no lateral control because, like the glider, the design placed faith

Handley Page's original glider at Barking in 1909 beside one of the dykes from which launches were allegedly attempted. Seated in the machine is Cyril Meredith, later to become works manager.

Frederick Handley Page in his first powered aircraft, the Type A *Bluebird*, with its original engine, a 20hp Advance vee-four. Straight hops were the best it could manage.

The *Bluebird* again, now fitted with a 25hp two-cylinder Alvaston engine and known as the Type C. It illustrates why Barking was not a very good aerodrome!

in the natural stability inherent in the crescent wing. Elevator and rudder control came from a movable cruciform appendage mounted on a universal joint at the rear of the fuselage. The early attempts to fly the *Bluebird* made clear the need for lateral control when the aircraft side-slipped into the ground during its first turn. While it was being repaired the aircraft had wing warping controls incorporated, the tail surfaces were enlarged and a new 25hp Alvaston flat-twin water-cooled engine was installed. It was redesignated the **Type C** but retained the name *Bluebird*. Despite the extra power of the new engine the Type C still only achieved gentle hops. Even when fitted with a 50hp Isaacson radial engine the aircraft remained reluctant to get into the air, but this engine was rather heavy for its power output.

By this time Handley Page had decided that he did not possess a natural aptitude for flying. When the Type C was put aside to make way for the next monoplane it also marked the end of his test-flying career. The *Bluebird* was handed over to the Northampton Institute in London (now City University). It was here that, besides running his business at Barking, he found the time and energy to lecture on aeronautical engineering two evenings a week. He was to set up and take charge of a specialised department there and it included one of the first aeronautical laboratories in the country. One of his pupils was George Rudolph Volkert, an Anglo-Swiss who, on completion of his training, would join Handley Page as chief designer at a salary of fifteen shillings a week.

HP's other significant interest was the Aeronautical Society, which he had joined in 1907. It was, at that time, governed by a self perpetuating Council. The young Handley Page was vociferous in his call for change and became a member of a committee charged with recommending reforms. The committee's recommendations were finally adopted, though not before some stiff opposition had been overcome, and at a meeting in September 1911 new rules governing elections were introduced and technical grades created. Handley Page was made an Associate Fellow and elected to Council. It was now set on course to become a respected, technically oriented professional institution.

Robert Fenwick seated in the Type B at Freshfield, Lancashire, with some extra horse power. It is in its later configuration with a single propeller. It made some successful flights from the beach at Formby.

The second aircraft in the HP type alphabet was the **Type B** biplane. This was not of Handley Page design but the brainchild of a Liverpool patent agent named W.P. Thompson. It was built at Barking with much of the work being done by Robert Fenwick, Thompson's assistant. The pilot sat below and in front of the wings with the engine just behind him. As originally built it had two propellers, driven by chains from the engine. Attempts at flight led to a buckled undercarriage and to make matters worse, while the aircraft was being repaired, a gale caused a partial collapse of the shed housing it, further damaging the biplane. HP considered the aircraft a failure and did not want to repair it referring to it as 'the scrapheap', but Fenwick persisted and took the rebuilt Type B to Freshfield in Lancashire. It now had ailerons, an improved tail unit and a single, direct driven propeller. It flew sufficiently well for Fenwick to qualify for his Royal Aero Club pilot's certificate, but by this time HP had completely dissociated himself from the aircraft. Fenwick was clearly pleased with it and on a post card to a friend in November 1910 he wrote 'I have now flown 74 miles and have remained up for 25 minutes and have done 17 miles at a stretch, including 2 turns'.

The **Type D** was the next of the crescent-winged monoplanes. It made its first appearance at the Olympia Aero Show in April 1911. Handley Page was assisted by Robert Fenwick in building the Type D, which was a beautifully crafted machine, having a monocoque fuselage with polished mahogany planking. It had an extra long skid below the fuselage which, as well as preventing the aircraft from nosing over, also supported the tail. Roll control was by wing warping operated by a handwheel in the cockpit. A Green engine of 35hp had been obtained on loan for the exhibition. The Type D was offered for sale for £450 but there were no takers.

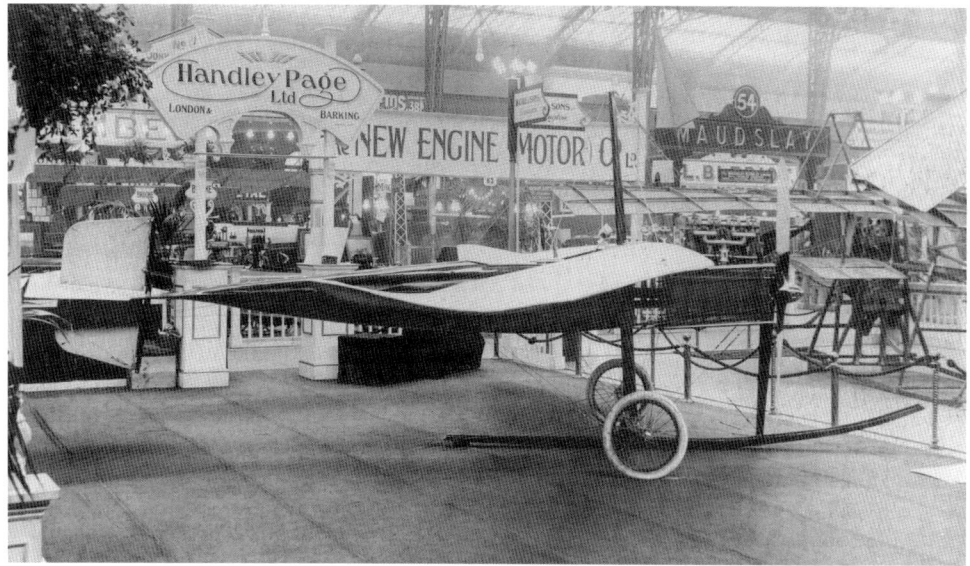

The Type D on display at Olympia in 1911 with its original highly polished mahogany-covered fuselage and a borrowed Green engine. The changing contours of its crescent wing can be seen well from this angle.

After the show it was taken to Fairlop, about six miles north of Barking, where Handley Page had rented part of a large playing field as a flying ground. It provided a large expanse of smooth grass, much more amenable to delicate aeroplanes than the rough surfaces at Barking. Fenwick was chosen to fly the aircraft but failed to get airborne on the power of the Green engine.

Handley Page decided to substitute the Isaacson radial engine from the Type C but this proved to be incompatible with the monocoque fuselage. The aircraft was therefore rebuilt with a more conventional fuselage comprising a fabric covered framework. In this form it was entered for the *Daily Mail* Circuit of Britain race which was to take place on 22 July 1911. Fenwick made a successful take-off in the Type D on 15 July but crashed on landing, to be immediately sacked by HP! The aircraft was repaired but was too late to participate in the race.

Meanwhile Edward Petre (known as 'Peter the Painter' after a well-known criminal of the day) had joined the company as a test pilot and made a few short flights in the Type D at Fairlop. During the aircraft's rebuild the fabric surfaces were varnished yellow and it was named *Antiseptic* by Petre and also known briefly as the *Yellow Peril*, a popular name at the time for Gold Flake cigarettes because of their yellow packets. This name, however, would become more associated with the Type D's successor. By this time more aerodynamic data were becoming available on wing sections and the Type D was set aside in favour of the much improved Type E.

With the additional benefit of the wind tunnel facilities at the Northampton Institute, Handley Page designed what was to be his first true success. The **Type E** was a two-seat monoplane with a 50hp Gnome rotary engine. It retained the crescent wing planform and wing warping control. The blue lacquered fuselage was

The Type E *Yellow Peril* after the fitting of ailerons to replace the wing warping controls. The earlier rectangular fin has also been replaced by a triangular one.

basically a fabric covered square section box but with formers and stringers added to give a streamlined appearance. It was of a generally more robust construction than his previous designs. The wings and tail were, like the Type D, yellow in colour and so it inherited the nickname *Yellow Peril*, by which it became widely known.

It made its first hops at Fairlop on 26 April 1912, which soon progressed to complete circuits. Once fully satisfied with its flying qualities Petre flew it the six miles to Barking, only to damage it landing on the rough surface there (he was in fact still teaching himself to fly at this stage – it was not until 26 July that he qualified for his Royal Aero Club certificate, using the *Yellow Peril* for the test). After rebuilding, the Type E, also known as the E/50 because of the engine horse power, was flown by Petre from Fairlop to Brooklands in fifty minutes on 27 July 1912. Handley Page was now to be seen at the very hub of contemporary British aviation!

Meanwhile, in 1912 a Government order had been obtained for a small number of Royal Aircraft Factory BE2a scout aircraft which had been designed by Geoffrey de Havilland. Only three were destined to be built by Handley Page because of the high cost of obtaining small batches of the high-quality steel required. HP made it clear he was not interested in further piecemeal orders. However, the potential for such production work emphasised the need for better facilities. September 1912 saw another move when Handley Page acquired some former riding stables at 110 Cricklewood Lane in north London. It was within fairly easy reach of Hendon Aerodrome where test flying could take place. All aviation activity then ceased at Barking. The old Handley Page site is today occupied by a large electricity generating station. The new Cricklewood address should not be confused with the later, purpose built factory with adjacent airfield which was to open in 1917 in nearby Claremont Road.

The *Yellow Peril* had remained at Brooklands for a few weeks while the company was concentrating on its relocation and on its new Type F monoplane. It was flown back from Brooklands to Hendon by Lt Wilfrid Parke RN who was most impressed with the aircraft and flew with a total of twenty-eight passengers over the following few days.

Following some accidental damage the Type E was rebuilt with a number of improvements, including a new triangular shaped fin. After more flying it was renovated to exhibition standard and displayed at the Olympia Aero Show in February 1913. At about this time George Volkert began his long association with the company when he joined in the capacity of chief designer. Almost immediately Volkert produced a design scheme to convert the wings of the Type E from warping to aileron control. It was first flown with the new controls on 1 May 1913 by Ronald Whitehouse, Handley Page's new pilot, who found it handled much better.

At the end of May 1913 Whitehouse took the *Yellow Peril* on a tour of England giving exhibitions and rides at many towns, extending as far north as Beverley in Yorkshire. By the end of this intense activity the Type E had carried several hundred passengers and flown several thousand miles cross-country, but events were moving on. HP had the aircraft modified in several ways including conversion to a single-seater and made it available to the Beatty School of Flying at Hendon where it stayed until the outbreak of the First World War. It was then requisitioned for military purposes but not used. It was returned, minus its engine, to Cricklewood, where HP had it placed in storage. It was never to fly again but it made a couple of public appearances in later years. The first occasion was the Victory Parade in July 1919. The second was in the Radlett hangar during the opening ceremony of the company's new aerodrome in 1930. By then it was very dilapidated and it subsequently languished in the rafters of

Handley Page pilot Ronald Whitehouse with passenger in the *Yellow Peril* at Hull during its tour of England in May and June 1913. From 1912 to 1914 several hundred people had their first flying experience in this aircraft.

Lt Wilfrid Parke RN in front of the Type F, built for the British Military Trials of 1912. Parke and Handley Page's works manager Arkell Hardwick died when the aircraft spun into the ground following engine failure.

the main shop at Cricklewood until 1940 when the then works manager, James Hamilton, required some space and had the remains burnt without obtaining Mr Handley Page's consent. History has not recorded the verbal exchange which took place, but it is known that HP was not pleased!

The final design in the series of crescent-winged monoplanes was the **Type F**. This was designed specifically for the British Military Trials of 1912, to be held on Salisbury Plain. The entrants had to meet detailed requirements in terms of take-off and landing distances, payload, endurance, climb rate and speed. The Type F was a side by side two-seater with a 70hp Gnome engine. It had normal hinged rudder and elevator controls but retained wing warping instead of ailerons.

The aircraft arrived by road, somewhat late for the trial and Edward Petre gave it a test flight on 21 August 1912. During another check flight the following day the engine failed and Petre had to land downwind in gusty conditions. While swerving to avoid people a wing dug into the ground and smashed. This put it out of the competition and it had to be taken back to Cricklewood by road for repair.

Following the repairs it was flown again on 9 November 1912 by Wilfrid Parke who was very impressed with it and wrote a good report on both this aircraft and the Type E. According to Parke the Type E had better lateral stability while the Type F was more stable in pitch. Parke flew it many times in the following weeks, taking many passengers for flights. There were frequent problems with the Gnome engine, however, and a complete failure due to a blocked fuel pipe resulted in a forced landing at Sunbury-on-Thames.

The troublesome engine was to be the downfall of the Type F when on 15 December 1912 Parke took-off from Hendon for a flight to Oxford with Handley Page's works manager A. Arkell Hardwick as passenger. The engine was producing less than its normal power and only a few hundred feet had been attained by the time the aircraft reached Wembley. Then the engine stopped and while attempting a forced landing Parke encountered a downdraft in the lee of some tall trees and the aircraft stalled and dropped a wing at too low a height for recovery. Both occupants died in the crash.

Frederick Handley Page was said to have been deeply affected by the loss of these two talented men at the start of promising careers. It may have provided the spur to his later research into slotted wings which proved to be pivotal in preventing many accidents of the kind which claimed the Type F. The crash also removed the very real chance that the aircraft might have been ordered as a scout by the Royal Navy.

This was a bad time for the pioneer flyers. Edward Petre was to be killed on Christmas Eve 1912 while he was test flying for Martin & Handasyde at Brooklands. Robert Fenwick had also died in a crash at the military trials flying his second aircraft, the Mersey monoplane.

The last of the Weiss-type crescent-winged Handley Page aeroplanes to fly was the **Type G**. Designed by Volkert, it was not a monoplane this time but a biplane although it was derived from the Type E, having a similar fuselage and upper wing, which was fitted with ailerons. The lower wing was essentially similar to that of the Type F. The fuselage was mounted mid-way between the two wings and it was powered by a ten-cylinder 100hp Anzani radial engine, hence its alternative designation, G/100.

A pupil at the Beatty School of Flying at Hendon saw the aircraft and agreed to buy it. He was Rowland Ding, a partner in the Northern Aircraft Co. in Windermere and the first customer for a Handley Page designed aeroplane. The first flight of the Type G took place on 6 November 1913 with Ronald Whitehouse at the controls. It performed well in trials, demonstrating a speed range of 35 to over

The Type G biplane was the last Handley Page aircraft to fly with the Weiss-type crescent wing. This picture was taken before the cockpit was separated into two sections by adding central decking.

Rowland Ding and Princess Ludwig of Löwenstein-Wertheim in front of the Type G at Hendon in May 1914, prior to crossing the English Channel. He is wearing his trademark seal skin helmet, while she wears a black fur coat and a hat held on by a silk scarf. Her hands are kept warm by the large ocelot fur muff.

80mph and on 12 December Whitehouse flew it to 3,000ft carrying two passengers. Following some official performance measurements at Farnborough the Royal Aircraft Factory suggested an increase in tailplane area. HP's immediate reaction was to remove both the fin and the tailplane and arrange for Whitehouse to demonstrate that the crescent wing's natural stability had little need for either!

Ding took formal delivery of the Type G on 29 April 1914. On 21 May he was asked by Princess Ludwig of Löwenstein-Wertheim to fly her from Hendon to Paris. She was formerly Lady Anne Savile, daughter of Lord Mexborough, and married to a German prince. She set off with Ding from Hendon (with considerable excess baggage!) but had to wait at Eastbourne for six hours because of fog. They finally landed at Calais late in the afternoon where the princess decided to continue by train. Ding returned to Hendon the following day.

Throughout the summer of 1914 Ding went on a barnstorming tour of the country giving displays and carrying numerous passengers. He would sometimes be accompanied on his travels by his wife and six year old daughter Aphra. Many years later, as Mrs Aphra Burley, she wrote down some of her memories of those days, recalling of one flight, 'I cannot have been strapped in because I remember standing up and looking down on a river and exclaiming that I could see a boat sinking. My mother, sitting on my right in the front passenger seat, explained that it was an illusion because we were so high up'. She also noted of Ding's return trip from Calais

Lost in the Clouds. A Contemporary Account by Rowland Ding of a Flight in the Type G.

The most terrifying flying experience I have had, and yet the most marvellous that any aviator could well have, occurred to me when flying from Bath to Harrogate. I set out early and intended to fly straight to Harrogate without a stop. Conditions were perfect.

Before long, however, I saw in the distance a little cloud just making its appearance. It looked quite thin and innocent, and I thought the best way would be to get over the top of it and continue by the aid of the compass. Having risen over the top of what appeared to be the little cloud, I found that it got larger and larger, the ground being quite hidden from sight; there was a sea of fleecy little clouds underneath me. I felt happy because the compass appeared to be doing its work and the engine was running beautifully.

Then the sea of white cloud began to rise gradually. I pulled up the nose a little and climbed up what looked like the side of a snowy mountain. As I got higher and higher, one of the plugs in the engine, probably fouled with oil, misfired. Thus having one cylinder cut off, the machine could not climb so rapidly, and as the surface of the cloud itself seemed suddenly to take a very steep ascent, this meant that I had either to come down below it or else continue on straight through the cloud. The extent of the latter being an unknown quantity, I thought the best thing would be to dive down until I was underneath it. Switching the engine off, I started diving down from a height of between 3,000-4,000ft, the cloud getting thicker and thicker until I could not see even the aeroplane itself. In fact, I could only just distinguish the instruments in front of me.

Of course I was watching the height recorder very intently and very anxiously, because it was a great surprise to find that the cloud was so deep. I thought I should soon be underneath it and have a clear view of the ground from about 2,000 or 3,000ft. I went on diving for a long time, until to my horror the height recorder registered nothing.

As I was unable to see anything at all I thought the best thing to do would be to make the machine fly as slowly as ever it could. I knew sooner or later I should have to hit something, and so the best thing was to hit it very slowly instead of very fast. Fortunately the engine I have – the Anzani – throttles down beautifully, and I managed to slow it down till the aeroplane was only travelling at about 35 miles an hour, and with teeth set I continued at this pace until suddenly – we hit the ground. Under such conditions a perfect landing could hardly be expected, and it is something to record that there was very little damage done to the aeroplane itself – in fact it was flying again in two days' time.

When the fog cleared I found that I had landed in a barley field, about a mile and a half outside Stroud in Gloucestershire, and the most wonderful part was that it was the only field for miles around on which a landing was possible. All round were forests and high hills. I had motored to Stroud many times previously, and scoured the whole district round to look for a suitable ground on which to give exhibition flying, but there was never a one to be found, and ultimately I had to give up. However, from the above it will be seen that my Handley Page biplane was more successful and found a ground of its own accord!

'My father found himself gliding down to the water after the engine cut out – but luckily it started up again'. The accompanying 'Lost in the Clouds' story tells how a routine flight in the Type G turned into a bit of a nightmare.

With the outbreak of war the Type G was commandeered by the Royal Naval Air Service for training and airship patrols. It survived being fired at by a 'friend' because of its likeness to the German Taube, but was eventually written off by a pupil pilot.

The Type G had been another very successful design for Handley Page and would have been the forerunner of more crescent-winged biplanes if war had not intervened. The **Type K** was a design for a small single seater for use by flying schools. It was not built but its layout was adopted for a more ambitious project. A doubling of the dimensions of the Type K created the **Type L**, or L/200 because of its 200hp Canton-Unné radial engine. It was built in the summer of 1914 to the order of none less than Princess Ludwig of Löwenstein-Wertheim to be entered for the *Daily Mail's* £10,000 prize for the first transatlantic flight. No original photographs or drawings of the aircraft exist but it was known to feature an enclosed cockpit with three seats. The princess wanted to be second pilot to Rowland Ding for the attempt at the prize (she had taken lessons at the Beatty School of Flying). However with war looming the Admiralty commandeered all 200hp engines and the Type L, although otherwise complete, never had the opportunity to fly. It became one of many potentially great 'might-have-beens' in the history of Handley Page Ltd.

The princess continued to harbour an ambition to be the first woman to fly across the Atlantic and in 1927, at the age of sixty-two, she bought a Fokker F.VII and hired two Imperial Airways pilots who were willing to attempt the flight with her. She occupied a wicker armchair behind the pilots. They took off from Upavon in Wiltshire and headed towards Ottawa. The aircraft was reportedly observed from a cargo ship well over half way across the ocean, but it never arrived at the destination and all aboard were presumed lost at sea.

An impression by Ralph Pointer of the Type L transatlantic contender of 1914, produced from the limited information which survives about it. The aircraft was built but never flew due to the outbreak of war.

Chapter 3

Big Bombers

The First World War broke out on 4 August 1914 and almost immediately Handley Page offered the use of his production facilities at the Cricklewood factory to both the Army and the Navy. The Navy expressed an interest and Frederick Handley Page and George Volkert were invited to a meeting with the Admiralty Air Department in London to discuss the Navy's aircraft requirements. The Department's Director, Cdre Murray Sueter, and his technical advisor, Harris Booth, were shown drawings of the L/200 and some twin-engined derivatives of it.

However, discussions turned to even larger seaplanes and landplanes, possibly prompted by a call from a Royal Navy task force commander in Belgium, Charles Rumney Samson, for a 'bloody paralyser of an aeroplane to stop the Hun in his tracks' (there are slightly different versions of the origins of the expression 'bloody paralyser', but it is a soubriquet which stuck to the resulting design). Handley Page offered to build a large landplane and a detailed specification was agreed and formally issued by the end of the year. The requirements included a top speed of 65mph and a load of six 100lb bombs. Four prototypes were ordered of what was to become the Handley Page Type O – a large twin-engined biplane patrol bomber with an initial wing span of 114ft. Because of its size it was also made a requirement that the wings should be foldable.

This represented a huge challenge for the company in several ways. Nothing as large as this had been seriously attempted in this country before and there was much scepticism in some quarters about the feasibility of such a large machine. The square-cube law was quoted as a reason why large aircraft would be unable to carry their own weight, let alone a useful payload. Isambard Kingdom Brunel had had to counter just such arguments over his big iron ships, arguments which subsequently proved to be groundless. There was also the matter of Handley Page's total experience of aircraft building, which was really just a handful of relatively small single-engined types. Other British companies which had been in existence for a shorter time had built aircraft in three figure quantities and were already gearing up for mass production.

Notwithstanding these possible difficulties, the order for four aircraft was received and design work commenced in earnest. Many new weight-saving techniques were being developed within the industry, such as built-up hollow spars and struts. This, together with careful detail design, stress calculations and structural testing, soon overcame any imaginary fetters of the square-cube law. The basic design, with the wing span now reduced to 100ft, was agreed on 4 February 1915. Gone was any influence of the earlier crescent wing theories, because for weight considerations these large structures demanded a more conventional approach. A straight wing layout was adopted, with the upper wing having a larger span than the lower one. The bomb load had increased to sixteen 112lb bombs.

The aircraft was now known as the **O/100**, either because of its wing span or because of the desire to maintain secrecy regarding its engine power, since Handley Page had up until then included the horse power figure in some of his aircraft designations. The engines were in fact Rolls-Royce Eagle vee-12s of 250hp each.

Towards the end of 1914 the Russian aircraft pioneer Igor Sikorsky (later to be a helicopter pioneer in the USA) had produced a four-engined aircraft of comparable size and power to the O/100. It had flown with fifteen passengers, but was very slow at 65mph compared with the 95mph which was ultimately achieved by the Handley Page machine. It was the *Ilya Mourometz* but only limited information about it would have been available to the Handley Page design team. Furthermore, just before the 1917 revolution in Russia the Imperial Russian Government were abandoning the Sikorsky in favour of a purchase of O/400s with Fiat A.12bis engines. However, this plan was never carried through because of the subsequent events in Russia.

The prototype, with the Handley Page constructor's number 1455, was completed at the Cricklewood factory in November 1915 and the major assemblies were transported to some large requisitioned premises in Kingsbury for erection. On the night of 9 November the assembled O/100 prototype with its wings folded underwent an adventurous three-quarter-mile journey along Edgware Road and Colindale Avenue to Hendon aerodrome. Teams of naval ratings provided muscle power amid many calls of 'two-six' from the chief petty officer. Arrangements had previously been made for the temporary removal of gas lamp standards, tram wires and other known obstacles. There were, however, some unexpected obstacles in the form of trees in people's front gardens and it was HP himself with a ladder and saw who carried out the necessary pruning, despite some loud protests from residents. When a bill later arrived from the gas company for the removal and replacement of the lamp standards, HP merely referred them to the Admiralty, insisting that it had been a naval operation! The Navy did in fact agree to pay.

The prototype O/100 at Hendon in December 1915 around the time of its first flight. The crew were fully enclosed behind the transparent nose panels. This was soon modified to the more familiar nose shape with open cockpits.

The first flight, actually a straight hop within the Hendon aerodrome boundary, took place on 17 or 18 December 1915 (reports from a number of reputable sources are at variance on this, but it seems to have been timed at 1:51 pm!). The crew were Lt Cdr J.T. Babington and Lt Cdr E.W. Stedman. Flight trials apparently progressed smoothly and a few modifications were introduced to deal with problems as they occurred. One of the first major changes was to the nose which for the aeraly flights of the prototype featured an enclosed cockpit behind transparent nose panels. For one thing the pilots did not like it and there had also been problems with condensation obscuring the view. There were also reports of structural failure or distortion of the nose panels on one flight. Thereafter O/100s had a lengthened nose with side by side seating in the open pilots' cockpit. Production aircraft had a gunner's position with a Lewis gun mounting in the extreme nose. There was another gunner's position at an opening in the upper mid-fuselage. Another early modification was to the radiators, which on the first flight were mounted above the engines, broad side on to the airflow. This caused excessive drag and the position was changed to the sides of the engines, parallel to the airflow. Production aircraft had honeycomb radiators installed across the front of the engines.

One problem which occurred during service trials at Eastchurch was an early manifestation of aerodynamic flutter. When the aircraft was flown above about 80mph the tail began to oscillate violently in a twisting motion. This required some stiffening of the rear fuselage structure, a torque tube linking the upper port and starboard elevators and deletion of the aerodynamic horn balance of the elevators which left them with their characteristic overhanging appearance.

Meanwhile orders for the O/100 were increasing in stages, first to twelve and later to twenty-eight. An indication of the load carrying ability of the big Handley Page was given in May 1916 when the second prototype, 1456, flew to over 7,000ft with twenty Handley Page employees on board. The pilot on this occasion was Clifford Prodger, an American instructor at the Beatty School of Flying who was also a freelance test pilot.

Production built up at Cricklewood during 1916 and deliveries to the Royal Naval Air Service began in September when the first examples arrived at the training squadron based at Manston in Kent. In November 1916 the first delivery was made across the Channel when aircraft No.1459, followed shortly by 1460, was flown to No.3 Wing RNAS based at Luxeuil, in the Vosges region of Eastern France. Deliveries were soon also taking place to other units based at Coudekerque, near Dunkirk.

An unfortunate episode occurred on 1 January 1917 when Lt Vereker was delivering 1463 with Lt Hibbard, Leading Mechanics Kennedy and Wright, and Air Mechanic First Class Higby, when a blanket of low cloud which had formed over northern France led to some uncertainty over their position, a situation exacerbated by a sticking compass. Descending to an indicated 200ft without any sight of the ground, they had to climb back to 6,000ft and fly in various directions for two hours until a break in the clouds was spotted. They were able to land in a field and left the aircraft to enquire of the locals where they were, only to find that they were twelve miles behind the German lines! When they tried to return to the O/100 to make a quick getaway they found that they were cut off by German infantry, and so 1463 was captured intact, an almost unimaginable prize for the enemy. It was taken away for detailed examination and flight testing but before a full assessment could be carried out it was destroyed in an accident caused by crossed control cables resulting from a maintenance error.

Views have been expressed that the German Gotha bomber was derived from the Handley Page O/100, but the two designs were very different and furthermore they were entering service within months of each other. It is therefore erroneous to suggest that one could have been significantly influenced by the other.

The first recorded action by an O/100 occurred on the night of 16/17 March 1917 when aircraft No.1460, based at Ochey and piloted by John Babington (who had first flown the prototype in December 1915) with Lt Cdr Stedman and Lt Hains bombed a railway junction south-west of Metz. They encountered searchlights and heavy ground fire but dropped eleven of the twelve 100lb bombs they were carrying. The twelfth bomb jammed in its cell and was later cleared manually by Stedman and Hains. After this raid Babington wrote a favourable assessment of the capabilities of the O/100.

Daylight raids followed against U-boat bases at Bruges, Zeebrugge and Ostende and also gun emplacements along the coast. On 25 April four O/100s bombed and sank a German destroyer, but aircraft 3115 was badly damaged by a Rumpler fighter and ditched in the sea off Nieuport. Three of the four crew were captured and one was rescued by a French flying boat. As a result of this loss daylight raids were suspended and all efforts were put into night operations.

Coudekerque receives its first O/100, serial number 3116, on 4 March 1917. There is obviously much interest in the new arrival as few would have seen an aircraft of that size before.

O/400 number C9704, one of the first batch produced by Handley Page, illustrates the wing folding which the specification called for. The engine nacelles are much shorter than those of the O/100 because they no longer had to accommodate fuel tanks behind the engines.

Forty-six O/100s were completed before production switched to the definitive model, the **O/400**, which embodied a number of modifications. The fuel system was much modified, in particular by removing the fuel tanks from behind the engines (which had given the O/100 its characteristic long nacelles) and replacing them by an extra tank in the fuselage. On the O/400 the propellers turned in the same direction whereas on the O/100 they turned in opposite directions. By October 1917 orders had been received for 450 O/400s and of these some 200 would be built by sub-contractors – Metropolitan Wagon Co., Birmingham Carriage Co., Clayton & Shuttleworth, Royal Aircraft Factory and Cubitts. The first machine to be designated an O/400 was powered by two Sunbeam Maori engines of 320hp each, but subsequent production machines had Rolls-Royce Eagles which by then were delivering 360hp. Maximum speed was now up to 95mph and the service ceiling was 13,000ft.

Coinciding with the introduction of the O/400 in 1917 was a move by the company to new premises in Cricklewood. The original premises in Cricklewood Lane and the requisitioned site in Kingsbury no longer had the capacity for the required level of O/400 production. A new quarter-mile long factory was built on eleven acres of ground alongside Somerton Road with an adjoining 160 acres of aerodrome occupying Clitterhouse Farm, which had been compulsorily acquired by the Crown. A design office occupied the Claremont Road end of the site. By the end of 1917 1,500 people were working for Handley Page at Cricklewood. The company were to occupy this factory until the mid-sixties, although the aerodrome was to close in 1930 when the new one at Radlett became operational.

O/400s had reached the squadrons in quantity by September 1918 and among those it equipped were numbers 58, 97, 100, 115, 207, 214, 215, and 216. They really began to inflict serious damage with the introduction of the 1,650lb SN bomb, a single example of which could be carried below the fuselage as an alternative to the normal internal load of sixteen 112lb bombs. The big bombs were frequently used against railway and industrial targets, for example one was dropped by No.58 Sqn on Valenciennes railway junction on the night of 28/29 September 1918. One O/400, C9861, was used in the Palestine campaign of the enigmatic Colonel T.E. Lawrence in support of his operations behind the Turkish lines. In one night raid on 19 September 1918, when flown by Capt. Ross Smith, it dropped sixteen 112lb bombs on the enemy headquarters and central telephone exchange, denying them intelligence on the movements of the main British forces which by then were on the offensive.

The big Handley Page bombers made a large contribution to the war effort with their sustained night bombing offensive in the closing months of the war. Furthermore, it established the principle of strategic bombing in the newly formed Royal Air Force. They were not used in the massed formations for area bombing as occurred in the Second World War but usually singly or in small numbers against specific pinpoint targets. Probably the largest number despatched on one night occurred on 14/15 September 1918 when forty Handley Pages from several squadrons attacked a number of aerodromes. Nine of the forty returned with engine trouble, one made a forced landing in friendly territory and three failed to return. Between June and November 1918 eighteen Handley Pages were reported missing and fifty-one were wrecked in accidents. Parachutes were not available to aircrew in the First World War.

What was it like doing night operations in an O/400? AVM Allan Perry-Keene (1898-1987) flew O/400s with 115 Squadron and in his later years recorded some of his memories in an interview for his old squadron. How did they navigate? 'Mostly by God and by guess I think, but inspection after the Armistice showed we often reached our targets. We had no form of direction finding, no radio communication and weather forecasting was somewhat poor. We had a chain of aerial lighthouses on our side of the lines and knew their bearings from one to the other and from each to home. They were our principal aids. I think fog and the Vosges mountains were a greater enemy than fighters, ack-ack and flaming onions. Flaming onions by the way were a string of pyrotechnics which were intended to set you on fire. They were easy to dodge and I never heard of them doing any trade.'

Eventually about 476 O/400s were recorded as being delivered by the war's end. Had the war continued some 1,500 Liberty-engined O/400s would have been built in the USA by the Standard Aircraft Corporation at Elizabeth, New Jersey. Many of these would have been based with the US Army Air Corps along the south coast of England at Ford, Tangmere, Rustington and Emsworth. The ending of the war meant that only about 100 of this order were completed, and only about seven of these were to fly in the USA. Other completed airframes were shipped to England.

An interesting demonstration of air power took place in the USA after the war when a unit of the US Army under the command of General William Mitchell conducted experiments with an O/400 against a heavily armoured German battleship. Other aircraft had already attacked it with bombs but the O/400 finished the

The *Bluebird* again, now fitted with a 25hp two-cylinder Alvaston engine and known as the Type C. It illustrates why Barking was not a very good aerodrome!

Frederick Handley Page addressing the workforce at Cricklewood in the summer of 1918 following presentations on the occasion of his wedding to Una Helen Thynne, who is seated with the feathered hat. O/400 wings can be seen in the background. Among the gifts on display is a silver tea service.

job by sinking the ship with a 2,000lb bomb. In September 1921 a 4,000lb bomb was dropped from an O/400 at a proving range in Maryland. These tests caused some serious concern in US Navy circles, where Mitchell was not exactly popular!

The 'Bloody Paralyser' in the shape of the Handley Page Type O bombers put the company firmly in the big league of aircraft design and manufacture and led to its name becoming synonymous with large aircraft. It even entered the Oxford Dictionaries which stated 'HANDLEY PAGE, n. Type of large aeroplane (maker)'.

Things did not rest following the success of the O/400, for something even bigger was afoot. The new concept of strategic bombing was to be taken a stage further with the massive four-engined **V/1500**, or 'Super Handley' as it was sometimes known. Its wing span was 126ft and the Rolls-Royce Eagle engines were arranged in a push-pull pair on each side. The front engine had a two-bladed propeller and the rear one had a smaller diameter four-bladed propeller. The V/1500 was a colossal undertaking for Handley Page and because Cricklewood was heavily committed with O/400 production, much of the manufacture of the V/1500 was to be undertaken by Harland & Wolff at Belfast and by Beardmore at Dalmuir.

The prototype, B9463, was assembled at Cricklewood from parts made at Belfast and first flew on 22 May 1918 with Capt. Vernon Busby at the controls. Initial flight testing was concentrated on harmonising the controls and this was being progressively improved when, on 8 June, during the aircraft's thirteenth flight, all engines stopped at 1,000ft over Golders Green. While Busby was trying to turn back to Cricklewood aerodrome the aircraft entered a spin and crashed. The only survivor was Col. Ogilvie who had been in the rear gunner's cockpit.

Despite this tragic set-back development progressed well. The second prototype, B9464, was experimentally fitted with aluminium engine cowlings of a streamline shape but they were found to detract from the handling and were removed with a saving of 500lb in weight. After much experimental flying to investigate directional and longitudinal stability, the tailplane was redesigned with a fifty per cent larger gap between the two horizontal surfaces, plus larger fins and rudders.

The prototype V/1500 taxies at Cricklewood in May 1918. It shows the original tail design, with low set upper tailplane. The aircraft was lost in a crash at Golders Green in June.

A production V/1500 at Cricklewood clearly showing the revised tail and the tandem engine arrangement, with two- and four-bladed propellers. The starboard wing has just been unfolded. Fitters are attaching the locking pins to the upper and lower wings while colleagues maintain tension on ropes at the wing tip. Others are at the port wing tip ready to haul that one forward.

The V/1500 was ready to enter squadron service in November 1918. It was able to carry thirty 112lb bombs internally, or two of the 1,650lb bombs, or a single 3,300lb bomb that was under development. Three aircraft were at Bircham Newton in Norfolk being made ready for a bombing raid on Berlin on 11 November when the Armistice was signed shortly before mid-day.

On 15 November 1918, which happened to be Frederick Handley Page's thirty-third birthday, a party of twenty-eight invited journalists arrived at the Cricklewood factory just before Clifford Prodger was to take aircraft No.F7136 on its very first test flight. Now that there was a partial lifting of the secrecy surrounding the bombers, HP suggested that they experience the joys of flying and they eagerly climbed aboard the vast empty fuselage, together with twelve Handley Page employees. They were all provided with leather flying clothing appropriate to the near freezing conditions. Two ladies shared the rear gunner's cockpit, HP's secretary, Miss Speiss, and Dorothy Chandler from the design office. Another two girls were in the nose gunner's cockpit. Frederick Handley Page's confidence in the machine did not seem to extend to finding a seat for himself!

Prodger took off and flew these forty passengers over Westminster and the City of London, reaching 6,500ft in the process. They returned via Buckingham Palace and the Edgware Road. A Canadian girl on board had a letter ready for posting. After adding a note for the finder to put it in the nearest letter box she dropped it overboard. It duly arrived at its destination in a couple of days with a Wembley postmark.

The landing took place in the dark with the aid of a large bonfire set up on the airfield at Cricklewood. This impromptu world record caught the public imagina-

Dwarfed by its 126ft wing span, these Handley Page workers lend some scale to the V/1500. The device attached to the nose is the aerial for the Marconi wireless.

tion with the promise of what civil aviation might offer in the future. However, it would be many years before such a large number of passengers would be carried in a commercial aeroplane.

One V/1500 was to see some real action, for there was once a time when an Afghan crisis could be solved by the use of just one Handley Page aeroplane. It was in May 1919 and the aeroplane was V/1500 No.J1936, named *Old Carthusian* because the pilot who captained the aircraft on its flight from England to India and a general who accompanied him had both attended Charterhouse School. Jock Halley was co-pilot on this outbound flight, a prolonged adventure in itself, and received the Air Force Cross in recognition of that feat.

At this time tribes in Afghanistan, united under Amir Amanullah, were attacking India along the North West Frontier and Capt. Jock Halley volunteered to fly an O/400 that was in the area to carry out a bombing mission on Kabul. Before the raid could be mounted the O/400 was wrecked in a sandstorm and the only hope of fulfilling the plan was to refurbish *Old Carthusian* for one more mission. It had been retired and dismantled, needed new engines and several major repairs but it was all achieved.

Halley and four other crew members finally set off for Kabul on 24 May 1919 with a load of 20lb and 112lb bombs. They cleared mountain ranges, struggled through an 8,000ft high pass despite a serious water leak from one engine and dropped bombs on Amanullah's palace and an arsenal from a few hundred feet. One bomb breached a wall in the Amir's harem, 'thus', commented HP, 'striking a blow for female emancipation in Afghanistan'. On the return leg the V/1500 had to negotiate the high pass again and soon after that the overheating engine had to be shut down. The whole flight covered 400 miles and lasted six hours. The Afghans, many of whom had never seen an aeroplane before, immediately sought peace with the Indian Government and the so-called Third Afghan War, which otherwise might have been long and costly in human life, was formally ended on 8 August 1919. *Old Carthusian* never flew again due mainly to termite damage in the wing main spars, but it had the distinction of being the only V/1500 ever to be put to warlike use. For this mission Capt. (later Group Capt.) Halley received a second bar to his DFC.

Another V/1500, F7140 named *Atlantic*, was prepared for an attempt at the still-unclaimed Daily Mail prize of £10,000 for the first non-stop transatlantic flight, the same prize that the L/200 had been designed to compete for some five years earlier. It was shipped out to Newfoundland and assembled at Harbor Grace in June 1919. The flight crew was to comprise the pilots, Maj. Herbert Brackley and Vice-Admiral Mark Kerr, a navigator, Maj. Tryggve Gran (the Norwegian polar explorer who had accompanied Robert Falcon Scott to the Antarctic in 1911) and Frank Wyatt from the Marconi Co. to act as wireless operator. With the extra fuel tanks which had been fitted, the aircraft had an endurance of up to thirty hours.

Two long test flights confirmed that the radiators were not performing well but they were not of the latest design and the replacements were already well on their way to Harbor Grace. Fog off the Newfoundland coast caused a day's delay in their arrival and just as they were being picked up from the harbour John Alcock and Arthur Whitten Brown took off in their Vickers Vimy and collected the prize. The V/1500 was then withdrawn from any attempt to cross the Atlantic but it made many flights in the USA. It suffered some mishaps during these flights including a seized engine with a connecting rod coming through the crankcase. This required Tryggve Gran and a fitter, H.A. Arnold, to climb out onto the wing to secure the damaged items. It was irreparably damaged in November 1919 during a landing accident. Brackley had been given only vague instructions as to the location of the destination aerodrome in Cleveland, failed to find it and, in semi-darkness and short of fuel, he landed on a racecourse. The wing tips were removed while attempting to steer between the judge's and timekeeper's stands, which were just too close together.

What if those radiators had arrived just one day earlier – would it be a V/1500 instead of the Vimy on display today at the Science Museum in London? We can but speculate!

Records of the time are a little inconclusive but it is probable that between thirty and forty V/1500s were delivered to the RAF. Other completed examples were flown

A scene at the RAF Pageant at Hendon in July 1920. It was probably the last public appearance of the V/1500. Three took part and incurred some Royal non-amusement when the lead aircraft, flown by Sholto Douglas, took off directly towards the Royal Box and thundered over the head of King George V. A 'Royal Rocket' was delivered to Douglas via Sir Hugh Trenchard.

but immediately put into storage at Hendon aerodrome. With the ending of the war there was little use for such a large and complex machine for military or civil use, and many that had been on order or partially completed were cancelled. Three took part in the first Aerial Pageant at Hendon in July 1920, one of which carried the intrepid Miss Sylvia Boyden in the tail gunner's cockpit, from which she descended by parachute. After that event the V/1500 seems to have faded from the scene.

For the O/400 however the ending of the war represented a new beginning. Eight of them were used by the RAF Communication Wing carrying passengers and mail between London and Paris during the 1919 Peace Conference. It was a step towards full commercial airline operations, but that's for another chapter.

Given the enormous commitment of Handley Page to the design and production of the big bombers it may seem surprising that they found the time late in 1917 to produce a contender for a Navy requirement for a small carrier-based reconnaissance fighter. It was the **R/200** and was produced in both landplane and floatplane versions. It was cleverly designed to have flaps and ailerons which were interchangeable, as were the rudder and elevators, and the fin and tailplanes. This was to simplify production and to reduce the spares requirements on board ship. Power was supplied by a 200hp Hispano Suiza engine.

The first two examples were completed as floatplanes and given the numbers N27 and N28. They were test flown at the Brent Reservoir ('Welsh Harp') near Cricklewood by Gordon Bell in December 1917. N29, the only landplane version completed, was test flown soon after the floatplanes. All three were delivered to the Isle of Grain for Admiralty testing, but a combination of engine unreliability and the obvious commitments with the O/400 and V/1500 meant that Handley Page did not get the production contract.

Despite their pre-occupation with the big bombers, Handley Page produced the Type R in 1917. It was a two-seat naval reconnaissance aircraft built in both landplane and floatplane forms. The latter was first test flown by Gordon Bell from the Welsh Harp reservoir near Cricklewood. It did not receive a production order.

Chapter 4

The Handley Page Slot – Aeronautical Panacea

'What did you do in the war, Daddy?
How did you help us to win?'
'Take-offs and landings and stalls, laddie,
And how to get out of a spin.'

In 1920 a device first took to the air which was to help prevent a very common type of accident – the stall and spin. It was the Handley Page slot, which was to save many lives in those early days and is still in widespread use today.

Throughout his career Frederick Handley Page was concerned about flight safety. It has been said that the loss of Wilfrid Parke and his works manager Arkell Hardwick in the Type F in 1912 concentrated his mind on developing a means of eliminating accidents due to stalling. If this were so then the fatal crash of the prototype V/1500 in 1918 would have added impetus to the research.

Frederick Handley Page had begun analysing wind tunnel data on the behaviour of wings at high angles of attack as early as 1911 when he delivered a lecture to the Aeronautical Society on the subject. Using his own wind tunnel at Kingsbury in 1917 HP and his aerodynamicist R.O. Boswall began experimenting with wings

What is a Stall?

When an aircraft reduces speed in level flight it still needs the same amount of lift from the wing to support its weight. This can be achieved by gradually increasing the angle at which the wing meets the airflow, i.e. by raising the nose of the aircraft. This is fine down to a lower limit of airspeed, at which point the wing angle relative to the airflow ('angle of attack') becomes so large that it reaches a critical value where the air is unable to maintain a smooth flow over the upper surface of the wing and breaks down into turbulent flow. The breakdown usually begins at the outer part of the wing and is referred to as the stall. It is associated with a sudden loss of lift, which means an equally sudden fast rate of descent. If this occurs near the ground then there is little opportunity to recover the situation. Recovery is usually achieved by applying power and lowering the nose to gain speed and reduce the angle of attack. If one wing stalls and drops before the other, as can occur in asymmetric flight, a spin can result. The aircraft then descends vertically while rotating about a vertical axis, rather like a sycamore seed in slow motion. There were many stalling and spinning accidents in the early days of flying, particularly during the take-off and landing phase where a sudden rapid descent often proved fatal. Even at higher altitudes, spin recovery techniques and the controls to effect them in those days were not always to be counted on.

The first aircraft to fly with Handley Page slots was this de Havilland DH9 in 1920. It had full-span fixed slats on each wing. Later the ground angle was increased by lengthening the main undercarriage legs.

The X4B, or HP20, was a much modified DH9A. It had a monoplane wing and slats which could be opened or closed by the pilot.

incorporating slots linking the upper and lower surfaces. At first the slots were chordwise (that is, parallel to the fuselage). They soon changed to the spanwise direction, with the slot parallel to the leading edge of the wing. It was immediately apparent that a significant increase in lift could be obtained with little penalty in extra drag. The angle of attack could be increased well beyond the value attainable without the slot before the airflow over the upper surface broke down. In practical terms this meant that an aircraft could maintain high lift down to a lower speed, effectively delaying the stall. And so, the 'Handley Page slot' was born and was destined to become universally adopted throughout the aviation industry. Great secrecy was maintained over the discovery while further research optimised the design of the slot. Patents were applied for in both Britain and the USA.

The ultimate test would come when the slot principle was tried on a real aeroplane and to this end HP acquired a surplus DH9 biplane in 1920, serial number H9140, at a knock-down price from the Aircraft Disposals Board. It was fitted with slats forward of the leading edge on both the upper and lower wings. Each slat comprised a narrow aerofoil section which formed a slot between itself and the wing. A series of flight tests commenced, the results from which would be compared with performance data measured before the slats were fitted. The DH9 came to be re-designated **HP17**.

Flight testing began on 31 March 1920 when Geoffrey Hill took it into the air for the first time with the slots blanked off with fabric. The fabric was progressively removed in subsequent flights and by the time all the slots were fully exposed the low speed flying qualities of the aircraft were shown to be much improved, with a significant reduction in stalling speed. Testing was also carried out by the Royal Aircraft Establishment, including some flights from the deck of an aircraft carrier. The aircraft had meanwhile been modified by having its undercarriage made longer to provide a more nose-up attitude on the ground. The slotted DH9 was demonstrated to the press at Cricklewood on 21 October 1920 and was soon the subject of enthusiastic reports worldwide. The demonstration had included controlled flight in the stalled condition.

The DH9 carried out all its testing with the slats fixed in one position. The next stage would be to have movable slats which could be operated by the pilot. The idea was that they should be opened only when required, typically during take-off and landing, or any other phase of flight where a low airspeed would be required. The ability to close the slot would allow a smooth aerofoil section to be retained for cruising and high speed flight. The aircraft chosen to test the movable slot was a DH9A, serial number F1632, but fitted with a completely new high mounted, plywood covered monoplane wing. This wing had full span slats and it also had slotted ailerons to increase their effectiveness. The aircraft was known initially as the X4B but later received the Handley Page designation **HP20**, with the serial number changed to J6914. Its first flight was on 24 February 1921 in the hands of Arthur Wilcockson. For its first few flights the slot remained closed and locked but was then made able to open by means of a worm drive linked to a handle in the cockpit. The mechanism was sometimes difficult to operate under certain air loading conditions, but despite this it was handed over to the Air Ministry for further trials on 25 October 1921.

Unknown to Handley Page at the time, a similar line of research was being pursued in Germany by Gustav Victor Lachmann, then a student at Darmstadt Technical College. He had had the misfortune in August 1917 to be injured in a flying accident soon after completing his flight training. Attempting a steep banked turn soon after take-off he overdid it, stalled and spun into the ground. This inspired him, like HP, to seek an answer to the problem of the stall and spin. Lachman began conducting experiments with wing sections incorporating a number of parallel slots between the leading and trailing edges. He applied for patents in 1918, some weeks before HP had applied for his, although it was to take a long time for the German Patent Office to accept the proposal as workable.

Lachmann's main problem was a lack of capital. His first serious wind tunnel experiments, using facilities at Göttingen University, had to be funded by his mother! It was not long before both HP and Lachmann became aware of the other's work and after some correspondence they arranged to meet in Berlin in August 1921. According to Lachmann they 'talked slots for hours.' The important outcome of the meeting was that they came to an agreement to collaborate on slot development and to share patent rights. Lachmann accepted a consultancy position with Handley Page Ltd which provided him with an income and funding for his research. For Handley Page it gave them access to data from the Göttingen wind tunnels, probably the best in Europe, where Lachmann would continue to work. This episode was a good illustration of the astuteness and charisma that HP showed in dealing with people – Lachmann became a devoted follower for over forty years.

In 1920 a specification was issued for a single-seat torpedo bomber to operate from aircraft carriers. Handley Page was quick to see this as a potential first application for slotted wings and put in a tender. This resulted in an order for three prototypes of the **Type T Hanley**, which would compete with the Blackburn Dart for a production order. During the early design stages in March 1921 George Volkert left for a two year stay in Japan with a naval trade mission and the position of chief designer passed to S.T.A. Richards. The Hanley was a fairly conventional biplane of wooden construction and powered by a 450hp Napier Lion. Movable slats were fitted across the whole span of both the upper and lower wings. Slotted ailerons were provided, but no trailing edge flaps. The three Hanley Is as they were designated all made their first flights with Arthur Wilcockson early in 1922. They carried the numbers N143 to N145 and were soon despatched to Martlesham Heath in Suffolk for trials by the Aeroplane and Armament Experimental Establishment (A&AEE). Initial performance measurements were disappointing and N143, which had suffered some heavy landing damage, was modified during the repairs to reduce its drag. It had fewer wing struts, a tidier undercarriage and other drag reducing modifications. It re-emerged as the Hanley II for flight test on 4 December 1922. Wilcockson took the aircraft to Paris and Brussels for demonstration flights and returned via Croydon for customs clearance on a windy day. With a good headwind he was able to make an almost vertical approach and landing, followed on departure by an impressive angle of climb. Top speed was now 115mph and the aircraft returned to A&AEE for more trials, including deck landings. Further modifications to the slot mechanism were made to improve the

The Handley Page Slot

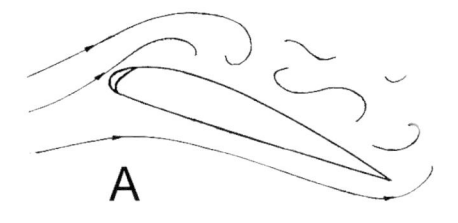

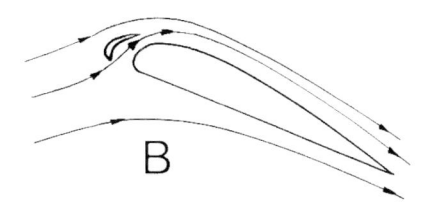

The effect of the slot in diagrammatic form. In A the wing is stalled at a high angle of attack with the slot closed. With the slot open at the same angle of attack, as in B, there is smooth air flow and hence controlled flight is maintained.

tightness of the fit of the slat against the leading edge of the wing when closed. When all the improvements were embodied on N145 it became known as the Hanley III.

One of the problems that had been encountered with the aircraft was that of pilot workload, with the manually operated slats (separate operating handles for upper and lower slats) adding to all the normal controls plus the tailplane incidence control which was necessary to counter the trim changes associated with the opening and closing of the slats. There was also quite a physical force required to move the slats under some conditions. This would later be solved by the introduction of the automatically opening slot. In the meantime, however, the Blackburn Dart had also performed well and won the production order. The Navy also preferred its structure which was more suited to the rigours of naval operations.

All was not lost for Handley Page as a specification was issued in 1923 for a two-seat torpedo bomber and the Hanley was adapted to compete with several other

The Hanley was the first aircraft designed from the outset to have slotted wings. This is the Hanley II and shows the slats in the open position.

designs. An order was soon received for six trials aircraft, which became the Type Ta, or Handley Page **Hendon**. They carried the serial numbers N9724 to N9729.

The Hendon had similar wings and controls to the Hanley III but had a longer fuselage to accommodate the observer and his Lewis gun. Fixed armament comprised a forward firing Vickers machine gun. Arthur Wilcockson flew the first of the six Hendons on 7 July 1924. They soon proved to be tail-heavy when carrying a torpedo and an early modification was to sweep the wings back five degrees to restore the balance.

Like the Hanley, the Hendon went through a series of modifications to improve performance and to increase the effectiveness of the slots. N9724 became the first Hendon II with improved slot operating linkages and a revised undercarriage. N9727 was further modified to become the Hendon III in August 1925. It had slotted flaps on both upper and lower wings, inboard of the ailerons and linked to the innermost slats. Linkages were also provided between the ailerons and the outer set of slats such that the slots were open with the ailerons down and closed with the ailerons up. The flaps enabled the Hendon III to approach and land with much less of a nose-up attitude, so improving the pilot's forward view. The interlinking of the slat with the aileron was the subject of much development work under George Volkert, who had by now returned from Japan. He was aided by draughtsman S.G. Ebel and wind tunnel engineer G.C.D. Russell.

The Hendon was a two-seat derivative of the Hanley and was also fully slotted. This view of the Hendon III shows the linkages below the wings joining the flaps and ailerons to the slats.

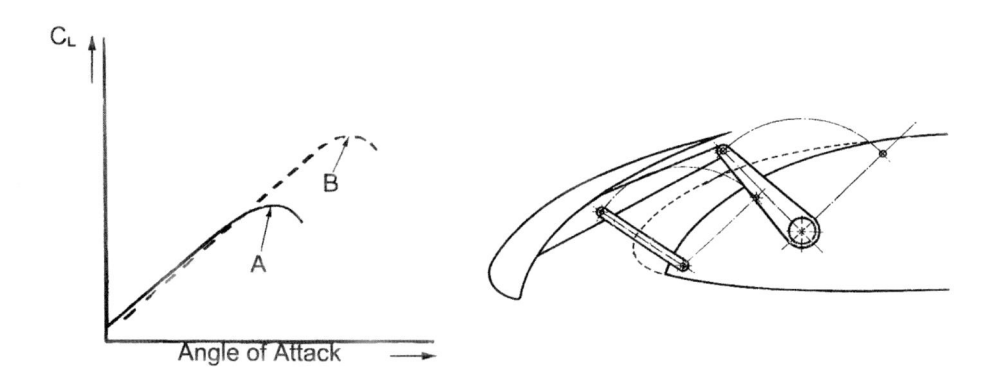

On the left is a so-called CL/alpha curve for a slotted wing with the slots closed (A) and open (B). It gives an increase of approximately fifty per cent in the lift coefficient CL (a measure of the lift obtainable from a particular wing section). On the right is a mechanism typical of those used for the early automatic opening slots.

A further refinement was a small hinged plate, known as an 'interceptor', fitted behind the outer sections of the slat and arranged by means of a linkage to lift as the aileron moved up, thereby blocking the slot. This produced a much more rapid response than moving the slat with the aileron and therefore much safer lateral control near the stall. (In slow flight the down-going aileron increased the overall angle of attack at the wing tip, requiring the slot to be open to avoid a tip stall whereas, conversely, the up-going aileron decreased the angle of attack and was found to be more effective with the slot closed.) The interceptor had its first flight test on the Hendon III in July 1926.

Meanwhile wind tunnel work continued at Cricklewood under George Russell. It was yielding results suggesting that with the right kind of linkage a leading edge slat system could be built that would be held closed for normal flight, but at a certain angle of attack it would automatically open due to the changing pressure distribution. Numerous model tests proved the concept of automatic operation. This was the final break-through in the development of a safety device which would soon be universally adopted.

Concurrently with the wind tunnel experiments, another two-seat torpedo carrying biplane was under development at Handley Page. It was the **HP31 Harrow**, designed to a specification which required a good load carrying capacity and long range. The engine was a 450hp Napier Lion, initially with a flat, front-mounted radiator. Two prototypes were ordered and they were built as N205 and N206 to compete against the Blackburn Ripon. They were built as landplanes but provision was made for conversion to floatplanes. N205 made its first flight on 24 April 1926 in the hands of Hubert Broad. Manually controlled flaps and slots were the order of the day and experiments with various configurations were carried out, including links between the slats and the trailing edge flaps, and between the slats and ailerons.

The commanding officer of the trials squadron at A&AEE where the Service trials were conducted was Sqdn Ldr Tom Harry England. During a meeting at Martlesham Heath in January 1927 HP made an offer to England to join the company as chief test pilot, which he accepted. Previous test pilots with Handley Page had been mainly freelance but they were becoming increasingly committed to other manufacturers or airlines. England's immediate task was to continue the Harrow development flying in the on-going competition with its Blackburn rival.

N205 had to be rebuilt at Cricklewood after sustaining heavy landing damage. In the process it was fitted with a more powerful Lion engine and given a completely new shaped cowling. The radiators were moved to the rear of the engine compartment, allowing the front end to have a pointed appearance, somewhat in the style of the Hawker biplanes of the early 1930s.

The next big step was the fitting of automatic tip slots to the Harrow in the summer of 1927. Gus Lachmann expressed the feelings on the occasion of the first demonstration of the automatic slot in his Handley Page Memorial Lecture at the Royal Aeronautical Society in 1964.

'The Harrow went up for a short flight during which England tried the aircraft with the slats controlled manually. All was well, and in an atmosphere of great expectancy, the worm drives were disconnected and the slats were free to move according to the dictates of the airstream. England took off again, climbed to a safe height and pulled the Harrow up to the stall. Out came the slats of their own accord and the Handley Page automatic slot was an accomplished fact. There was no hesitation about their working. Until the critical stalling angle was approached the resulting vector of the air forces acting upon the slat passed ahead of the instantaneous centre of the linkage and the slat was firmly held in place against the leading edge. As the stall was approached the vector rotated and its line of action passed on the other side of the instantaneous centre – and out came the slats.

This demonstration was so tremendously encouraging that, after the incorporation of a few detailed improvements, HP arranged a demonstration for Air Ministry technical officials. This took place a month after the first successful flight test. By great good fortune it was discovered that the new automatic slot could be fitted to the standard Bristol Fighter wing. This aircraft, so equipped, flew at the beginning of October 1927 and from then on the technical and commercial career of the slotted wing ran willy-nilly from triumph to triumph.'

Sadly for Handley Page, the Blackburn design yet again won the competition and no order was forthcoming for the Harrow, but it did continue with slot development work. In 1928 N205 was fitted with floats for trials at Felixtowe, but attempts to get the RAF to adopt it were not successful and the Harrows were finally scrapped.

None of the three designs of torpedo bomber discussed above made it into production. However, the Hanley (HP19), Hendon (HP25) and Harrow (HP31) had great significance for Handley Page, and for the aviation business generally because of the contribution they made to the development of the slotted wing, not forgetting the slotted flaps and ailerons which followed from it. It was doubly satisfying for HP because all the work was paid for by Government contracts!

The HP31 Harrow was originally flown as a landplane and was the first aircraft to demonstrate automatic slot opening. The first of the two prototypes ended its days at Felixtowe in 1928 for trials as a torpedo-carrying seaplane.

No discussion of slot development could finish without a mention of one more Handley Page aeroplane, the HP39 which appeared in 1929. It was built to take part in the Guggenheim Safe Aircraft Competition to take place that year at Mitchel Field on Long Island, New York. Known initially as the 'Guggenheim Competition Biplane' it was nicknamed **Gugnunc** by *Flight* magazine after a catch-phrase from the *Daily Mirror* strip cartoon 'Pip, Squeak and Wilfrid.' It soon became the HP39's official name. The engine was an Armstrong Siddeley Mongoose of 150hp.

The requirements of the competition included a top speed of at least 110mph and the entrants had to demonstrate the following:

a. level flight with engine on at not more than 35mph.
b. three minutes glide with engine off at not more than 38mph.
c. landing over a 35ft barrier within 300ft, and a ground roll no more than 100ft.
d. taking-off in 300ft and clearing a 35ft barrier 500ft from the start.

There were other requirements relating to glide angle and stability, all amounting to a stringent test of the aircraft's (and pilot's) capability.

The design featured a sesquiplane layout, in which the upper wing was considerably larger than the lower one. The wings had all-strut bracing with no external wire bracing. Both the upper and lower wings had full-span leading edge slats. The outer slats on the upper wing were automatic and independent of any other control. The

The HP39 Gugnunc at Mitchel Field, New York, in 1929 for the Guggenheim Safe Aircraft Competition. The engine is fitted with a Townend ring which was removed after its return to England. The Gugnunc is now preserved by the Science Museum at Wroughton, near Swindon. *(Science Museum)*

remainder of the slats were also automatic but were linked to the trailing edge flaps so that when a critical angle of attack was reached the slats opened and lowered the flaps, with no action required by the pilot.

Tom England made the first flight on 30 April 1929 and the next few flights concentrated on control and slot harmonisation. Further refinements followed to reduce drag, with the test flying being shared by England and his assistant test pilot Maj. James Cordes. The most noticeable external change to the aircraft was the addition of a Townend ring surrounding the radial engine to reduce the turbulence from the cylinders which occurred when they had been fully exposed to the airstream.

In September 1929 Cordes set sail for New York with the Gugnunc and carried out a test flight at Mitchel Field before handing it over to the Guggenheim pilots for the competition flying. There were originally twenty-seven entrants but a series of withdrawals, crashes and eliminations left just two aircraft, the Gugnunc and the Curtiss Tanager. The Gugnunc was struggling to achieve one of the gliding requirements (to maintain 38mph for three minutes with the engine switched off) and details were sent by cable to HP in Cricklewood. Cordes also mentioned that he had sneaked a look at the Curtiss in its hangar and found that it had slats of a design covered by the Handley Page patents. HP immediately set sail for New York and openly expressed his anger that the Tanager was sporting fully slotted wings for which they had not sought permission, let alone paid the royalty. A fierce legal battle followed which was eventually ended by mutual consent. The Tanager took the prize, but Handley Page could feel satisfied with the performance of the Gugnunc, with its demonstrated speed range of 33-112 mph, and a landing distance of just 21 yards.

After the competition the Gugnunc returned to Cricklewood to continue with its development under the eyes of Lachmann, who recommended several improvements, including the fitting of interceptors which time had not permitted before the competition. The Townend ring was removed and not fitted again. Cordes flew demonstrations in France in June 1930. On 7 July at the official opening, by Prince George, of Handley Page's new aerodrome at Radlett, England put on a show. With the engine started inside the hangar he began the take-off run and was airborne as he went out the doors!

The Gugnunc was passed to the Air Ministry for further development of high lift devices. It acquired military markings, with the serial number K1908 replacing the civil registration G-AACN. It made several appearances at the RAF displays at Hendon before it was retired in 1934. Frederick Handley Page then presented it to the Science Museum in London where it was put on display suspended from the roof. Following the outbreak of war it was put in storage for many years, making only rare public appearances. One such occasion was Handley Page's fiftieth anniversary celebrations at Radlett in 1959 when it was placed on static exhibition. In the 1990s it underwent a thorough restoration and now resides at the Science Museum's storage centre at Wroughton, near Swindon. It is now occasionally viewable by the public on open days. It is the oldest complete Handley Page aeroplane in existence.

Gus Lachmann had moved to England as a full time employee of the company in 1929, taking charge of aerodynamics and stressing, as well as looking after slot development. He became chief designer for a few years in the 1930s. In 1953 he was appointed Director of Research, a post he held until his retirement in 1965. The only serious drawback to his Germanic origins came during the Second World War when he had to spend much of the duration as an internee on the Isle of Man.

During the 1920s many British and foreign aircraft were fitted with slats. The improvement in flight safety was so significant that in 1928 the Air Ministry ordered that all Service aircraft should be so equipped. They paid Handley Page £100,000 for

A Flight Test Experience

In 1964, Reginald Stafford, then Technical Director of Handley Page Ltd, recalled an incident during the development of the Gugnunc. 'At that time I was an aerodynamicist-cum-flight observer. After much difficulty I persuaded our lord and master to invest in some highly expensive flight test instrumentation and we acquired an air log with which to measure true air speeds, at the enormous cost of about £100. The Gugnunc had a very narrow cockpit and the air log was longer than the width of the cockpit, as was the board on which its cable was looped. Launching the air log and paying out the cable presented real difficulty and during this operation I got the cable wound round my neck with the air log already trailing out. This presented the choice of struggling with the cable at some risk of strangulation or cutting the air log loose and facing the awful rage of Sir Frederick. I confess that it was this fear rather than heroism which prompted me to retrieve the air log.'

Single Slotted Flap   Double Slotted Flap

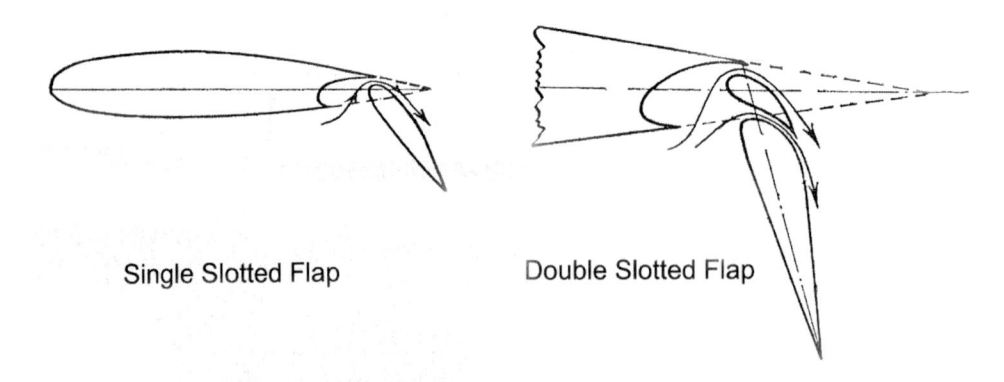

Examples of single and double slotted flaps, showing the air flow through the slots. Triple slotted flaps are also in common use.

the rights. Later that year the US Navy adopted it and paid $1 million for the rights. The founder and first editor of *The Aeroplane* magazine, C.G. Grey, rated the importance of the slot to aeronautics as similar to that of the pneumatic tyre to the motor industry. It was certainly important to Handley Page because in the lean inter-war years the royalties more than anything else kept the company afloat. Total royalties up to the time the main patents expired in 1938 amounted to approximately £750,000.

This period up to the Second World War was the heyday of the slot. Development of the thicker monoplane wings in the 1930s and other aerodynamic improvements made wings less prone to tip stall and the leading edge slat began to disappear, although slotted flaps remained the norm. However, when the swept wing came into use with the introduction of high-speed jet aircraft after the war, interest in the slot revived because swept wings are more prone to tip stall than straight wings. So now there is once again widespread use of slotted wings.

The next time you are on a Boeing 737, for example, take a look along the leading edge of the wing during the approach to landing. Outboard of the engine you will see leading edge slats deployed. They can be manually extended on their own, or they can be automatically extended whenever trailing edge flap is selected. Other high lift devices are used on the leading edge inboard of the engine. These are Kruger flaps which comprise a section of the wing lower surface which is hinged at the leading edge and swung forward to increase the camber. They are less effective (and less complex) than slats, but that part of the wing is less critical from the stalling point of view. If you are seated aft of the wing look out for the triple slotted trailing edge flaps. The slots in the flap allow larger deflection angles, hence more lift at low speed, with the added bonus of less of a nose-up attitude during landing.

Handley Page's explanation of how the slot worked, by directing high energy air from below the leading edge to re-energise the sluggish air on the upper surface, was not questioned for many years, or even decades. It was supported by numerous leading aerodynamicists, including the great Ludwig Prandtl. The real change in thinking came with the work of a leading American aerodynamicist and scientific

The double slotted flaps on the Handley Page Hermes V at Radlett in 1949. On the left is chief test pilot Hedley Hazelden and with him is chief designer Reginald Stafford.

researcher, the late Dr A.M.O. Smith in the 1970s (*High Lift Aerodynamics*, AIAA Wright Brothers Lecture 74-939, August 1974). The theory, well beyond the scope of this book, involves the effect of the slot on inviscid pressure distributions, and mutual interference between the various elements, i.e. the wing, slat, and slotted flaps, and the wakes behind them. Although HP's explanation of the slot principle was over-simplified, he showed that it was workable and drew up the rules for its application, so perhaps it was not surprising that the underlying principles were not questioned for so many years.

A final thought from HP himself came when Lachmann reminded him shortly before his death in 1962 how successfully the slotted wing gospel had been spread throughout the world. He gave a sad and wistful look and said 'But Lachmann, the patents have expired!'

Chapter 5

The Dawn of Civil Aviation

During the latter stages of the First World War minds were turning to the potential peacetime uses of the aeroplane. In the immediate post-war period flying remained the sole preserve of the armed forces, under the Defence of the Realm Act, until domestic civil aviation legislation was enacted and agreements put in place to regulate international flights.

Handley Page were well placed to be in at the very beginning of commercial aviation with their experience of large aircraft. However, the first O/400s to carry passengers belonged to the RAF's 86th (Communications) Squadron which from early 1919 operated on the London-Paris route in support of the Versailles Peace Conference. They carried goods and mail and were provided with simple bench seats in the fuselage, but at least two were fitted out to carry up to six VIP passengers, with windows on each side of the cabin and upholstered seats. They were known as H.M. Airliners and the first of these was D8326, named *Silver Star*. They had an overall silver finish which gave them a very distinctive appearance in comparison with the matt dark green 'Nivo' finish of most O/400s.

Frederick Handley Page was not slow off the mark and in a typical entrepreneurial move he bought back four unused O/400s at less than cost price for conversion into passenger carrying aircraft. He also acquired twelve nearly completed surplus airframes. The first four were to become registered under the new system as G-EAAE, F, G and W. G-EAAF was awarded British Certificate of Airworthiness Number 1. A new company, Handley Page Transport Ltd (HPTL), was formed on 14 June 1919 to operate the aircraft. Meanwhile a civilianised mock-up of an O/400 with luxurious leather passenger seats had been exhibited at Selfridges' Oxford Street store in March 1919. It was not, however, very representative of the true interior of the early passenger cabins which were rather spartan and equipped with wicker chairs.

The first true passenger service to be flown by Handley Page was with G-EAAE (still at this time having to wear its military identity D8350) on 1 May 1919, the day that commercial flying became legal with the passing of the Air Navigation Bill. The O/400, flown by HPTL's chief pilot Lt Col Sholto Douglas, took eleven passengers from Cricklewood to Manchester in three hours and forty minutes against a stiff headwind. Later that year international agreements allowed cross-Channel services to commence and HPTL began regular flights between Cricklewood and Paris on 2 September 1919. The first service was flown by Sholto Douglas in G-EAAF *Vulture*. A Brussels service commenced on 23 September. It must have been slightly galling for HP to be beaten by his rival Holt Thomas whose Air Transport & Travel company had begun a scheduled Paris service from Hounslow on 25 August with de Havilland DH4s converted to carry two passengers. Actually an O/400 did fly passengers to Paris that day, but they were invited journalists.

Modifications to the basic O/400 design soon followed to improve its passenger appeal. There were no windows and the internal fuel tanks and tie rod bracing in the fuselage did nothing for accessibility and comfort. The **O/700**, soon to be given the shortened title O/7, retained all the main structural features of the O/400 but had some significant changes to improve the passenger accommodation. The fuselage fuel tanks were removed and tanks were re-installed in the rear of the extended engine nacelles, as on the O/100. The fuselage cross bracing was replaced by a vee arrangement of tubular struts which were relatively easy to step between. Five wicker seats were fitted along each side of the cabin and windows were provided. Seats were also installed in the former nose gunner's cockpit for two additional hardy passengers. Access to the cabin was via an entry door on the fuselage side instead of a ladder to a trap door under the front fuselage. Other similar variations on the O/400 theme were known as the **O/10** and **O/11**. Handley Page Transport's London-Paris service introduced the first in-flight meals, in the form of lunch baskets. A season ticket in 1920 on that route cost £120 for twelve single flights.

In 1919 Handley Page were invited to tender for an order from China for a long range civil transport. The result was an order for six O/7s which were converted from the twelve airframes already acquired by HP. On 5 July 1919 the first of these was tested by Geoffrey Hill, taking eighteen passengers to 1,500ft as part of the process. With an all-up weight of 12,800lb he was able to demonstrate level flight with one engine throttled back. The aircraft were given the numbers HP-1 to HP-6 and by the end of September all six had been shipped to Shanghai. They were successfully employed during 1920 in passenger, freight and mail services, linking many outlying areas to Peking until the on-going civil war rendered these services inoperable.

Towards the end of 1920 British airlines were experiencing serious difficulties because of the heavily subsidised European competition on the same routes. By March 1921 things started to recover when subsidies were forthcoming from the British Government for passenger flying, but not for freight. The return fare to Paris was reduced to twelve pounds.

Services with the O/400 continued from Cricklewood until May 1921, when HPTL were requested by the Air Ministry to transfer their terminal to Croydon, which was to become established as London's airport in the inter-war years. This was much to the relief of the residents around Cricklewood because the climb performance of the O/400 was such that they were often to be seen too close for comfort. One newspaper reported, perhaps with just a little tongue in cheek, that it was dangerous to stand up on the top deck of a tram on Cricklewood Broadway! As far back as 1919 there had been a complaint from the MCC of a Handley Page flying low over a cricket match at Lord's. HPTL pilot Robert McIntosh wrote that they hoped to achieve 500ft by the time they reached Marble Arch.

The All Weather Mac

Capt. (later Wg Cdr) Robert Henry McIntosh joined Handley Page Transport on 21 September 1919 and the following year became the company's chief pilot. He had previously served with the RAF's 214 Sqn on O/400s and had also flown these aircraft with the communications squadron on the London-Paris peace conference service. Some of his adventures with HPTL illustrate how different commercial flying could be in those days compared with today's relatively trouble free and routine experience. On one London-Paris flight in bad weather he had to make nine forced landings, as the weather dictated, and even that was not the record in the company. Fortunately the low landing speed of the O/400 was a great blessing when getting into small, unfamiliar fields.

On one famous occasion in October 1921 he was bringing the O/10 G-EATH with six passengers back from Paris to Croydon as fog was thickening. He was assisted in the cockpit by engineer/wireless operator Freddy Dismore. As he passed Sevenoaks he noticed that a low layer of cloud had formed at about 250ft altitude. He turned back and returned under the cloud, sometimes being forced down as low as 50ft. This led to the trailing radio aerial becoming snagged on a tree and parting company from the aircraft. From that moment he had no further radio communication.

He tried various approaches to Croydon under the cloud but it became so low that it was impossible to continue in the zero visibility. This was now FOG! His last chance, barring returning to the coast, was to climb above the fog and look for the twin towers of the Crystal Palace, which thankfully appeared protruding through the fog. He had mentally prepared for just such an occasion in the past during clear weather and knew that if he flew along the imaginary line passing through the towers in a south-westerly direction, then after four and a half miles he would be directly over the aerodrome. He now put this to the test and let down to 200ft, levelling off as a precaution, knowing that at 65 mph it would take two and a half minutes from the towers to the aerodrome. He finally recognised some familiar glazed roofs below and as he was too high to land he flew straight and level for a further 30 seconds, easing slightly to the right then pulling the O/10 into a sharp left turn onto a reciprocal heading. He 'felt his way' to the boundary hedge, cut the engines and touched down, with no small sigh of relief. They then sat in the middle of the fog-bound aerodrome for a further ten minutes before a car found them and led the way back to the terminal.

The press the next day used headlines like 'McIntosh for All Weathers' and were full of praise for the Marconi radio and the controllers who had talked him down. It was only many years later that Mac revealed that he did not have a functioning radio. He was also known as 'All-Weather Mac' for the rest of his eventful life!

The last of the civilian O/400 family in service was HPTL's O/10 G-EATH which flew its last passenger service in September 1923 when it completed the London-Paris-Basle-Zurich run. By this time Handley Page's new airliners, the W.8 series, were in service.

Although the O/400 and its derivatives did an excellent job in laying the foundations of mass air transport, as a practical airliner it had distinct drawbacks. It was a large aircraft for the limited passenger capacity in its rather obstructed cabin, despite

O/400 D4631 was converted to civilian O/10 standard and became G-EATH with Handley Page Transport in June 1920. It was the aircraft in which Robert 'All-Weather Mac' McIntosh made his dramatic landing in fog at Croydon on 20 October 1921. It survived until 1924 and was probably the last airworthy civilian example of Handley Page's classic First World War bomber design.

Film stars rarely miss out on a photo opportunity. American-born Pearl White, a well-known silent movie actress of the time, was no exception. Here she is about to take a draughty ride from Cricklewood to Paris in the former front gunner's cockpit of an O/400 conversion in 1920. The crew are the pilot R.H. McIntosh (left) and engineer A.P. Hunt.

the improvements which had been made with the introduction of the O/700 version. What was wanted was a more compact aircraft with greater capacity. Before the war had ended Volkert was investigating improvements to the layout, in particular by reducing the wing span. He proposed having upper and lower wings of equal span and this was tested on a modified O/400, C9713, which had its wing span reduced from 100ft to 85ft. It was given the type number **W/400** and it also featured a monoplane tail unit in place of the twin tailplane of the O/400. In this form it first flew on 22 August 1919 with Sholto Douglas at the controls (under protest since there was no bonus for Handley Page Transport pilots undertaking test flying!). Its predicted performance was confirmed but there was no intention of producing it in this form. However, it served as a development aircraft for Handley Page's first purpose designed airliner, the W.8.

The **W.8** prototype, G-EAPJ, first flew from Cricklewood on 2 December 1919, piloted by twenty-year-old HPTL pilot Robert Bager. Geoffrey Hill was unfit at this time and Sholto Douglas had resigned to return to the RAF (he would later succeed Lord Dowding as C-in-C of Fighter Command in 1941 and, as Lord Douglas of Kirtleside, he was Chairman of British European Airways from 1949 until his retirement in 1964). The W.8 was a biplane with a wing span of 75ft and power was provided by two Napier Lions. Fuel was gravity-fed to the engines from small tanks under the upper wing, as had been provided on the O/7. The fuel was pumped up to them from the main tanks behind the engines. There were seats for twelve passengers in the unobstructed cabin, but the two crew still sat out in the open. The cabin had eight circular windows along each side.

Two days after the first flight the W.8, with a fully furnished interior, was flown to Le Bourget from where it was towed, wings folded, to the centre of Paris for an aeronautical exhibition at the Grand Palais on the Champs Elysées. It returned to Cricklewood on 22 January 1920 and resumed development flying in March. It gave a good demonstration of load carrying on 4 May 1920 when Geoffrey Hill set a record by flying to 14,000ft with a load of 3,690lb. In July it underwent another long tow, this time from Cricklewood to Olympia for the Aero Show. After that it went into service with Handley Page Transport and flew the Paris route until written off in 1923 when a serious fuel leak shut down one engine. The crew, Arthur Wilcockson and A.P. Hunt, had to land downwind in a cornfield. All was going well until the end of the landing run when the aircraft nosed over into a sunken road. There were no serious injuries.

The first production version of the W.8 was the **W.8b**, which had Rolls-Royce Eagles because the more powerful Lions were proving difficult to obtain at the time. Another obvious external difference was the adjoining rectangular windows on each side of the cabin. Unlike the original W.8 there was no provision for wing folding. This was to simplify the structure of the wing root and save weight. Continuing in the tradition of the O/400, but contrary to the accepted convention elsewhere, the pilot was still seated on the right hand side of the cockpit.

The W.8b first flew on 21 April 1922. Three were built for HPTL, G-EBBG, H and I, and one for the Belgian airline Sabena. Others for Sabena were built under

The Dawn Of Civil Aviation

W8b G-EBBG was named *Bombay* when it first went into service with Handley Page Transport. Within two weeks it was renamed *Princess Mary* in a VIP ceremony at Croydon, after which a number of joy-riding flights were carried out. On one of these it flew with twenty-five passengers!

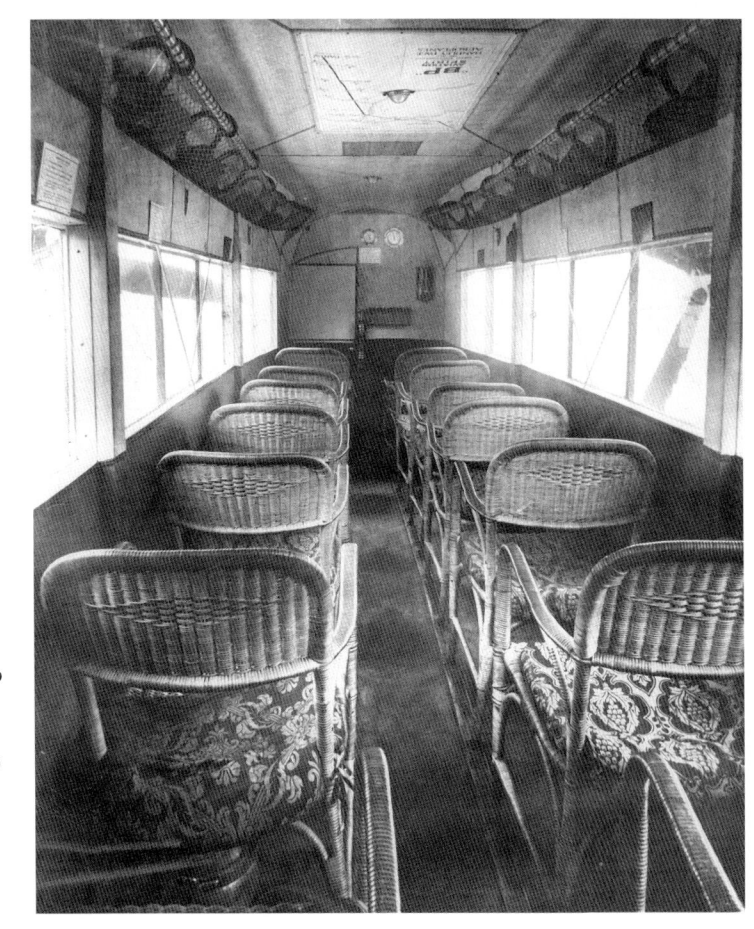

The interior of a W.8b after revision from a twelve to a fourteen seat layout. A map on the ceiling shows the London to Paris route going via Tonbridge, Boulogne, Abbeville and Beauvais.

licence by SABCA in Belgium. Following a naming ceremony at Croydon on 16 May 1922 the W.8b's made a number of joy-riding flights. On one of these G-EBBG went aloft with no less than twenty-five passengers! They gave Handley Page Transport and its successor, Imperial Airways, many years of service. The last one, G-EBBI, was retired in 1932. In its ten years of service it flew half a million miles in 5,473 hours.

Handley Page's ventures into civil aviation after the First World War were not confined to large multi-engined transports. The company became involved with the other extreme in 1923 when the *Daily Mail* offered a number of prizes aimed at very light aircraft. The competition was to be held at Lympne in Kent in October of that year. The biggest prize of £1,000 was offered for the greatest distance flown around a 12.5-mile triangular course on a gallon of petrol.

Capt. W.H. Sayers, technical editor of *The Aeroplane* magazine, came up with three different designs for the competition and Handley Page built them at Cricklewood. They were known as **Sayers-Handley Pages** and initially were only identified by their competition numbers which were 23, 25 and 26. Of the three only No.25 (later recorded as the HP22) showed any promise, although it needed some attention from Handley Page's senior designer Harold Boultbee. He lowered the wing and increased its angle of incidence. He also applied a fairing around the 397cc ABC engine to blend it into the fuselage. For good measure the pilot was also faired in below a hatch in the top of the fuselage with a small oval window each side which gave only a minimal forward view. The smallest, lightest pilot available was Gordon Olley of Handley Page Transport. Olley sought additional remuneration for this extra task and was so persistent that HP finally agreed that he could have one third of any prize money he might win.

Frederick Handley Page seemed to relish the atmosphere of the competition and the difficulties some of the entrants were having. He remarked 'This reminds me of the early days, lots of enthusiasm but no flying!' His own enthusiasm might have

Sayers-Handley Page No.25 built for the *Daily Mail* light aircraft competition held at Lympne in October 1923. A small elliptical window on each side provided the pilot's only view of the outside world. Despite a temperamental engine it made some successful flights but did not win a prize.

been somewhat tempered by the troublesome engine on No.25 and its inclination to kick back during starting. While he was starting it by hand it did indeed kick back and broke one of his fingers.

Olley's first outing around the official course achieved forty miles before engine trouble forced him down. On the next attempt, in gusty conditions, the aircraft dropped to the ground just after take-off and damaged a wing which put paid to Handley Page's attempt at the prize (and to Olley's bonus). The main prize was to be shared by the English Electric Wren and the ANEC 1, both of which achieved eighty-seven and a half miles to the gallon. No.25 was repaired and did some further flying at Hendon and is believed to have bettered the competition-winning fuel consumption, but by then it was too late.

In 1923 a Government-appointed committee was looking into the future of subsidies for the airlines. Its main recommendation was that the various companies should be merged into a single strong company to qualify for continued subsidies. This led to the formation of Imperial Airways Ltd (IAL) on 31 March 1924 by the merger of Handley Page Transport, Instone Air Line, Daimler Airway and the British Marine Air Navigation Co. HPTL then lost its identity but it provided the major proportion of the seating capacity of the new airline.

To improve the performance of the W.8b in the event of a single engine failure, particularly over the remote African routes, a three-engined derivative was introduced in 1924 for Sabena. This was the **W.8e** which had two wing-mounted Siddeley Puma engines plus a Rolls-Royce Eagle in the nose. Handley Page built one of these and further examples were built in Belgium. The very similar **W.8f Hamilton** was the final aircraft in the W.8 series. One, G-EBIX, was built by Handley Page for IAL and first flew on 20 June 1924. Others were built under licence for Sabena, who ultimately bought a total of fifteen of the W.8 series airliners.

A further refinement of the three-engine concept came with the **W.9a Hampstead** which had the wing span increased from 75ft to 79ft and was powered by three 385hp Siddeley Jaguars, later changed to 450hp Bristol Jupiters. It flew for the first time on 1 October 1925 and was delivered to Imperial Airways in March 1926. It could carry fourteen passengers and cruised at 100mph. Heating was provided in the cabin and also for the two crew, who still occupied an open cockpit reached by an external ladder. For the first time in a Handley Page airliner the pilot sat on the left. Only one W.9a was built and after several years of service it was sold to a company in New Guinea in 1929 but crashed in bad weather in 1930.

The final development of the 'W' series of airliners was the Napier Lion powered **W.10**. It was a step back in a way because it reverted to the twin-engine layout with the inability to maintain height if one engine failed. Two were indeed to be lost in the English Channel for just this reason. The three-engined W.9a had certainly survived more than one engine failure, including one over the Channel and another just after take-off from Croydon. The design of the W.10 was a response to an urgent request from Imperial Airways for an improved W.8 when they were short of aircraft for their cross-Channel services. It was mostly derived from the Hyderabad bomber but with a W.8 front fuselage 'grafted on'.

The sole example of the W.9a Hampstead served with Imperial Airways from 1926 until 1929. The crew reached the open cockpit by means of the ladder suspended from the nose. This picture was taken at Filton just after the original Jaguar engines had been replaced by Jupiters in July 1926.

The W.10 had seating for fourteen passengers in a heated cabin. It had the new angular style of fin and rudder which had first been tried as a modification on the W.8f Hamilton. It flew for the first time on 10 February 1926 and a total of four were built for Imperial Airways. They were registered G-EBMM, R, S and T. On 30 March they were all at Croydon together with the W.9a for a naming ceremony. Their entry into service was timely because the General Strike began on 4 May 1926 which meant that train and boat services were severely disrupted.

The first W.10 to be lost in the Channel was G-EBMS *City of London* in October 1926. Capt. Freddy Dismore was carrying ten passengers when a sudden engine failure left him with no alternative but to ditch. All on board were rescued by a nearby trawler. Not so lucky was G-EBMT nearly three years later when Capt. Brailli had to ditch three miles off Dungeness on 17 June 1929. Four of the eleven passengers drowned, the first fatalities among passengers with Imperial Airways' Handley Page fleet. From then on the airline introduced a policy of only using three-engined aircraft on cross-Channel routes. The twin-engined aircraft were restricted to overland routes and cross-Channel freight services. The remaining two W.10s were finally sold off in 1933 to Sir Alan Cobham's air display company. G-EBMM was modified by Cobham in 1934 as an airborne tanker for his early in-flight refuelling experiments. It suffered a fatal crash in September 1934 following a failure of the tailplane bracing attachment at 800ft. The surviving aircraft, G-EBMR, was sold in Malta in November 1934 but was not used for much longer.

None of the aircraft so far covered in this chapter had slotted wings. There had been a proposal in 1920 to build a slotted wing W.8 with Bristol Jupiter engines, to be known as the **W.8a**, but it was not proceeded with.

A small monoplane airliner was produced in 1926 to an Air Ministry requirement. It featured manually operated leading edge slats as well as slotted flaps and ailerons. This was the **HP32 Hamlet** and it had the distinction of being the first British civil aircraft with a modern style enclosed cockpit, complete with a windscreen wiper. It could accommodate four to six passengers, depending on the standard of comfort to be provided. It was powered by three Bristol Lucifers but later modified to have two Armstrong Siddeley Lynxes.

Registered G-EBNS, it first took to the air on 19 October 1926, flown by Arthur Wilcockson. The slats were locked in the open position for the first flight, but on the second flight foreman W.H. MacRostie was on board to check the slat and flap operation. He had to turn the slat operating handwheel himself because the mechanism was too stiff for the pilot alone.

The slat mechanism was adjusted in time for a visit to Croydon on 21 October where it was shown to visiting prime ministers from the Dominions. More development flying followed and eventually in March 1927 it was re-engined again with three Armstrong Siddeley Mongooses, but did not fly because it was awaiting a cure for a roll control problem reported by chief test pilot Tom England. It was finally bought as it stood by the Air Ministry for research purposes and taken by road to Farnborough but it does not appear to have flown again. It was scrapped in 1929.

Watched by Sir Samuel Hoare (Secretary of State for Air), The Hon. Peter Larkins (Canadian High Commissioner), Sir Eric Geddes (Chairman of Imperial Airways) and numerous guests, Lady Maud Hoare officially names the four W.10s and the W.9a at Croydon on 30 March 1926.

With full-span leading edge slats plus slotted flaps and ailerons the HP32 Hamlet of 1926 was built to an Air Ministry requirement for a small air taxi and charter aircraft. It first flew with three Bristol Lucifer engines but is seen here after they were replaced by two Armstrong Siddeley Lynxes. Only one example was built.

Radlett aerodrome was used during the 1930s by aircraft taking part in the Hendon displays. Here two Harts of 601 Sqn await their turn in June 1936. On the right is Harold Hurlock, owner of nearby Springfield Farm, who helped Maj. Cordes park the Avro Avian in 1929 when Cordes 'discovered' the aerodrome. Beside Hurlock is Mr G.H. Cullen, tenant farmer at Springfield. In the front with his sisters Antoinette and Natalie is Gerald Cullen who became Chairman of the Handley Page Association in 2002. *(G. Cullen)*

By the late 1920s it was becoming obvious that Cricklewood was going to be inadequate as an aerodrome before very long. It had a noticeable slope and there was no room for expansion, which would have been necessary as higher performance aircraft came along. The 'suburban sprawl' was moving rapidly across north-west London and there was demand for ever more land. Furthermore the local councils were becoming increasingly vociferous about low flying and noise. The aerodrome was eventually sold off for £100,000 with an agreed closure date of 8 November 1929.

Meanwhile the search had been going on for another suitable airfield and it was much influenced by a chance incident that befell test pilot Jim Cordes on one of his first tasks with the company in 1928. He was ferrying an Avro Avian from Woodford in Cheshire down to Cricklewood, where it was to be used for auto slot development. He had completed most of the journey using the railway system for navigation (or 'Bradshawing' as it was termed in those days after the famed railway timetable publication), when a thickening fog layer and impending darkness made him decide on a precautionary landing. He chose a large field just south of St Albans in Hertfordshire between the LMS railway and the A5 road ('between those two ancient avenues of communication' as Frederick Handley Page would later describe it). Once on the ground he made contact with the farmer, a Mr Slaughter, and the aircraft was parked and secured for the night, with assistance from a neighbouring farmer, Mr Hurlock.

The next day when he reached Cricklewood, Cordes told HP of the field and how he thought it would make a good aerodrome. Little more was done about it for a few months, by which time the situation at Cricklewood was becoming most pressing and negotiations began with Slaughter. The outcome was the purchase by Handley Page Ltd of around 154 acres of land, more than adequate for the aircraft of the day. At the southern end of the field a large assembly and flight test hangar was built.

Back at Cricklewood the 8 November deadline to quit the airfield meant a bit of a scramble to get all the remaining aircraft out. Building operations had actually commenced while flying was still taking place. This undesirable state of affairs led the local authority to forbid the use of the area as an airfield and, presumably knowing something of HP, they had a fence built separating it from the factory. There were strict warnings about unauthorised removal of any part of the fence. Unfortunately there remained one aircraft which had to be flown out. It was a French Latécoère biplane (also reported as a Bréguet) which had been fitted with slats. Having been warned of the dire penalties of interference with the fence, HP arranged for the chippies to construct a pair of ramps. They were placed either side of the fence very early one morning and the biplane was manhandled over, flown away and the ramps removed, leaving little evidence of the undercover operation!

Radlett aerodrome was officially opened on 7 July 1930 by HRH Prince George, later Duke of Kent, in the presence of high ranking ministers, foreign air attachés and Lord Trenchard. The occasion was enlivened by England's demonstration of the Gugnunc, where he started the take-off run in the hangar and was airborne before leaving it. On display in the hangar were the rather tattered remains of the 1912 *Yellow Peril*. Also on display was the main fuselage section of *Hannibal*, the first example of Handley Page's legendary airliner of the 1930s, the HP42.

The **HP42** owed its origins to specifications issued by Imperial Airways in 1928. The airline were keen to develop routes to India and other far flung parts of the British Empire, as well as further developing the European services. Tenders were invited for three and four-engined aircraft, for which IAL would provide the engines and radio equipment. The specification called for minimum performance guarantees in respect of stalling speed, fuel consumption, range and ability to maintain height with one engine failed. It even detailed the type of structure and the crew accommodation, which was to be in an enclosed cockpit. There were also strict delivery dates specified ranging from September 1930 to March 1931, with bonuses for early delivery and penalties for late delivery.

Handley Page tendered for both the Eastern and Western requirements with a large biplane powered by four Bristol Jupiter engines. They were known respectively as the HP42E and HP42W. The designations HP42 and HP45 have also been used and originated from revisions to IAL's specification for the Western type, including a different type of engine, but eventually it was only a matter of internal layout which distinguished the two versions. So although the type number HP45 appears in some records of the time, it is simpler to use the generic HP42 for both types, especially as some individual aircraft changed roles.

The first HP42 G-AAGX *Hannibal* at Radlett in November 1930 around the time of its first flight. Leading edge slats are in evidence on the 130ft span upper wing. No flaps were fitted because the 50mph landing speed was sufficiently low. The diagonal strut at the outer wing section was soon replaced by cross-bracing wires and a window was added to the crew entry door in the nose.

Hannibal on final approach, still with the additional outer strut. Its reputation for exceptional passenger comfort brought forth the comment 'As steady as the Rock of Gibraltar, and just as fast!' – perhaps a reference to its modest cruising speed of 100mph.

The Western version had accommodation for thirty-eight passengers, while the Eastern model, which needed to carry more fuel and baggage, could accommodate eighteen to twenty-four. They were split between two cabins, forward and aft of a central area which was used for baggage, toilets and stewards' accommodation with a galley and a bar. This central area was beneath the wings and in line with the engines, and therefore noisier. The forward cabin was 16ft 6in long and the rear one 17ft 4in. With soundproofing material and soft furnishings the passenger cabins provided a relatively quiet environment as well as a feeling of luxury, reminiscent of the Pullman carriages of the railways.

It was a large aircraft for its day, with a wing span of 130ft (the largest of any Handley Page aeroplane in the company's sixty-year history). George Volkert was in charge of the design, assisted by Harold Boultbee. They opted for an all strut braced wing to facilitate rigging maintenance. The vee arrangement of this 'Warren-girder' strut bracing resulted in the upper wing having a much larger span than the lower one – the sesquiplane layout already employed on the Gugnunc and Hare. The lower wing was attached to the top of the fuselage but the inner section was cranked downwards, which allowed shorter and sturdier undercarriage legs. Automatic slats were fitted to the outer section of the upper wing, which also held up to 500 gallons of fuel.

The fuselage comprised two main sections. The larger forward part, which accommodated the crew and passengers, was an all-metal monocoque structure with a corrugated duralumin outer skin and a plywood inner skin. Kapok soundproofing was sandwiched between these two skins. The rear section of the fuselage was a fabric covered steel tube structure. It was angled up slightly at the joint giving the fuselage a characteristic 'banana' shape. This served the useful purpose of placing the passenger entry door nearer the ground.

The first of the total of eight aircraft (four of each version) was G-AAGX *Hannibal*. After a few straight hops on preceding days, it flew for the first time on 14 November 1930 from Radlett, with England and Cordes on board. Because the enclosed cockpit was in the extreme nose, with little of the airframe visible for reference purposes, England had requested an external 'artificial horizon' bar mounted ahead

Capt. Dismore goes aboard *Heracles* at Croydon in 1937 via the crew door, just before completing the aircraft's millionth mile in the air. It was the first commercial aircraft to achieve this distinction. The passenger door was at the rear of the fuselage and was just three steps up from the ground.

of the windscreen as an aid to keeping the wings level. This was removed after a few flights when the pilots had become familiar with the aircraft.

The Western fleet, with its flagship G-AAXC *Heracles*, operated the services from Croydon to Paris, Le Touquet, Brussels, Cologne, Basle and Zurich. A typical airborne time between Croydon and Paris Le Bourget was about two and a quarter hours, ample time for an excellent in-flight meal. The Eastern Hannibal class operated from Cairo eastwards to Karachi and southwards to Kisumu on the shores of Lake Victoria. There were a few mishaps and forced landings from time to time, but in nearly nine years of service with IAL leading up to the Second World War not one passenger was killed or seriously injured in an HP42.

The HP42 was most elegant, even stately, in appearance. It did not, however, represent a great step forward in aerodynamics or performance, with its 'built-in headwind' of large biplane wings and struts (in the USA the much faster DC-2/DC-3 series airliners of a more modern appearance were being produced from 1934). What the HP42 brought to Imperial Airways was passenger appeal, with its unprecedented comfort, quietness, reliability and, perhaps above all, a growing reputation for safety. Each one logged over 12,000 flying hours in service. The HP42 can be justifiably claimed as the world's first true airliner and deserves a special place in aviation history.

The main drawback from Handley Page's viewpoint is that, in spite of the enviable reputation of the aircraft, they did not make the company any money. All were delivered later than the contract called for, and the penalty clauses effectively meant that IAL received the last of the eight free of charge! This was not a very palatable situation to the financially prudent Frederick Handley Page. In 1933 the airline

The End of an HP42 Sqn Ldr E.G. Libbey

One morning in August 1940, whilst serving at RAF Doncaster, I was ordered to fly to Ringway (Manchester), pick up a full load of mixed ammunition in boxes and take it on to a base in the outer islands of Scotland. I set off early in my HP42 (Horsa) with a co-pilot and two crew. Our load was duly collected at Ringway and piled up in the aircraft. We were soon off again in lovely weather, on a north-westerly course, and continued on our stately way (airspeed about 90mph indicated!) passing over Morecambe Bay and on to St Bees Head. Here I intended to leave the land temporarily and head out across the Solway Firth towards Stranraer.

However, the next thing I knew was that the top starboard engine suddenly stopped. Whilst my co-pilot was vainly trying to rectify this situation by checking switches and petrol cocks, I decided that, although I knew the HP42 would cope quite well on three engines, discretion was the better part of valour, and I would continue my journey over the land and around the coast.

At that moment my fellow pilot, who had happened to put his head out of the cockpit window and look backwards, hastily announced that the top starboard engine and part of the fabric covered upper wing was on fire. Almost immediately the bottom starboard engine also decided to stop.

I decided then that the outlook for the immediate future was rather dim. If I went by the book, throttled back and tried to land into wind, I would end up amongst the rocks at the foot of high cliffs in the midst of a very rough high tide. By now I was only about a 1,000ft up, wallowing on the point of a stall, wing slats right out, and some horrible airspeed showing on my indicator. I managed to keep going slowly round to the right (about north-east) with both port engines going flat out, gradually losing height until I was approaching some reasonably level ground, some three miles north-east of Whitehaven. I remember passing very low over a bus running along a quiet country road, and I am not sure who was the more frightened, the bus passengers or myself!

By this time both starboard wings were well on fire, and so we must have made quite a spectacular sight trailing a large cloud of black smoke and flame. I was relieved to find that I had made a good initial landing downwind (!), but shortly after touchdown I saw that we were going to hit something ahead resembling a grass covered wall, about 4ft high. This we did, smashing off the undercarriage and sliding the rest of the way on the fuselage.

After coming to a sudden halt, without any injuries to anyone, I suddenly remembered all the boxes of ammunition sitting in this burning aeroplane. I decided it was high time we all vacated the spot pretty quickly. The two of us in the cockpit could not go to the rear via the main cabin since the boxes were all piled up against the communicating door, so the only alternative was to bale out of the small side windows. This we somehow managed to do. We then rushed to the rear to see how the crew had got on and found them running to see what had happened to us. The aircraft had ended up in a slight depression which helped us shortly afterwards when all the ammunition started to explode and go off in all directions!

A platoon of soldiers exercising by chance nearby came in useful as a temporary guard. The local policeman then arrived and was at first quite sure that I was a German parachutist just landed. However, I managed to persuade him otherwise and he escorted me to the nearby village of Distington to fill in acres of the usual paperwork. I telephoned the nearest RAF unit at Carlisle and requested them to take over the burned out wreckage which was all that remained of a once proud Horsa. We all returned safely to Doncaster the next day. I heard many years later that a fractured main petrol pipe was to blame for the disaster.

requested another two HP42s and they were quoted £42,000 each, double the original price. Imperial Airways declined the offer and ordered two landplane versions of the Short Kent flying boat instead. Named *Scylla* and *Syrinx*, they never equalled the comfort or flying qualities of the HP42s.

The outbreak of war in 1939 spelt the end of commercial flying in Europe for several years. The HP42s were immediately pressed into RAF service as transports. Their shiny aluminium finish was replaced by matt dark earth and dark green camouflage. None survived the war. *Hannibal*, with eight passengers and crew aboard, disappeared on a flight from Jask to Sharjah in March 1940. No trace was ever found and it was presumed lost in the Gulf of Oman – the only fatal accident to an HP42.

HP42 Production List

HP42E	G-AAGX	*Hannibal*	Crashed, Gulf of Oman 1.3.40
	G-AAUC	*Horsa*	Crashed, Whitehaven 7.8.40
	G-AAUD	*Hanno*	Wrecked in gale, Bristol 19.3.40
	G-AAUE	*Hadrian*	Wrecked in gale, Doncaster 6.12.40
HP42W	G-AAXC	*Heracles*	Wrecked in gale, Bristol 19.3.40
	G-AAXD	*Horatius*	Crashed, Tiverton 7.11.39
	G-AAXE	*Hengist*	Destroyed in hangar fire, Karachi 31.5.37
	G-AAXF	*Helena*	Scrapped, Donibristle 1941

A typical passenger cabin layout in an HP42, often likened to the Pullman carriages on the railways. There were no economy class passengers in those days, and no seat belts.

Chapter 6

Military Aircraft Between the Wars

With the return of peace late in 1918 the O/400 was not further developed as a bomber. Its place in the RAF was gradually taken over by the smaller and faster Vickers Vimy and de Havilland DH10. By the end of 1921 O/400s had disappeared from the front line squadrons but a few examples soldiered on in lesser roles for a number of years (F5431 was reliably reported as visiting Duxford on 30 March 1925). The big and complex V/1500, with its high maintenance costs, was not required in the post-war RAF and had disappeared from the scene by the end of 1920.

Handley Page's first new military aircraft design after the war was the slotted winged Hanley, which was described in Chapter 4 (as also were the Hendon and Harrow because of their importance to slot development). Next came the completely different **Type S**, or HP21. It was a small single-seat, single-engined, low-wing monoplane fighter built to a 1921 order from the United States Navy. Power was supplied by a 230hp Bentley rotary engine.

S.T.A. Richards led the team on this advanced looking design which would have to operate from aircraft carriers or as a seaplane. The wing and the front half of the circular section fuselage were built as an integral structure. Full span leading edge slats were fitted.

The HP21 Type S naval fighter in its original form with a small, unbalanced rudder and no dihedral on the wings. It has full-span ailerons which were arranged to droop symmetrically when the leading edge slots were opened.

Construction of three aircraft was commenced and the first example, known as S-1, made its first flight with Arthur Wilcockson at the controls on 7 September 1923. Flight tests went well once directional stability had been improved by introducing dihedral to the wings and increasing the rudder size. The second example, S-2, was taken by road to Martlesham Heath where the project pilot, F.P. Raynham, confirmed a maximum speed of 146mph on its first flight.

On his second flight in S-2 Raynham had a very lucky escape. He lost elevator control at 2,000ft and managed to trace the cause to a disconnection of the elevator push-rod at the base of the control column. He controlled the descent by holding the end of the push-rod with one hand and using the other hand to blip the magneto switch. As his head was mostly down in the cockpit the landing was heavy and the aircraft bounced. It finished up on its back, fortunately without injury to Raynham. The aircraft was repaired at Cricklewood but wrecked again when the undercarriage collapsed during heavy load trials. Unfortunately, the US Navy cancelled the order in 1924 and S-3, the third aircraft which was being completed with floats, was not flown.

Notwithstanding their ongoing developments in the civil aviation field and the pursuit of perfection in slotted wing research, Handley Page were not long out of the big bomber business. Their first new bomber design after the First World War was the W.8d **Hyderabad**. As its designation suggests, it was closely related to the W.8 series airliners and retained the basic wooden structure but had a redesigned nose to accommodate two pilots and a wireless operator/gunner. There were also mid-upper and rear ventral gun positions. It was powered by two Napier Lion engines and the prototype was first flown by Arthur Wilcockson in October 1923. Forty-six were built.

The Hyderabad of 1923 was Handley Page's first multi-engined bomber to appear after the First World War. This example, J8813, was the only one to be fitted with leading edge slats during experiments with automatic slots in 1928.

Early examples of the Hyderabad had a rounded type of fin and rudder as used on the W.8b but later production machines had the W.10-style angular fin and rudder. Bombs were carried externally in carriers below the wings and fuselage. The Hyderabad first went into service in December 1925 with 99 Squadron at Bircham Newton. No.10 Squadron at Upper Heyford re-equipped with the Hyderabad in January 1928 and it was also used by two auxiliary squadrons. It was a popular aircraft with its crews due to its pleasant handling characteristics and manoeuvrability. Accidents occurred but the Hyderabad had what must be a unique record among RAF service aircraft of the inter-war period – not one was involved in a fatal accident in its career which lasted until 1933, when the last example was retired. One Hyderabad, J8813, became the first large aircraft to be fitted with automatic leading edge slats when it was used for slot development in 1928.

One former Hyderabad crew member retained a love of this aircraft from his first acquaintance with it in 1926 until the end of his days in the 1990s. Denis Newman wrote some wonderful articles about it for the Handley Page Association newsletter in his very individual style. The accompanying extract gives a flavour of his thoughts on the Hyderabad.

Denis Newman's Memories of the Hyderabad

My RAF career began with three years training near Winchester, with nearby Worthy Down supplying the flying scene. On my sixteenth birthday came my first flight – in a Bristol Fighter. But there seemed to be something missing, for during the Great War there were occasions when harsh reality penetrated my young mind. The sight of Mother silently going through the casualty lists in the daily papers, for my father and my elder brother were both serving officers. Surely nothing could touch them? There were too many sombre periods when adults gathered. Then suddenly, the great morale booster, the name of Handley Page! Aeroplanes which would teach the evil enemy a thing or two and the name assumed magic proportions in my young mind.

In 1925, under a newspaper heading 'Leviathan of the Air', was the announcement that the RAF had accepted a new giant Handley Page bomber into its fold which was to be named Hyderabad. There were no photographs, but when at Worthy Down next year for air experience with radio in Bristols, I had my first sight of the new machine, conspicuous with its vivid green colour. We had no opportunity for a close inspection but I noted that, like the Vickers Victoria, it boasted a cabin and, although the span was less than the Vickers, it was a Handley Page aircraft and that was good enough for me! A little later I saw a flight of them at the Hendon display, but imagine my feelings when posted to 99 Squadron at Bircham Newton, the first to be equipped with them.

In September 1926 I was introduced to J7746, 'my' aeroplane, although the first pilot made it clear that he had no use for radio and said bluntly that he did not wish to see me again. However, at first it was enough to clamber all over, sit in every seat and examine every detail. My pilot's attitude greatly restricted my flying compared with that of my friends, but my first experiences were remarkable enough. On 10 September I managed to sneak on board for two short flights, to feel the power of the two Napier Lion engines, admire the taut, smooth fabric of the wings, the stability and the freedom of movement within the machine. Then followed an order to fit radio and be prepared for a flight to Northolt with another machine. The pilots were seated in tandem with the nose gunner's cockpit below and in front, with a crawlway from the cabin. The radio was fitted at floor level so that the operator was obliged to lie upon his right side to use the Morse key – decidedly uncomfortable. A waving hand with a message from the second pilot/navigator to attract attention was frequently changed to a kick on the head from a heavy flying boot. The advantage of the flying position was quickly learned, that in fine weather the operator could stand up in the nose cockpit with an ideal view, leaving his open log book resting against the rounded portion betwixt him and the navigator above, the steady wind pressure holding the book firmly in place.

I was in the cabin when our arrival at Northolt was announced by the closing of throttles followed by a series of stresses and strains which had me baffled, just hanging on tight as the aircraft was slung about. No fear at all, simply wondering what on earth was going on. Then came agonising pain in my ears until happily I swallowed, and with a pop the pain vanished. I learned after that we had descended in a series of stall turns.

For the return flight the next day I was allocated the other aircraft J7741 with no radio duties, standing in the nose cockpit all the way. The captain of the aircraft was Sgt Mitchell, but the flight commander, Sqn Ldr Hargrave, had taken over the first pilot's cockpit, an event which could easily have made this my last flight. As we glided in to land there was no attempt to level out and we hit with a mighty bump, with the nose shooting up at a sharp angle. Both engines burst into life and we proceeded with a succession of lessening bumps until coming to rest. After a long silence, apart from the engines ticking over, the conversation went something like this:

'A bad landing Mitchell'.
'Yes sir'.
'Can't understand what you were doing'.
'Me sir? I didn't land it'.
'You are the captain of this machine and it was your duty to land and I left it to you'.
'But you took over my cockpit and flew us here and I naturally left it to you'.
No further comment!

The next time that I experienced stall turns was when arriving back at Bircham at 3,000ft with me in the nose looking down at a football match. The throttles closed and we flew steadily on. I turned to look up at the pilots, one gazing ahead and the other over the side. Suddenly the nose fell away and I grabbed frantically at the gun ring as my feet left the floor. I stood looking straight down at the football pitch when suddenly the floor lifted and my legs gave way and then I was looking at cloud. A swing over to port and down went the nose again and so on until low enough to resume normal flight and approach for landing. In later years I flew in many faster and highly manoeuvrable aeroplanes and, when it came to aerobatics, went through the book. But, for thrills, the Hyderabad won hands down. The great strains upon the wings, repeated again and again, assured our faith in the stamina of this remarkable aircraft.

The third HP28 Handcross J7500 at Cricklewood in 1925. The holes in the engine cowling were introduced to cure overheating during ground running and taxiing.

On 6 December 1924 the Handley Page **HP28 Handcross** took to the air for the first time, piloted by Hubert Broad. It was a large biplane with a wing span of 60ft and powered by a 650hp water-cooled Rolls-Royce Condor. Several designs were competing for an Air Ministry order for a two-seat long range landplane bomber. The Handcross carried bombs externally under the wings and also semi-buried in a fairing under the forward fuselage. The total bomb load was 550lb. Three prototypes were ordered, serial numbers J7498 to J7500.

After completing manufacturer's trials the first aircraft was delivered on 25 January 1925 to Martlesham Heath for service evaluation. The second aircraft, J7499, went to the Royal Aircraft Establishment at Farnborough for radio trials, while the third aircraft remained at Cricklewood to test modifications arising from the Martlesham trials. One such modification was the cutting of a number of circular holes in the engine cowling to improve cooling during ground running and taxiing, but some of these had to be blanked off again when problems arose with coolant freezing at high altitudes. The speed range of the Handcross was from 53mph to a maximum of 120mph.

The Handcross failed to win the competition, the winner being the Hawker Horsley. J7500 remained at Cricklewood until 1926 as a general trials aircraft and J7499 moved from Farnborough to Martlesham Heath where it flew with the Armaments Trial Flight until 1928.

Hinaidi II K1075 illustrates the slight sweep back on the outer wings, the main external difference from the Mk.I. The Mk.II also had a metal structure beneath the fabric covering whereas the Mk.I was all wood.

Following on from the Hyderabad came the HP33 **Hinaidi I** night bomber (named after an RAF base near Baghdad) which was very similar in external appearance to the earlier aircraft, apart from a change to 440hp Bristol Jupiter radial engines in place of the Napier Lions. The first Hinaidi I was actually a conversion from an early Hyderabad, J7745, and it first flew on 26 May 1927. Other conversions took place and the last six Hyderabads on the production line were completed as Hinaidi Is, making a total of fifteen of this model.

A significant design change came with the introduction of the HP36 Hinaidi II, which had a fabric covered metal structure in place of the wooden airframe of the earlier version. The change of material coincided with the arrival at Cricklewood of Ray 'Sandy' Sandifer, a specialist in steel and aluminium alloy structures (he finally retired from Handley Page in 1968 as assistant chief designer). The new model was also distinguished by a five degree sweepback on the outboard wing sections. This was to compensate for the rearward shift of the centre of gravity resulting from the change to the lighter Jupiter engines. Complaints had been received from the RAF of tail-heaviness with the Mark I version. The Hinaidi II also had automatic wing tip slots, which had been tested on Hyderabad J8813 but not used in production because the wooden front spar had not been designed for the additional stresses. The prototype Mark II aircraft made its first flight on 25 November 1931 with Tom England at the controls. Thirty-three production aircraft followed.

The first squadron to receive the Hinaidi in both its Mark I and Mark II forms was 99 Squadron and the type served until October 1935 when the Special Reserve 503 Squadron retired its last one. The Hinaidi had a largely unsung career, making few appearances at the Hendon shows, but 503 Squadron's aircraft took part in the RAF Jubilee Review on 6 July 1935.

The original Hinaidi I, J7745, distinguished itself in an unexpected role in Afghanistan in 1929. This silver painted Hinaidi was based with the RAF on the North-West Frontier of India in 1928. British residents in Kabul were advised to leave in December 1928 during the rebellion against King Amanullah and a large scale evacuation commenced. In company with Vickers Victorias of 70 Squadron the Hinaidi helped to fly out 586 people by the end of February 1929. Kabul is over 6,000ft above sea level and the route to Peshawar involved crossing a 10,000ft high mountain range. J7745 made eight return flights to Kabul carrying up to thirty-eight passengers at a time, with their luggage too. Compare this with the maximum of fourteen passengers carried in Imperial Airways' very similar W.8s and W.10s. Thereafter J7745 continued serving in India until 1934 with the RAF's Heavy Transport Flight.

Another single-engined design made its first flight on 24 February 1928, flown by Tom England. This was the HP34 **Hare**, built to a specification for two-seat high altitude day bomber. The engine was a Bristol Jupiter of 485hp. It was the first Handley Page aeroplane to use the combination of the sesquiplane layout and the Warren-girder struts in its 50ft span wings. In a system patented by the company there were no external rigging wires. Hawker, Gloster and Westland produced competing designs but none of these four contenders was destined to receive a production order.

An unfortunate incident occurred on the Hare's third flight when the seat collapsed during a steep turn. England made a heavy landing back at Cricklewood, followed shortly by the collapse of the undercarriage. The aircraft was repaired and changes made to the rudder and elevator to improve handling. At a later stage manually operated leading edge slats were fitted to the outer section of the upper wing, but there were never any trailing edge flaps fitted. Eventually automatic slots replaced the manual ones.

While the Hare was being prepared for trials at Martlesham Heath in the torpedo bombing role another serious crash occurred at Cricklewood when England landed fast after a flight with the slats locked. Although the touchdown was quite gentle the port undercarriage failed and the aircraft cartwheeled, badly damaging the wings. England finished up hanging in the inverted aircraft with petrol pouring everywhere, but fortunately he had switched off the ignition in time and no fire resulted.

The Hare was rebuilt yet again with further control modifications and it flew to Martlesham Heath on 10 June 1929. It returned to Cricklewood in October for a more powerful Jupiter engine to be fitted, together with full span slats. It performed some short take-off and landing trials at the new Radlett aerodrome in November (it was probably the last Handley Page aeroplane to fly out of Cricklewood aerodrome). More trials were conducted at Martlesham but the new Hawker Hart ruled out any further interest in the Hare as a day bomber. It also marginally lost out to the Vickers Vildebeest as a torpedo bomber.

Following a final modification to fit an Armstrong Siddeley Panther engine the Hare was sold to a Mr J.N. Addinsell and appeared on the civil register as G-ACEL in March 1933. Addinsell was planning a long-distance flight in the Hare but dropped the idea. The aircraft was abandoned at Hanworth and, following much attention from vandals, was scrapped in 1937.

Built in parallel with the Hinaidi was a transport derivative, the **HP35 Clive**. The Clive I, J9126, first flew in February 1928. It was powered by two Bristol Jupiters and used the basic wooden structure of the Hyderabad, but with the wing configuration of the Hinaidi II with its slightly swept back outer section. The front fuselage was longer than the Hinaidi's and windows were fitted in the cabin. It could carry seventeen troops or, if required, it could be fitted with racks under the wings for up to 1,300lb of bombs. Lewis gun positions were provided in the nose and mid-upper fuselage.

Two more Clives were built. They were known as Clive IIs and had the metal structure of the Hinaidi II. J9948 was the first and it took to the air for the first time in March 1930. They were used by the RAF in India. The Clive I was eventually furnished for passenger carrying as the Clive III for a proposed London to Belfast service. This did not come to pass and in April 1933 the aircraft was sold to Sir Alan Cobham for joy-riding and flight-refuelling experiments as G-ABYX. On one busy day it carried 1,008 passengers in forty-eight flights. By the time it was scrapped in November 1935 it had carried over 120,000 passengers.

The HP34 Hare featured an all strut-braced wing and leading edge slats. It was a contender for separate requirements for a high altitude bomber and a torpedo carrier, but no production order was received.

The Clive was a bomber-transport derivative of the Hinaidi. This is J9948 in March 1930, one of two Clive IIs with a fabric covered metal structure. The bomb racks below the wing are each carrying three bombs in tandem.

One more large biplane bomber was to be produced by Handley Page, and it was destined to be the last of the RAF's biplane bombers. The HP38 **Heyford** prototype, J9130, made its first flight at Radlett on 12 June 1930. It was a radical departure from the conventional biplane layout. In the interests of aerodynamic efficiency, George Volkert, assisted by Harold Boultbee, sought to achieve an uncluttered upper surface on both upper and lower wings. This was done by attaching the fuselage to the bottom of the upper wing. The two Rolls-Royce Kestrel engines were also slung below the upper wing. The lower wing was therefore placed in relatively undisturbed air below the fuselage. Two large main wheels were enclosed in neat fairings below and ahead of the lower wing. The question of where to put the bombs was resolved by thickening the centre section of the lower wing between the wheels to provide for internal bomb stowage. Additional external bomb racks could be fitted outboard of the undercarriage. The general structure followed the convention of the time – fabric covering over a metal framework, except that the front fuselage was a metal monocoque 'bathtub' design. The overall design resulted in a good performance, although there was a limit to the size of bomb which could be carried.

Another novel feature of the Heyford was the lower gunner's position. He would climb into a cylindrical 'dustbin' equipped with a Lewis gun and the whole thing would be lowered from within the fuselage. It was rotatable and gave the gunner a large field of fire. One interesting point about the lowering mechanism is that it made use of bungee cords. When testing the system on the ground it was important to have a man or equivalent weight inside otherwise the turret would be forcefully catapulted against the top of the fuselage! (It has been said that all Handley Page aeroplanes had bungee somewhere – even the early Jetstreams had it in the door counterbalance system.) Other defensive gun positions were in the nose and mid-upper fuselage. All the gunners and the two pilots in their open cockpit had an excellent all-round view.

The aircraft went into production as the HP50 Heyford Mk.1, which differed from the HP38 prototype in having uprated Kestrels and a cleaner design of engine nacelle. Thirty-eight of this model were built and the first squadron to receive them was, like the Hyderabad and Hinaidi before, No.99 which was then based at Upper Heyford in Oxfordshire. Minor improvements to later aircraft in this first batch led to their being termed Mk.1As.

The last Mk.1A off the production line, K3503, was used by Handley Page in 1934 to further refine the design. Drag reducing modifications and more powerful Kestrel engines increased the maximum speed from around 138 to 154mph. An enclosed

A Heyford I on display at Hendon in 1933 shows its unusual design. The lightweight ladder was a necessary piece of equipment for many maintenance operations and was stowed on board the aircraft. The photo also shows the sides of the engine cowling hinged down for use as working platforms. Just visible behind is the HP39 Gugnunc.

Heyford Mk.I serial number K3500 of 99 Squadron. It shows the rotatable 'dustbin' gun turret in the lowered position. The Lewis guns in the nose and mid-upper fuselage positions are also manned.

cockpit for the pilots was also tried but not adopted for production. This aircraft became the prototype of the Heyford Mk.II, of which sixteen were built. The final production version was the Mk.III, which again used K3503 as a prototype. It had uprated Kestrels with improved steam condenser cooling. Seventy Mk.IIIs were built.

The Heyford was well liked in service. It had no vices in the air and was even looped on several occasions, notably by one of 102 Squadron's aircraft at the RAF Display at Hendon in 1935, where the spectators could hardly believe their eyes. It was also easy to maintain in service, even if some of the maintenance operations had to take place well above the ground.

At the Royal Jubilee Review in July 1935, Heyfords led the massed flypast at Duxford in front of King George V. Earlier that year the Heyford had the honour of taking part in the first demonstration of the use of radar to detect an aircraft in flight. Dr Robert Watson-Watt in association with the BBC's transmitting station at Daventry detected echoes from K6902 using an early form of radar receiver.

One incident that occurred in December 1936 showed up the vulnerability of aircraft to airframe icing. Some of 102 Squadron's aircraft were returning to Finningley from an armament practice camp at Aldergrove when they encountered intense icing in cloud over the Pennines. Only one arrived at its destination that day. Two successfully force-landed and flew home the next day. Two were badly damaged during attempted forced-landings. One crew had to bale out when severe icing made the aircraft uncontrollable and K6900 suffered a fatal crash on a hill top, with three of the four crew killed. Subsequently the Mk.III Heyford K5184, which had been engaged in flight-refuelling experiments at Farnborough, came to be used in early trials of the TKS liquid de-icing system. This aircraft later participated in catapult launching experiments at Farnborough in December 1940.

The Heyford never had to drop bombs in anger but up to the start of the war several were still in use as navigation and gunnery trainers. Two (including Farnborough's K5184) remained on RAF charge until April 1941 when they completed towing trials with the General Aircraft Hotspur glider. One of these

The HP43 bomber-transport of 1932 shows its close resemblance to the HP42 airliner. The wing span was reduced by removing the centre section of the upper wing. Three Bristol Pegasus engines replaced the four Jupiters of the HP42. The fuselage was a new much simpler fabric covered design.

Heyfords was put in store, but not flown, at Cardington until at least August 1944. It was even kept under armed guard!

A few more one-off designs were produced in the 1930s, with varying degrees of success. When Handley Page tendered for the HP42, they also offered Imperial Airways a smaller three-engined version. With the acceptance of the HP42 the company was left with the smaller design just as the Air Ministry issued requirements for a bomber-transport. It was built as the **HP43** and first flew with Jim Cordes at the controls on 21 July 1932. It had a simpler fuselage than the HP42 with a fabric covered metal tubular structure. The upper wing was similar to the HP42 but had the centre section removed and a single Bristol Pegasus engine mounted below the mid point. The anhedral inner sections of the lower wings were correspondingly shortened and the two lower Pegasus were in similar positions to the Jupiters of the HP42. The low cruising speed did not make it an attractive proposition for the customer, but the HP43 was later to re-emerge in another guise.

One of the company's least successful designs to take to the air was the **HP46** naval torpedo bomber, built to a 1931 Air Ministry requirement. It was a 50ft span biplane (the company's last biplane design) with a flat upper wing and the lower wing downswept as far as the undercarriage, as with the HP42. This was to provide a reasonable gap between the wings and to keep the undercarriage short. It was powered by a Rolls-Royce Buzzard and from its first flight in October 1932 it was beset by control problems. Although the requirement was soon superseded the Air Ministry wished the HP46 to continue with research into low speed flight controls – it was fully slotted and flapped. The control difficulties were never satisfactorily resolved and the aircraft had faded into obscurity by 1935, after only five and a half hours in the air. The only known photographs of the HP46 are some clandestine ones taken by an apprentice of the time, Bert 'Corny' Cornthwaite. This may well be an indication that the company was keen to forget it!

The next single-engined design from Handley Page was the **HP47**. It was designed to a requirement for a general purpose aeroplane to undertake a multiplicity of tasks to include day and night bombing, dive bombing, torpedo bombing, reconnaissance, army co-operation and casualty evacuation. Several companies built contenders and Handley Page's entry was a low wing monoplane designed under the leadership of Gus Lachmann. It featured a highly tapered wing, a hallmark of Lachmann's monoplane designs of the 1930s, and the engine was a Bristol Pegasus. The wings were fitted with full-span leading edge slats, slotted flaps and ailerons. The pilot sat well forward in an open cockpit and an observer/gunner occupied an aft-facing cockpit amidships. The space in the fuselage between the two crew members could be used for stretchers. Aft of the wing the fuselage tapered to a narrow boom.

Structurally the aircraft was an advance over previous Handley Page types with the increased use of metal in the wing structure. The leading edge skin formed a 'D' torsion box with the main spar and the inner section of the wing was all metal skinned. The outer wing sections were fabric covered aft of the main spar. The front fuselage was a semi-monocoque structure, covered in a thin aluminium alloy skin with corrugations in the Junkers style (Lachmann was very familiar with this from his work in Germany).

The HP47 was flown for the first time on 27 November 1933 by Tom England and early flight trials showed that the rudder and elevator control loads were too heavy. These were progressively improved by increasing the size and adding aerodynamic or mass balances where necessary.

The HP47 went to Martlesham Heath in April 1935 where the A&AEE criticised its longitudinal stability and trimming ability, which had to be cured. All the effort was to no avail, because the Handley Page monoplane narrowly missed out on the produc-

Not many photographs exist of the HP46 torpedo bomber which proved to be a difficult beast in the air. It was one which Handley Page were happy to forget!

tion order to the Vickers 253 biplane (Vickers subsequently had the order transferred to their newer monoplane, the Wellesley). The HP47 was delivered to Farnborough in March 1936 where RAE continued investigations into its slow flying abilities. After a final spell of engine development work the HP47 was scrapped in May 1937.

The HP43 bomber-transport referred to earlier was developed from the HP42 and was itself to be further developed as a contender for a later bomber-transport specification. Monoplanes were now in the ascendancy and so the HP43 fuselage, still with its front and rear gun positions, was fitted with a new design tapered monoplane wing (again showing the Lachmann influence). It had two cleanly cowled Armstrong Siddeley Tiger engines of 700hp each and the tail unit was similar to that of the HP43 but of larger span. Known as the **HP51**, it retained the serial number J9833 of its predecessor and was first flown on 8 May 1935 by Jim Cordes, who was now chief test pilot following the departure of Tom England.

The HP51 could carry thirty troops in bench seats in the fuselage or 4,000lb of bombs externally. Various modifications took place including replacement of the engines by more powerful Bristol Pegasus and refinements to the fins and rudders. It did not go into production as such (the Bristol Bombay won that particular contest) but it led to the very similar Harrow bomber-transport of 1936. The HP51 was used for early flight refuelling trials in 1937 and continued to serve as a military trials aircraft until 1940.

The late 1930s saw an interesting piece of research by George Volkert into the concept of the high speed unarmed bomber. As proposed it was a twin-engined aircraft of very clean aerodynamic design and powered by two Napier Sabre engines. This was 1937 and at least a year before de Havilland presented their proposal for what was to become the Mosquito. A memorandum to the Air Staff summarised the advantages of the unarmed bomber over the twin-engined 'heavies' being designed to Specification P13/36 (which eventually led to the four-engined Halifax and Lancaster).

The memorandum emphasised the superior performance and manoeuvrability, the

The HP47 general purpose bomber/reconnaissance aircraft of 1933. It is seen here at Radlett with Slaughter's Farm in the background. The farm was demolished early in the Second World War to make way for aerodrome expansion.

The HP51 was produced from the HP43 by replacing the biplane wings with a new monoplane wing. The design was further refined to produce the Harrow bomber-transport.

increased bomb load and the fact that fewer crew members were required. For example, the Volkert (as it has been called) over a 3,000 mile range would carry 7,000lb of bombs against the P13/36's 3,500lb. The aircraft would also be lighter and faster. Much correspondence followed and official opinion varied from partial acceptance to rejection. In due course the negative view prevailed and work on the Volkert ceased. The eventual acceptance of the Mosquito might well have been assisted by the thought provoking correspondence on the Handley Page proposal a year or two earlier.

Three more Handley Page bomber types were to make their debuts in the 1930s, and these are the subject of the next chapter.

Chapter 7

The Second World War – More Big Bombers

Apart from the relatively minor roles played by the Heyford described in the previous chapter, three other Handley Page aeroplanes were to participate in RAF operations during the Second World War. The Harrow, ordered to a specification for an interim bomber-transport in 1935, saw service as a transport throughout the war years. The Hampden medium bomber was one element of the RAF's front line bomber force at the outbreak of war in 1939, and the Halifax four-engined heavy bomber played a major role in the RAF's strategic bombing campaign from 1941 until the end of the war. It also served in other roles and operated in all the war theatres.

The previous chapter showed how the HP42 airliner evolved first into a biplane bomber-transport (HP43) and then into a monoplane version (HP51). A further clean up of the design resulted in the **HP54 Harrow**, which retained the highly tapered wing with a slight reduction in span to 88ft 5in. It was originally submitted for a bomber-transport requirement but the call for rapid re-armament in the mid 1930s resulted in the Harrow being ordered as a stop-gap bomber to make up a shortfall in the number of bomber squadrons. This required the provision of under-floor cells for up to 3,000lb of bombs without compromising its ability to carry twenty troops in a secondary transport role. The prototype first flew on 10 October 1936 with Cordes at the controls and with an order for 100 machines already signed. Service trials at Martlesham Heath began at the end of November.

New features on the Harrow included power operated gun turrets in the nose and tail, variable pitch propellers and steam heating for the cabin. There was also a mid-upper gun position under a plexi-glass cupola which was rotatable but not powered. The whole design was aimed at rapid production using Handley Page's newly developed 'split-construction' method. The engines were Pegasus Xs on the Mk.1 Harrow and more powerful Pegasus XXs on the Mk.II. Some Mk.1s were later converted to Mk.II standard.

Deliveries to 214 Squadron at Feltwell commenced on 13 January 1937. One of this squadron's aircraft, K6940, had to return to Radlett on 25 March and during its final approach the main wheels hit the top of a passing LMS express train. The aircraft eventually came to rest among the gravel pits beyond the airfield, fortunately with no serious injuries to the crew. Nobody in the train was hurt despite the kitchen car losing most of its roof. The Harrow was a write-off.

The final Harrow was delivered in December 1937 and by then Nos 37, 75, 115, 214 and 215 Squadrons were equipped with the aircraft. They served as bombers

The Second World War – More Big Bombers

The Harrow fulfilled an interim role as a bomber during the years of re-armament in the late 1930s. It is exemplified here by Mk.1 K6947.

Replacing the front and rear turrets of the Harrow with smooth fairings produced the *Sparrow* transport which served throughout the Second World War. The Harrow was unusual in having the main entry door on the starboard side.

until the early weeks of the war by which time the squadrons had re-equipped with Wellingtons. The Harrows did not take part in any bombing operations and soon went into temporary storage where many were converted back to the full transport role. Others continued to be used for crew and gunnery training. Some of the transports joined the newly-formed 271 Squadron at Doncaster whose duties included supporting the allied forces in France and Belgium in the weeks before the Dunkirk evacuation. Some of these transport Harrows were further modified by having their nose and tail turrets replaced by smooth fairings. They then became unofficially known as 'Sparrows'. The transports remained in service until the end of the war and were often in the thick of the action after D-Day on casualty evacuation duties. On 1 January 1945 several of them were destroyed on the ground at Brussels airport during a German air attack.

Harrows were also used for a number of special trials, some interesting and some slightly bizarre. Before the war three aircraft were given civil registrations and used by Sir Alan Cobham's Flight Refuelling Ltd for aerial tanker development work. They were used to refuel Imperial Airways 'C' Class flying boats on experimental transatlantic mail services.

In the 'slightly bizarre' category was the formation of 93 Squadron in 1940 to test aerial mines as a defence against bomber formations. Five Harrows were modified to carry 'Long Aerial Mines' (LAMs) under the code name 'Pandora.' These were small explosive devices released along 2,000ft of cable trailing from the aircraft in the path of an approaching bomber stream. The idea was that the bombers would strike the long wires and the charges would be released to slide down the wires and explode on impact with the aircraft. They were deployed in October 1940 and the Harrows, with only the pilot aboard, waited at 17,000ft under the direction of ground control. On intercepting the enemy they would turn across their path and try to entangle them. Four or five kills were officially credited (though this is doubted) but it seems that the LAMs did more damage to the Harrows when chain reactions of exploding mines came right up to the aircraft. Fortunately all the Harrows returned safely, usually with large areas of fabric missing! The experiments continued with Douglas Havocs but were soon abandoned.

While the Harrow was being pressed into service as an interim solution to ease the bomber shortage, another twin-engined bomber design was progressing at Handley Page. Designed to a 1932 specification (number B9/32) for a day bomber the HP52 **Hampden** introduced more advanced features such as an all metal monocoque construction. It was also the first Handley Page aeroplane to have a retractable undercarriage. Once again a sharply tapered monoplane wing design was chosen which had a span of 69ft and, in another reminder of its HP47 predecessor, the crew were housed in a deep forward fuselage. The lower part of the front fuselage contained the bomb bay, which could hold a 4,000lb bomb load. Aft of the wing the fuselage tapered to a slim boom which carried the twin-finned tail unit. Two Bristol Pegasus engines drove three-bladed de Havilland variable-pitch propellers.

Split-construction techniques had been further developed for the Hampden. George Volkert and works manager James Hamilton worked closely together to

Memories of the Harrow. By Sqn Ldr E.G. Libbey

I met up with the Harrow in 1939 at RAF Evanton, north of Inverness. I was given a quick conversion (two circuits and landings) and then did a lot of flying on them with loads of would-be air gunners trying their luck on towed targets. I had several narrow squeaks with various mechanical failures, but especially with a particularly keen gunner who all but shot the tail off the aircraft!

Early in 1940 I was posted to 271 (Transport) Squadron at RAF Doncaster which had a mixed bag of aircraft including HP42s and Harrows. The Harrows came to us completely stripped inside. The turrets, dual controls, bombing equipment, etc, had all been removed. Some were Sparrows with nose and tail streamlined into points. The stability of these aircraft in the air was remarkable. Nothing seemed to affect it, the proverbial herd of elephants could rush from front to rear and back again without causing any undue upset! I made numerous flights all over Great Britain and into France (before it was overrun) with mixed loads, without too many qualms.

I did, however, have one unfortunate occurrence which resulted in the loss of a Harrow. I collected a replacement aircraft from a Maintenance Unit in the south and proceeded to head north. The compass was not all it should have been and the weather was deteriorating rapidly. I ended up at about 200ft in fog with one engine packing up. I had little alternative therefore but to force-land. I hurriedly picked a field and landed surprisingly well but soon discovered that the field had a slope down towards a main road and my brakes were no longer working. We ended up with a bang against a high grass bank in a corner of the field with most of one wing across the road. Luckily neither I nor the solitary airman who had accompanied me were injured. I was rather amused shortly afterwards when a police car arrived on the scene and an angry sergeant emerged and demanded that I remove the wing right away as it was blocking the traffic! It was of course later removed along with the rest of the aircraft by the RAF.

ensure that a smooth flow of major components reached the assembly line when and where needed. This may seem an obvious thing to do now but in the 1936 aviation business it was an innovation. The narrow tail boom was made in two halves, as though sliced vertically down the middle. The halves were only mated together once all the control runs and wiring had been installed. The wing centre section acted as the foundation upon which were attached the outer wings, engine nacelles, fuel tanks, undercarriage and the completed front, centre and rear fuselage sections. There were no power operated gun turrets in the Hampden. Single hand-aimed Vickers K-guns were fitted in the nose and in the upper and lower rear gunners stations which occupied the position where the fuselage narrowed to the tail boom. The rear guns were later doubled up to twin gun mountings.

The pilot sat in a fighter type cockpit in the deep but narrow front fuselage. The narrowness would sometimes cause difficulties during emergency situations on operations, but an incapacitated pilot could be removed from his seat by lowering the back of the seat.

The first flight of the prototype, K4240, was carried out by Maj. Cordes on 21 June 1936. Within two weeks it had been shown in the New Types Park at the

RAF Display at Hendon. The nose glazing had been discreetly covered to hide the 'secret' equipment inside. 'The Aeroplane' editor C.G. Grey remarked to Jim Cordes that it looked like a flying suit case. 'Oh yes', said Cordes, 'it's a perfect Revelation'.

A second prototype was also constructed. It was known as the **HP53** and had its origins in a Swedish requirement for a coastal patrol aircraft to be equipped with floats, wheels or skis. Continued indecision by the Swedish government led to a change in the contract whereby the fifth production aircraft would be supplied which the Swedes could modify as they saw fit. It was delivered to them in 1938. Plans to build seventy Hampdens in Sweden were dropped.

Production aircraft differed from the two prototypes in having a more rounded perspex moulding on the nose and increased dihedral on the outer wings to improve lateral stability. To complement production by the parent company orders were also placed with English Electric at Preston and the Canadian Associated Aircraft Group. The first production aircraft was L4032 which Cordes first flew on 21 June 1938. It was used for the official naming ceremony at Radlett on 24 June when Viscountess Hampden declared 'I name you Hampden, and may the spirit of John Hampden, defender of civil liberties, inspire all those who fly in you'. A union flag falling from the nose and a wire guided bottle of champagne completed the ceremony, after which everyone went outside to watch Cordes give a flying demonstration.

The sole example of the HP53 had first flown with Pegasus engines but was taken over by Short Brothers & Harland in Belfast to be re-engined with Napier Daggers. This was to lead to an order for 150 of a version of the Hampden with these engines. It was known as the **Hereford** and retained the Hampden's designation HP52. The

The Hampden prototype at Radlett in 1937 being made ready for despatch to Martlesham Heath for service evaluation trials. On production aircraft the nose glazing was more rounded and smooth, not like the birdcage arrangement of the prototypes. The outer wings were also given more dihedral.

An unusual view of an early production Hampden photographed in March 1939 from the nose of another by flight observer Ginger Wright.

Dagger was an air-cooled in-line engine with four banks of six cylinders in 'H' formation driving twin crankshafts. It proved to be very difficult to cool the rearmost cylinders, leading to unreliability. The Hereford therefore was not used on operations and had to be restricted to training duties. It was probably better that they were limited to shorter flights because the scream from the high-revving Daggers would not have been popular on long operations. Twenty Herefords were later converted to Hampden standard. In another investigation into alternative powerplants there was a trial conversion in 1941 to produce the HP62 **Hampden II** with American Wright Cyclone engines, but it did not go into production.

The first two production Hampdens went to Martlesham Heath in August 1938 for acceptance trials. Production built up rapidly and by the end of the year thirty-six had been delivered to Nos 49 and 83 Squadrons at Scampton and 50 Squadron at Waddington. When war broke out on 3 September 1939 ten squadrons had been equipped. The two Scampton squadrons were despatched on the very first day on an abortive search for the German fleet. One of No.83's aircraft was piloted by Guy Gibson, later of 'Dambusters' fame. It was not to be very long before the defensive firepower of the Hampden was found to be hopelessly inadequate for daylight operations. On 29 September 1939 five out of eleven aircraft of 144 Squadron were shot down by fighters during an anti-shipping patrol off the coast of the Heligoland Bight. The Air Staff were then convinced that the Hampden and other twin-engined bombers in the RAF inventory could not defend themselves against fighters in daylight, and they were switched to night-time only operations.

An early Hampden on test with chief test pilot Maj. James Cordes at the controls. The dihedral introduced on the outer wings and the production standard nose are evident.

Hampdens continued in the bombing role until 1942 and helped to make up the psychologically important number of 1,000 bombers for the big raids that year on Cologne, Essen and Bremen. The last bombing raid by Hampdens was on 14/15 September 1942 when 408 Squadron of the Royal Canadian Air Force attacked Wilhelmshaven. By then many had been modified to carry torpedoes and undertook anti-shipping tasks until the end of 1943, after which they faded from front line RAF service. Total production, including the Herefords, had amounted to 1,582.

The solitary Hampden bought by Sweden in 1938 was used for various duties during the war and in 1945 it was acquired by SAAB and given the Swedish civil registration SE-APD. It was used in the development of electronic equipment until 1947, making it the longest serving Hampden of them all. Another Hampden was retained by the Air Ministry in the UK as a possible museum exhibit, but sadly it was deemed to be taking up too much space and was broken up at Bovingdon in 1956.

The Hampden played its part in establishing the RAF's offensive capability in the early stages of the Second World War, but Handley Page's greatest contribution to the war effort was the **Halifax** four-engined heavy bomber. It arose from specification P13/36 issued in 1936 for a twin-engined medium bomber able to carry a maximum of 8,000lb of bombs for a distance of 2,000 miles at a cruising speed of

For Valour – The Hampden VCs

Two Victoria Crosses were awarded to Hampden crew members out of a total of nineteen for the whole of Bomber Command. The first was to Flt Lt (later Wg Cdr) **Roderick Learoyd** *and it was also the first to be awarded to any member of Bomber Command.*

At 8 p.m. on the night of 12 August 1940 eleven Hampdens of 49 and 83 Squadrons set off from Scampton to raid a heavily defended aqueduct on the Dortmund-Ems Canal. Four of the aircraft mounted a diversion raid elsewhere and two others failed to locate the target. Learoyd's aircraft, P4403, was the last of the five which carried out the attack. Of the four which went before him two had been shot down and two managed to limp home after being damaged. Learoyd pressed on regardless through a hail of flak and, although blinded by searchlights, he attacked the target in a dive at 300ft, dropping a delayed action bomb near the aqueduct. The aircraft's hydraulic system was badly damaged, leaving it without operable flaps or undercarriage. Learoyd nursed the Hampden back to Scampton where he arrived at 2 a.m. As he would not risk a belly landing in the dark he continued to circle the airfield until first light at about 5 a.m., when he finally achieved a smooth landing.

*Sgt **John Hannah** was the second Hampden VC, in another Scampton-based aircraft, this time P1355 from 83 Squadron. On 15/16 September 1940 the aircraft, under the command of Pilot Officer Connor, was attacking barges at Antwerp. During its second bombing run at 2,000ft the Hampden was hit by several shells and a fierce fuel fire erupted. This soon spread to the rear fuselage where a large hole appeared in the floor when the aluminium melted. The rear gunner baled out through this hole. The navigator in the front of the aircraft also baled out. Eighteen year old Hannah, despite his burning clothes and parachute, remained with the aircraft and smothered some of the flames, with ammunition exploding in the heat. He then forced open a jammed door, grabbed two fire extinguishers and when they were exhausted beat out the remaining flames with his log book.*

Although badly burned he went forward to assist Connor who brought the aircraft home, despite two holed fuel tanks. Hannah was awarded the VC, the youngest airman ever to receive the award. Connor received the DFC but was killed on operations a few weeks later. Hannah's health never really recovered and he was invalided out of the RAF in 1942.

L6002, the first production Hereford built by Short Brothers and Harland which first flew at Belfast in May 1939. The Napier Dagger engines distinguish this model from the standard Hampden. Only 150 were built because of the unreliability of the engine.

not less than 275mph. Service ceiling was to be a very optimistic 28,000ft and defensive gun turrets were to be fitted. There was a long list of other requirements including a multi-role capability. A particular powerplant was specified – the Rolls-Royce Vulture 24-cylinder X-type engine of 1,760hp.

Avro submitted a design which was to go into production as the Manchester. Handley Page's equivalent was the HP56, a slightly smaller development of the projected HP55 designed to a 1935 specification (B1/35). Two prototypes of the HP56, L7244 and L7245, were ordered. The Air Staff took a huge risk with the undeveloped but very powerful Vulture and it was a risk which did not pay off. Once it became clear that the Vulture was going to be a troublesome engine and subject to delays in delivery, Volkert produced schemes for other engine installations and eventually obtained approval for a design with four Rolls-Royce Merlins. A contract was awarded in September 1937 and the result was the HP57 Halifax. It was a twin-finned design with a wing span of 98ft 10in and a length of 70ft 1in. Meanwhile Avro continued with the Manchester which was to be plagued in service by the unreliability of the Vulture. They did however get the opportunity later to do a major redesign with four Merlins which was also free of some of the constraints of P13/36. It was to become the Lancaster.

The prototype Halifax, L7244, was built at Cricklewood and transported to Bicester where it made its first flight on 25 October 1939 with Maj. Cordes at the controls, accompanied by E.A. 'Ginger' Wright as observer. No major problems came to light and the second prototype, L7245, first took to the air at Radlett on 17 August 1940. This second aircraft was more fully equipped internally and was

The prototype Halifax, L7244, which first flew at Bicester on 25 October 1939. No gun turrets were fitted to this aircraft.

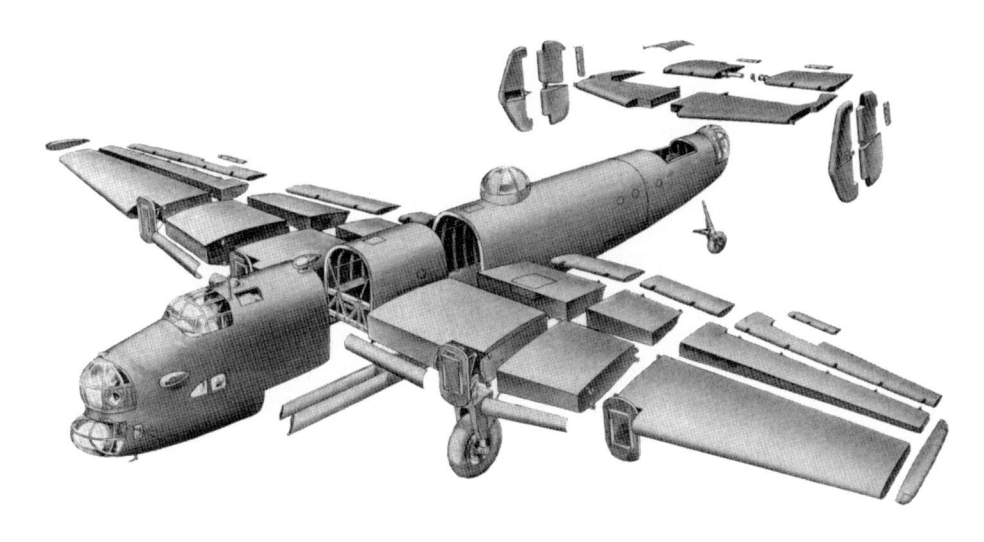

The main sub-assemblies of the Halifax showing how it all came together on the final assembly line using the technique of 'split construction'. The Halifax used for this illustration is an early B.II with the nose turret, the large Hudson type mid-upper turret and triangular fins.

fitted with 2-gun front and 4-gun rear Boulton-Paul power operated gun turrets. It was followed on 11 October by the first production Halifax B.I, L9485, which was soon despatched to Boscombe Down for trials. The total production of Mk.I Halifaxes was eighty-four. The original production model was known as the B.I Series 1. It had Merlin X engines and an all-up weight (AUW) of 55,000lb. Later machines were B.I Series II and III with the AUW increased to 60,000lb. The later Series IIIs had Merlin XXs and some B.Is had beam mounted machine guns for added defence. Early examples had leading edge slats on the outer wings but they were soon deleted to make way for barrage balloon cable cutters. Slotted wings were not seen as essential for the Halifax and any loss of landing performance was more than made up for by increasing the maximum available flap deflection angle.

The Halifax, like the Hampden, was designed for split construction. This was of great assistance in setting up production at several major sub-contractors who received large orders for Halifaxes. There was English Electric at Preston, Fairey Aviation at Stockport and Rootes Securities at Liverpool. There was also the London Aircraft Production Group (LAPG) which comprised bus and coach body builders around North London – Park Royal Coach Works, Express Motor & Body Works, Chrysler Motors and Duple Bodies. The LAPG aircraft were assembled and test flown at Leavesden, just a few miles from Radlett.

Another aid to production developed by Handley Page was photo-lofting. This entailed covering sheet metal in light sensitive emulsion so that templates could be reproduced photographically to a consistent accuracy by eliminating marking-out errors.

The first Halifax squadron was No.35 which became operational in March 1941 at Linton-on-Ouse in Yorkshire (the county where most of the Halifax squadrons would ultimately be based). This was about three months after the entry into service of the Short Stirling, the first of the RAF's Second World War 'heavies.' Halifaxes made their first operational sortie on the night of 10/11 March with a raid on Le Havre. There was some difficulty in locating the target and one Halifax received flak damage. Worse luck befell the crew of L9489. It had bombed the target but on its return it was misidentified by an RAF night fighter over Surrey and shot down. The following night two of 35 Squadron's Halifaxes attacked Hamburg. The last Halifax B.I, L9608, was completed on 12 September 1941 and was used for the official naming ceremony at Radlett by Viscountess Halifax. This was watched by many VIPs from the aviation world including Lt Col Moore-Brabazon, Minister of Aircraft Production and holder of the first British aviator's certificate to be awarded, and some of the early Handley Page pilots like Brackley, Douglas and Babington (who had first taken the O/100 'Bloody Paralyser' into the air in 1915).

Following on from the B.I was the HP59 Halifax B.II Series 1, first flown by Cordes on 3 July 1941. The beam guns were dispensed with and replaced by a mid-upper Boulton-Paul Type C twin-gun turret. This was the type of turret fitted to the Lockheed Hudson. It was large and added much weight and drag to the aircraft with a consequent loss of performance (the effect on the relatively small Hudson must have been even more severe). An interim 'clean-up' of the exterior resulted in the B.II Series I (Special). This had the nose turret removed (which was of limited defensive capability) and replaced by a plain aluminium fairing, known as the 'Tempsford' nose. The large mid-upper turret was either completely removed or replaced by the much more compact Boulton-Paul Type A four-gun turret, as fitted to the Defiant fighter. A further improvement came with the B.II Series 1A which had a clear all-perspex nose of better aerodynamic form and which also incorporated a hand-aimed Vickers K 'scare gun.' The Series 1A was also the first to introduce the larger 'square' fins and rudders to replace the original style triangular fins. A number of accidents to early Halifaxes had been attributed to the fins stalling at large yaw angles, as might occur during asymmetric flight with one or more engines shut down, particularly on approach to landing when airspeed would be reduced.

The different variants described above should not give the impression that a firm dividing line existed between them. Modifications were often tried on a small scale before becoming standardised in production. For example, some B.II Series 1As were delivered with triangular fins while others had square fins.

Changes were also happening within Handley Page because Jim Cordes resigned in July 1941 and his place as chief test pilot was taken by Flt Lt James R. Talbot.

Another significant variation on the Halifax B.II theme was meanwhile being produced by Rootes and Fairey. The large magnesium alloy castings for the Messier main undercarriage legs were not being produced as fast as required and Dowty were approached for an alternative. The result was a lighter (and correspondingly less robust) design of tubular construction and the Halifaxes with this undercarriage were known as B.Vs. These had equivalent variants to the Mk.II, namely the Series 1,

Series 1 (Special) and the Series 1A. The first B.V flew in October 1941. Total production of the B.II models was 1,977 aircraft. B.V production totalled 904.

At the beginning of 1942 concern was rising over the threat imposed by the German naval fleet to Allied shipping. The Tirpitz was known to be sheltering in a fjord near Trondheim and Prime Minister Winston Churchill was insistent that it should be a priority target. Among the RAF squadrons chosen for the task were the Halifax II equipped Nos 10, 35 and 76. They were despatched to Lossiemouth in Scotland to prepare for an arduous sortie which would involve a near maximum range flight over the North Sea. The target itself would be difficult to find in the desolate coastline with the possibility of fog and snow adding to the problems. After a number of abortive sorties thirty-two Halifaxes set out on 27 April 1942 carrying mines and bombs. The heavily defended battleship was attacked but unfortunately not put out of action for long. Two Halifaxes were lost. The crew of one aircraft, captained by Wg Cdr D.C.T. Bennett, baled out. The other, W1048 'S' of 35 Squadron, crash landed on the frozen surface of Lake Hoklingen, which allowed the crew to get out. The burning aircraft eventually sank through the ice and lay on the lake bed for the next thirty-one years. In 1973 it was raised by a group of volunteers, led by an RAF sub-aqua team, and brought back to England. It is now on display at the RAF Museum at Hendon in the condition in which it was raised.

LAPG-built Halifax B.II Series 1A at Leavesden. It has the smooth contoured all-perspex nose but still has the triangular fins. Later aircraft of this Series were fitted with square fins. Below the fuselage is the radome for the H2S radar scanner in its early transparent form. This aircraft is also fitted with flame dampers over the engine exhausts.

The last of 710 Halifaxes built by the London Aircraft Production Group, a B.III serial number PN460, was formally named *London Pride* on 16 April 1945. After the ceremony the guests were treated to a short flying display, some of which was clearly at a very low level!

Excluding the two prototypes a total of 2,965 of the Merlin-engined Halifaxes, the Marks I, II and V, were built. While doing an excellent job they were slightly lacking in performance. Weight increases without corresponding increases in power meant less of a margin in take-off performance. There were also penalties in climb rate, ceiling and cruising speed. They were, however, able to be used in North Africa and the Middle East under hot tropical conditions for which neither the Stirling nor the early Lancasters could be adapted. The introduction of the HP61 Halifax Mk.III brought about a marked improvement in performance. The major change was the replacement of the Rolls-Royce Merlins with Bristol Hercules radial engines. Other changes included the standardisation of the Defiant-type mid-upper turret and the introduction of a retractable tail wheel. Maximum AUW was increased to 65,000lb and most Mk.IIIs were built with rounded wing tips, which added over 5ft to the wing span. An H2S ground mapping radar scanner was mounted in a radome beneath the rear fuselage but this was sometimes replaced by a Frazer-Nash ventral gun turret. The first one, actually a converted Mk.II, R9534, first flew on 12 October 1942, while the first true production Mk.III, HX227, made its first flight in August 1943.

With all the modifications the Halifax Mk.III was transformed into a formidable aircraft, loved by its crews and with a capacity for other significant improvements which were to be denied it. For example all the stress calculations were done for a simple modification to the bomb bay roof beams comprising twenty-four gauge stiffening plates over lightening holes. This would have enabled the Halifax to carry the largest bombs, including the 22,000lb 'Grand Slam.' However, decisions made within the walls of the Air Ministry meant that the modification was not approved so the largest bombs that the Halifax could carry remained the 8,000lb 'Blockbusters.' The Mark III was built in greater numbers than any other version – 2091 in all.

The first Mk.IIIs to go into service were delivered to Nos 433 (Canadian) and 466 (Australian) Squadrons in November 1943 and were ultimately to equip forty-one operational squadrons. Later versions of the Mk.III with more powerful Hercules and improvements to the fuel system were known as the Mk.VI and Mk.VII.

Several Halifaxes went on to complete more than 100 operations. The most famous of these was B.III LV907 'F' of 158 Squadron based at Lissett in Yorkshire. It was taken on charge on 10 March 1944. The squadron code letter 'F' was allocated despite eight previous Halifaxes on the squadron carrying the 'F' code being lost in the preceding twelve months. Most crews on the squadron considered it an unlucky code except for its first allocated pilot, Sgt Smith. He insisted on keeping the code and had the Halifax named *Friday the 13th*. Not only that, the squadron artist adorned the nose with an upside down horseshoe, a ladder over the entry door, a broken mirror and a skull and crossbones. Near a scythe dripping blood was the legend 'As ye sow, so shall ye reap.' A bomb symbol on the nose was added after each operation, except for the 21st which was marked by a key (from the days when 21 signified the coming of age marked by presentation of the key to the door). It went on to complete 128 missions and was honoured after the war by being included in the 'Britain's Aircraft' exhibition on the bomb site that was once the John Lewis store in Oxford Street. It was scrapped soon afterwards and all that survives is a section of the nose skin with the artwork. This is in the RAF Museum at Hendon. The aircraft has more recently been honoured by the Yorkshire Aircraft Museum because their reproduction Halifax has been painted to represent *Friday the 13th*.

For Valour – The Halifax VC

The Nuremburg raid of 30/31 March 1944 saw Bomber Command suffer its worst disaster, with 96 out of 795 aircraft failing to return. Halifax B.III LK797, named 'Excalibur' and flown by P/O **Cyril Barton**, *was one of twelve aircraft from 578 Squadron which took off that night from their base at Burn in Yorkshire. About seventy miles from the target an attack by a Ju88 followed shortly by an Me210 put the Halifax's guns and intercom out of action and caused serious damage to an engine and fuel tanks. In the confusion the navigator, bomb aimer and wireless operator baled out and, although unable to contact the remaining crew, Barton continued to the target and released the bombs himself.*

As he turned for home the propeller detached from the damaged engine but he pressed on, steering by the stars and compass and his captain's map. He finally crossed the English coast low on fuel at Sunderland, about ninety miles north of Burn. Suddenly the two port engines died and, too low to bale out and with only one engine remaining, he crash landed at Ryhope Colliery in County Durham and hit a row of houses. Barton died soon after the crash but the other three remaining crew survived. Cyril Barton received a posthumous award of the Victoria Cross, the only crew member of a Halifax to do so.

Woodbridge aerodrome, Suffolk, in March 1945 during preparations for the Rhine crossing, 'Operation Varsity'. The station was closed for five days while two Halifax squadrons towed in sixty-eight Hamilcar and Horsa gliders. Here they have all been carefully positioned for take-off in quick succession.

It was not only as a bomber that the Halifax was successful. It proved to be easily adaptable to other roles such as maritime reconnaissance where, for example, the equivalent of the B.V bomber version would be called the G.R.V, the 'G.R.' standing for General Reconnaissance. It also excelled with the airborne forces as a paratroop carrier and glider tug, making light work of the General Aircraft Hamilcar heavy assault glider. The Halifax was the only aircraft cleared for towing the Hamilcar. The airborne forces aircraft were designated A.VII and A.IX, the latter having a better arrangement for paratroop and supply dropping with an exit door in the lower rear fuselage. A dedicated transport version was known as the C.VIII. In this model a large removable pannier was fitted underneath the bomb bay.

The 'missing' Mark of Halifax was the B.IV which was a modified B.II with Merlin 65s and the inboard engine nacelles extended aft to protrude beyond the wing trailing edge. It had an improved performance over the Mk.II but did not go into production. The grand total of all models was 6,176 plus the two prototypes.

With the end of hostilities in 1945 the Halifax bomber squadrons were soon run down but Halifaxes continued in use as transports and for reconnaissance duties. The last ones in squadron use were the G.R.VIs of 224 Squadron Coastal Command based at Gibraltar. These served in the meteorological reconnaissance role until March 1952. The very last Halifax in use was an A.IX, RT936, which served at Henlow with the Parachute Test Unit until 1954.

Dinkum – The Flight Observer Spaniel

Ginger Wright, wind tunnel engineer turned flight test observer, had a pet dog going by the name of Dinkum. This very portly black spaniel was very much a member of the experimental flight test team in the latter stages of the Second World War. Most of the effort was then on the further military development of the Halifax and its peacetime variants such as the Halton.

When two or more of the flight observer team – Ginger Wright, Noel Brailsford, Jimmy Steel and Geoffrey Ratcliffe – carried out flight test duties along with the pilots, Messrs Talbot, Mitchell, Marsh and Sanders, Dinkum, alias 'The Dinkum Dog' or 'Fat Dog', occasionally accompanied them. This did not include higher altitude missions when he would have looked a bit stupid in an oxygen mask! Dinkum would usually commandeer the prone bomb aimer's position in the Halifax nose and lie, head on paws, looking at the countryside below for the whole flight. If not on flying duties Dinkum would be taken by the flight test team for lunch time walks to the local gravel pits where he enjoyed a swim in the River Ver.

Probably the most famous Halifax of all was B.III LV907 *Friday the 13th* of 158 Squadron based at Lissett in Yorkshire. Despite all the 'unlucky' nose artwork it survived the war with 128 missions to its credit, as indicated by the bomb symbols on the nose.

Halifax Production Summary
Total – 6176 plus 2 prototypes

1 – By Type
Prototypes	2
Mark 1	84
Mark II	1977
Mark III	2091
Mark V	904
Mark VI	468
Mark VII	407
Mark VIII	100
Mark IX	145

2 – By Manufacturer
Handley Page	1592
English Electric	2145
LAP Group	710
Rootes	1070
Fairey	661

3 – By Engine
Rolls-Royce Merlin powered	2967
Bristol Hercules powered	3211

Hampden Production Summary
Total – 1580 plus 2 prototypes

1 - By Type
Hampden	1432
Hereford	150

2 – By Manufacturer
Handley Page	502
English Electric	770
Canadian Associated Aircraft Group	160
Short Bros (Hereford)	150

Chapter 8

The Post-War Transports

Just as the O/400 was adapted for civilian use at the end of the First World War so it was with the Halifax in 1945. The first to appear on the civil register was B.III NR169, which became G-AGXA. It was bought by an Australian who named it *Waltzing Matilda* and flew it out to his homeland in June 1946 with fifteen fellow countrymen as passengers. The C.VIII transport with the freight pannier beneath the fuselage was to see service with the budding airline companies, mostly in the freight transport role. Some B.VIs and A.IXs also acquired civil registrations. The C.VIII derivatives, most notably the **Halton**, were also developed to carry passengers. The Halton had some concessions to passenger comfort, including spacious seats and a row of square windows along each side of the cabin. The transparent nose was replaced by a 'solid' fairing and the whole nose compartment was made into a baggage hold. One special conversion was G-AGZP which was known as the Halton II. It retained the perspex nose and was flown out to India to become the luxury personal transport of the Gaekwar of Baroda and his family.

Twelve Haltons with a ten-passenger cabin layout were ordered by British Overseas Airways Corporation in 1946 for their African and Indian services. They were sold off early in 1948 but in July they were pressed into service with various operators on the Berlin Airlift in the company of many other civilian Halifaxes. During the Airlift forty-one Halifaxes and Haltons flew more than 8,000 sorties, carrying 54,000 tons of essential supplies during the fifteen months of the Soviet-imposed blockade. This was about one third of the total carried by civilian aircraft. The Berlin Airlift helped several Halifax operators to become established as independent airlines – Eagle Airways was one example. Another entrepreneur of the time was Freddie Laker, whose career in the air transport industry began when he bought converted Halifaxes. He operated these on the Airlift under an arrangement with Bond Air Services.

Their availability for the Airlift was timely but the Halifaxes were really only a stop-gap as far as the airlines were concerned. More than ninety appeared on the civil register but most of them had been withdrawn from use by 1950, by which time more suitable post-war designs were available.

While the Second World War was still in progress thoughts within the industry were turning to the post-war requirements of British civil aviation. In the USA aircraft like the Douglas DC-3 and DC-4 and the Lockheed Constellation were already flying as military transports and were readily adaptable to passenger carrying after the war. Avro had produced the York in 1942 by adapting the Lancaster wings and tail unit to a new square section fuselage. Various major modifications to the

The sole example of the Halton II was G-AGZP which was converted from Halifax C.VIII PP336. It was used as a personal transport for about a year by the Gaekwar of Baroda. It did not have the square windows which were provided on BOAC's Haltons. This aircraft later served with Lancashire Aircraft Corporation and was scrapped in 1953.

Halifax were also examined. These mostly featured a larger circular section pressurised fuselage, one of which was the **HP64** military and civil transport. There was also a similar proposal for a bomber but none of these were built. George Volkert and Sir Frederick Handley Page (he had been knighted in 1942) finally agreed to concentrate on a single finned military transport derivative of the HP64 with similar wings to the Halifax but with the span increased from 104 to 113ft. This design was approved and two prototypes were ordered of what was to become the **HP67 Hastings**.

Following the go-ahead for the Hastings, a civil counterpart was soon underway. Known as the HP68 **Hermes I** it was similar in appearance to the Hastings but it had structural provision for fuselage pressurisation which the Hastings did not. It was completed as an unfurnished shell ahead of the Hastings prototypes and was ready for test at the beginning of December 1945. Registered G-AGSS the Hermes I began taxiing trials on 1 December and was due to embark on high speed taxi runs the following day. At 3.40 p.m. on Sunday 2 December the aircraft, with Jimmy Talbot and Ginger Wright aboard, lined up on Radlett's runway 21 for a fast run. As it accelerated it was seen to bounce at the intersection with runway 15/33 and became airborne, much to the surprise of onlookers. It was immediately apparent that the crew were experiencing severe control difficulties because the aircraft began a series of pitch oscillations which increased in amplitude as the aircraft headed towards the village of Radlett. To the south of the village the Hermes reached an almost vertical nose up attitude and then fell to the ground, killing Handley Page's two very experienced and valued crew members.

The most likely cause of the accident, although never completely explained in terms of the final extreme flight attitudes, was considered to be the result of elevator overbalance, that is the combined trim and geared balance tab on the elevator trailing edge overcompensated for the control forces and tended to drive the elevator towards either the up or down stop. Whatever the explanation, the development programme for the Hastings and Hermes could not have got off to a worse start.

A Premonition Come True

Ginger Wright was Handley Page's chief flight observer in 1945. He and chief test pilot Jimmy Talbot made up the crew of the ill-fated Hermes I prototype which crashed on 2 December 1945. Some weeks beforehand Wright had an uncanny premonition of his own death which his flight test colleagues Geoffrey Ratcliffe and Noel Brailsford revealed more than forty years after the event.

In the late summer of 1945 Ginger Wright changed suddenly from his usual ebullient self, becoming very morose. He locked himself away for much of the day in a flight observers' instrument room at Park Street. For some weeks no one dared question him about his odd behaviour, although it was known that he was doing some work in the locked room. Then Geoffrey Ratcliffe had the temerity to broach the matter during an informal moment. The only thing Ratcliffe revealed at the time was that Wright was troubled and depressed following a vivid and bad dream. That conversation took place a few days before the accident.

Ginger Wright had narrated the story in a strange way that can only be described as shy. He said he had had a disturbing dream about going to Cricklewood to see works manager MacRostie and that while driving his car along Watling Street towards Elstree on the south side of Radlett village he saw an aircraft come down and crash in the fields between the road and the railway on his left. He stopped the car, ran across the fields, pulled someone out of the wreckage and dragged him to a safe distance. It was only then that he saw who it was – it was himself.

On the afternoon of the accident Jimmy Steel and Geoffrey Ratcliffe were called up at home by Ginger Wright and asked to come and observe the taxi and brake runs of the Hermes. They had a cine camera and recorded the aircraft moving out from the apron at Park Street. Having a car to use, they positioned themselves at the south-west end of the main runway so that the fast taxi runs might be readily recorded. During the first fast run the aircraft was allegedly thrown into the air at the hump in the surface where the secondary runway intersected. It passed the two flight observers well airborne, still at full throttle but pitching markedly. The pitching motion worsened while the aircraft climbed away. It turned south as it passed Radlett seemingly to make a circuit and land back at the airfield. The end came suddenly with a steep dive, leaving a stunned silence back at the airfield. The firm's fire tenders started off straight away, heading for the plume of black, oily smoke.

After a minute or so Ratcliffe and Steel went back to the car and set off to follow the rescue vehicles. Their route was through Radlett along Watling Street. The wreckage was on the left not far from the road, between the road and the railway near Kendall's Farm, so they stopped the car and ran through a gateway into the field. Some of the wreckage was not burning, the airframe being well broken up. It was soon apparent that there was nothing helpful either of them could do so they drove back to Park Street in a rather distressed state. In terms of the premonition a significant fulfilment, apart from the preciseness of the crash site itself, was that it was Ginger Wright's car which they drove that afternoon. He had loaned it to them as it had an airfield pass.

The ill-fated prototype Hermes I G-AGSS during preparations for its first flight. The aircraft was very similar in appearance to the Hastings but had less cockpit glazing.

In 1946 and 1947 the SBAC Show was held at Radlett, before the venue changed to Farnborough in 1948. This is a scene at the 1946 show with the BOAC Halton G-AHDS *Freemantle* in the foreground and the Hastings prototype behind.

Hastings TG531 of No.47 Squadron at Radlett in 1953. It is a C.1A, one of many converted from the C.1 with the provision for underwing fuel tanks.

Work was temporarily stopped on the second Hermes prototype, G-AGUB. Meanwhile the Hastings prototypes were well advanced and the first one, TE580, was ready for flight test in May 1946, after modifications to the trim and balance tabs. It was decided that a longer runway than Radlett's should be used for the initial testing so the prototype was transported by road to RAF Wittering, near Stamford. A successor to Talbot as chief test pilot still had to be appointed and so Sqn Ldr Maurice Hartford was seconded from the RAF. The first flight took place successfully on 7 May 1946 and by the end of the month ten hours flying had been completed with no major snags. The second prototype, TE583, was flown for the first time by Hartford at Radlett on 30 December 1946 and both aircraft underwent Service acceptance trials at Boscombe Down. A production order was already in place for one hundred Hastings C.1s.

Maurice Hartford had wished to join Handley Page as chief test pilot but it seems he did not have an easy relationship with Sir Frederick and the job went to another ex-RAF man and Hartford's fellow graduate from the Empire Test Pilots School No.1, Sqn Ldr Hedley George Hazelden. 'Hazel', as he would become universally known, took the first production Hastings, TG499, on its first flight on 25 April 1947.

The on-going handling trials had been highlighting a problem of longitudinal instability under certain loading conditions and there began a series of tests of different tailplane configurations. The original prototype, TG580, did much of the testing which included flights with the tailplane at various dihedral and anhedral angles. Production aircraft TG501 and TG502 were also modified respectively with

Hastings C.2 WD479. Compared with the Hastings C.1 and the prototypes the C.2 had a larger span tailplane which was lowered to the fuselage centreline.

a lower set tailplane and one of increased span. These two modifications when combined in October 1948 were found to give much improved longitudinal stability and were later embodied on the Hastings C.2.

Before the original Hastings acceptance trials had been completed in 1948 the Berlin Airlift had begun in June and urgent steps were taken to get a Hastings squadron formed in order to take part. Number 47 was formed at Dishforth in October 1948 and effectively continued with Service trials on the Airlift, operating alongside its Halifax brethren. It really was a case of getting thrown in at the deep end and by the end of the Airlift Hastings had carried out 12,396 sorties in 16,385 flying hours.

The Hastings C.2 with the modified tailplane started coming off the production line early in 1951. The C.2 also incorporated modifications to increase the range and the AUW. Additional fuel tanks were fitted in the outer wings. Forty-two of this model were produced and the last of these was delivered to the RAF on 17 October 1952. In the middle of the C.2 production run four special aircraft were produced, known as the HP94 Hastings C.4, sometimes referred to as the 'VIP.4'. They had lavishly equipped interiors for the long range transportation of VIPs and carried the serial numbers WD500 and WJ324 to 326. They were externally distinguishable by having highly polished natural metal surfaces instead of the sprayed aluminium paint finish of the normal transport variant.

The Royal New Zealand Air Force was the only export customer for the Hastings and they took delivery of four modified versions of the C.2, which were also the last to come off the line. They had more powerful Hercules engines and this model was known as the Hastings C.3.

In parallel with the production of the Hastings during 1950 and 1951 a number of Hastings C.1s were modified to become Met.1s. They were painted with dark sea grey upper surfaces and were used until 1964 by 202 Squadron based at Aldergrove for meteorological reconnaissance, a task they took over from Halifaxes. These weather observation duties involved flights of up to nine hours duration at altitudes ranging from 200 to 18,000ft. After the production line closed about fifty C.1s were returned to Radlett for modification to C.1A standard which had the provision for carrying external fuel tanks under the outer wings.

The two prototypes had long and useful lives. TE580 was used in the early 1950s for propeller icing research by de Havilland Propellers at Hatfield. The second prototype TE583 carried out towing trials in 1947 with the Hamilcar glider and in 1950 it was modified by having its two outer Hercules engines replaced by Armstrong Siddeley Sapphire turbojet engines. The Sapphire was the chosen powerplant for Handley Page's jet bomber then under development, the HP80 Victor. The Hastings test-bed was used to gain flight experience with the Sapphire, which was also to power the Gloster Javelin fighter in 1951 and also some versions of the Hawker Hunter. In 1953 TE583 was further modified by having a Victor-type crew door fitted on the starboard side of the rear fuselage for in-flight filming of escape procedures. To assist with this an outline of the Victor wing root was painted on the fuselage side.

Most of the jobs done by the Hastings in RAF service were routine and mundane, carrying men and materials to any part of the world where British forces were stationed, from Europe to the Far East. The most warlike use of the Hastings occurred

The second prototype Hastings TE583 after its two outboard Hercules engines had been replaced by Armstrong Siddeley Sapphire turbojets. These engines were to power the Victor B.1.

The Hermes II G-AGUB was over 13ft longer than the Hermes I and Hastings, but retained the tailwheel undercarriage. It was developed into the Hermes IV for BOAC.

in the Suez War of 1956 during the brief confrontation with Egypt by Britain and France. The Egyptian Air Force had already been put out of action when Hastings and Valettas took off from Cyprus on 5 November loaded with paratroops and equipment for dropping at El Gamil airfield. The equipment dropped from the Hastings' under-fuselage racks ranged from small containers to 106mm guns. A single Hastings later flew over Cairo on a leaflet dropping mission.

The Hastings had a long and distinguished service career with the RAF as the backbone of Transport Command. It was popular with its crews and provided them with comfortable and spacious accommodation. The last of the transports were formally stood down on 6 January 1968, by which time the Lockheed Hercules was entering service. The longest serving of all the Hastings were the special conversions known as T.5s which were originally built as C.1s. They were transformed in the late 1950s into flying radar classrooms and replaced the Avro Lincolns of the Bomber (later Strike) Command Bombing School to train V-Bomber crews in the use of radar and other electronic systems. Once equipped with the Hastings the unit became affectionately known as '1066 Squadron'. The Hastings T.5 was readily identifiable with its large radome beneath the fuselage. One of these aircraft, TG511, made the last ever flight by a Hastings when on 16 August 1977 it flew from RAF Scampton to Cosford where it is now preserved.

Returning to 1946, the parallel civil programme was then coming to terms with the loss of the prototype Hermes I, which resulted in the suspension of work on the second aircraft. Work resumed with modifications made to the elevator tabs because of the conclusions from the Hermes I crash investigation. A bigger change was a lengthening of the fuselage. This was agreed by the Ministry of Supply with a new BOAC requirement in mind. The length was increased from 88ft 2in to 95ft 6in and was achieved by inserting 80in plugs forward and aft of the wings. This would allow the carriage of up to sixty-four passengers using a five-abreast layout.

The new design took shape as the **HP74 Hermes II** and it first flew on 2 September 1947. Flight trials were satisfactory but the Hermes II was destined to remain a one-off because the discussions which had been taking place between Handley Page, the Ministry of Supply and BOAC led to an order for twenty-five of a development of the Hermes II with a tricycle undercarriage and other more advanced features. The Hermes II therefore served as an aerodynamic prototype for the final production version, the **HP81 Hermes IV** (the Hermes III was a proposed development of the Hermes II with Bristol Theseus turboprop engines). The fuselage proportions were changed slightly on the Hermes IV, with less ahead of the wing and more aft of the wing because BOAC wanted a galley at the front end of the cabin and this would have resulted in nose heaviness with the original layout.

Among the new features introduced to BOAC with the Hermes IV, apart from the tricycle undercarriage, were fuselage pressurisation and air conditioning, and an AC electrical system. For the latter the two inner engines drove 125V alternators. Later a third alternator was fitted to the starboard outer engine.

The first Hermes IV, G-AKFP, was not a prototype in the normal sense, but the first of twenty-five production aircraft. Sqn Ldr Hazelden made the first flight on

Some early production Hermes IVs lined up at Radlett in their original, rather plain, BOAC livery. G-ALDF *Hadrian* is nearest.

A Flight Testing Tale

It was a Sunday, 19 September 1948 to be precise. The flight and ground crews had been hanging around for most of the day for the prototype Hermes IV, G-AKFP Fox Peter, to be made ready for flight, the 11th since its first flight on 5 September. It was finally ready after 6 p.m. but dusk would be setting in at around 7 p.m. Perhaps there would be time to do a quick check on the longitudinal stability with an estimated aft CG limit. With hindsight, a wrong decision was taken when Sqn Ldr Hazelden elected to fly.

It was 6.50 p.m. when Fox Peter lifted off from Radlett aerodrome. The crew included four flight observers, Noel Brailsford, Ian Bennett, John Pitt and Jimmy Steel. Their jobs were to operate and read the special instrumentation which had been fitted and also to look after the engine controls and monitor the health of the four Hercules 763 engines. There was also some concern about the electrical system which needed monitoring also.

The flight testing never happened. What looked like possible flying conditions proved not to be. With a low, near setting sun, the mist that looked OK from the ground became quite opaque from above and they were almost immediately lost. That was bad enough to worry any pilot, even Hazel was a bit put out! There was no radio operator because the radio was not fitted, and so Hazel could not call for a position fix. The navigation lights were not operational so there could be no night flying. Moreover, the fuel load was quite modest, being only intended for a short flight.

All crew were summoned to look-out positions in order to improve the chance of spotting a landmark. This went on for some time and was a dispiriting task as glimpses of the ground were fleeting and infrequent. They began to wonder how they were going to get out of this fix. It was even thought that most of the crew would have to bale out before the fuel was exhausted. But then a minor miracle occurred. One of the observers standing just behind Hazel briefly saw a large white cross marked on the ground. There was a shout and Hazel reacted so quickly that this marker (indicating a disused airfield, not available for landing!) was spotted again. Such was the poor state of the light and the mist that Hazel took a chance and made a direct approach to land, thirty-five minutes after leaving Radlett.

The place certainly looked deserted and there were no obstructions on the runway. Near the far end of it buildings were spotted slightly to the right, so Fox Peter was turned towards them, moving very slowly on a taxi way. The crew were then astounded to see a crowd of young people ahead of them, all seemingly quite demented as they jumped up and down in great excitement. Some were waving model aircraft as they crowded in on the Hermes. It was clearly the highlight of their day and, perhaps, even a planned surprise for them, an extra treat, a real aeroplane! Hazel ordered the outboard engines to be shut down to minimise the chances of youngsters being decapitated by propellers. Very soon he had to shut down all engines and come to a halt because the crowd was not clearing a way for them.

They were now on an unknown airfield, surrounded by countless young aeromodellers, and with no sign of any official reception. The forward door was opened with the hope that someone would bring a ladder. No chance. The sill of the door was some 12ft above the ground, too high to jump from. Hazel wanted to find a phone and was not going to endure the humiliation of being trapped in such a high-tech prison.

They made a rope using all the parachute harnesses. Hazel was no lightweight and it took four of the crew to hang on at the top while he climbed down, ending up on the roof of a car that came along at just the right moment. Hazel was away for some time, during which the Law arrived on his pushbike. This he parked against the starboard main wheel and proceeded to do a good job in keeping the crowd back. Then came reinforcements of police in a dark saloon with loudspeakers mounted on the roof. Lots of orders to everyone came from these speakers. 'Will the owner of the bicycle leaning against the aircraft wheel remove it.' This was repeated a number of times before a rather sheepish copper took his bike away and was not seen again. Men with a ladder arrived with Hazel who informed everyone they were at Fairlop, near Hainault in Essex, and that transport would be coming from Radlett to pick them up. By a strange coincidence it was at Fairlop that the early Handley Page monoplanes were being test flown in 1911 and 1912. The police in the car turned up trumps. Their car was pressed into service as a taxi to a local pub, and the Radlett transport did not turn up until after closing time.

When Hazel went to Fairlop the next day to fly out Fox Peter he was asked, for the first time ever, to produce his flying licence, failing which he could not take the aircraft away. However, permission was eventually granted on the understanding that a valid document would be shown at the local nick within so many days. So it came to pass that, on the following day, an astonished and bemused desk sergeant at South Mimms was asked to verify this rather uncommon certificate.

5 September 1948. On 7 September he flew it to Farnborough and performed two demonstration flights at the SBAC Show, returning to Radlett on the 10th. Testing progressed at Radlett followed by trials at Boscombe Down. Deliveries to BOAC commenced in 1950 and the first passenger services took place on the African routes in August. The cabin was equipped to carry forty first class passengers. The total service life with BOAC was relatively short because Comets took over the African services in 1952 and the Hermes was gradually withdrawn from the Corporation's fleet. There was a brief, unplanned, extension of their life following the Comet tragedies. BOAC's last Hermes flight was from Nairobi to London on 2 December 1954.

The life of the Hermes with BOAC was not without incident. The most notable was that which befell G-ALDN *Horus*. A serious navigation error on a flight from Tripoli to Kano put it too far west leaving it short of fuel over the Sahara Desert in what is now Mauritania. After eleven hours in the air it was forced to land in a remote part of the desert, tearing off a wing in the process. The co-pilot received head injuries in the landing and died of heat exhaustion five days later during a protracted rescue operation. The aircraft remains there to this day in the shifting sand dunes, having provided occasional shelter to wandering tribesmen. Early in 2002 an expedition led by Rob Watt visited the site and some small items were recovered. It has since been established that some nomadic scrap dealers set fire to the wreck in 2000 and carried away much of the remaining metal.

Despite its early retirement from BOAC life was far from over for the Hermes because the growing independent airline industry was looking for just this kind of aircraft. Trooping contracts and the emerging package air tour business were to keep the Hermes IV going for another ten years. For trooping flights the cabin was fitted with rearward facing seats. One of the modifications required was to change the engines from Hercules 763s to 773s which could run on 100 octane fuel instead of the 115 octane required for the 763. The higher octane fuel could be made available on scheduled airline routes but for the more ad hoc destinations it was not so easy. The aircraft thus modified were known as Hermes IVAs. From 1957 the 115 octane fuel was more widely available and the remaining aircraft were converted back to Hermes IV standard.

Among the operators of the Hermes IV were Airwork, Britavia, Skyways, Silver City Airways, Air Safaris, Falcon Airways and Air Links. The last airworthy example was G-ALDA which spent its last two years with Air Links. It made its last flight on 22 December 1964 when it was ferried to Southend, where it was scrapped in 1965. Other than G-ALDN, which still languishes beneath the sands of the Sahara Desert, the only Hermes survivor is the fuselage of G-ALDG. After service with BOAC it was used by Airwork, Falcon and Silver City. Following its retirement in 1962 it was used by British United Airways at Gatwick as a cabin crew trainer until 1975 when it was moved to the fire training area. Fortunately it was not seriously damaged and thanks to the good offices of Gatwick's chief fire officer it was made available to the Duxford Aviation Society. It is now exhibited at Duxford in the colours of BOAC.

There was another promising line of development with the Hermes which began in 1949 with the first flight on 23 August of G-ALEU, the first HP82 **Hermes V**. It was very similar to the Hermes IV but it was powered by four Bristol Theseus turboprop engines of 2,540hp each. A second prototype, G-ALEV, flew on 26 August 1950. This differed from the first one in having double slotted trailing edge flaps. On a test flight from Boscombe Down on 10 April 1951 G-ALEU suffered a triple engine failure and Handley Page's pilot 'Monty' Burton attempted a landing at the disused Chilbolton aerodrome but had to land just short of the runway with the wheels up. The aircraft was later declared a write-off.

The first Hermes V G-ALEU getting airborne from Radlett under the power of four Bristol Theseus turboprop engines.

The prototype Hermes IV G-AKFP was leased to Airwork by BOAC in 1952 and eventually sold to them for trooping contracts. It was written off at Calcutta on 1 September 1957 when it struck a taxiing Dakota while landing. *(T. Chapman)*

G-ALEV was temporarily issued with a Special Category Certificate of Airworthiness in May 1951 in order to undertake some demonstration flying in Paris. It was flown there by Dougie Broomfield with eighteen invited passengers at a ground speed of 300mph. The demonstrations had to be cut short when one of the engines suffered a bearing failure. It was the continuing unreliability of the Theseus which denied the Hermes V any chance of entering production and although new versions with Bristol Proteus and Napier Eland engines were proposed, none were built. Nevertheless the Hermes V was the largest and fastest turboprop powered aircraft of its time and remained one of Handley Page's 'might-have-beens'. G-ALEV ended its days in a fatigue test rig at RAE Farnborough.

It might come as a surprise to some that the last airworthy Hermes of them all was none other than G-AGUB, the sole example of the Hermes II. After completion of trials and geophysical survey work with the Elliott Sun Compass in 1953, it spent the remainder of its life at the Royal Radar Establishment, first at Defford and then at Pershore. With the military serial number VX234 it was used for radar development until June 1968, by which time it had accumulated 1,346 flying hours since its first flight more than twenty years earlier. It was scrapped in 1969.

The Hermes II had visited Radlett in 1965 to ferry a Hastings crew. When the author mentioned this to Hazel a few days later he got the reply 'G-AGUB? You mean "Utter Bastard"'. It is not recalled whether this was its unofficial call-sign or a reference to its flying characteristics!

Chapter 9

The Victor

At the end of the Second World War two important developments were having a profound effect on aircraft design. These were the swept wing and the jet engine. Soon after the war had ended Handley Page's research engineer, Godfrey Lee, was given a military uniform and sent to Germany as part of a Ministry of Aircraft Production mission. Lee's task was to discuss tailless aircraft and their swept wings with German engineers and scientists at their research facilities at Volkenrode and Göttingen. He subsequently described this as one of the most important visits of his life. The German research showed that by giving sweep back to a wing the speed, or more precisely the Mach number, at which the drag started to rise rapidly due to compressibility effects was raised significantly, as compared with an equivalent unswept wing. The swept wing therefore brought the prospect of much higher performance.

The significance of the jet engine, was that it was only efficient when going fast. Hence sweep plus jet was a formula for success and in the immediate post-war period it led to a revolution in aircraft design. Godfrey Lee had a very serious attack of pneumonia after returning from Germany and while convalescing late in 1945 he produced a design study for a 50-ton aeroplane capable of carrying fifty passengers at 500mph non-stop across the Atlantic. Within a year this concept had transmuted into a proposal for a bomber which ultimately became the Victor.

Early studies were of a tailless nature with wing-tip fins and rudders. This layout was inspired by Handley Page's own tailless research programme of the early 1940s in which Godfrey Lee had played a major part (the HP75 Manx research aircraft is described in Chapter 11). In a later proposal the wing tip fins were formed by curving up the tips to produce something which very much resembled the modern 'winglet.' By this time the design was being further refined to include a fuselage with a tailplane mounted on top of a very short fin. Further evolution of the design resulted in the wing tip fin idea being dropped. An Air Ministry Specification B.35/46 had meanwhile been issued to cover the official requirement for a new bomber. In another submission to meet this specification, A.V. Roe were adopting a completely different approach which culminated in the Vulcan.

George Volkert had retired soon after the end of the war and his place as chief designer was taken by Reginald Stafford. Gus Lachmann had also returned from wartime internment on the Isle of Man to look after research projects. Stafford was to become more concerned with the Hermes and Hastings developments (vital bread-and-butter work for the company at that time) and left the bomber design

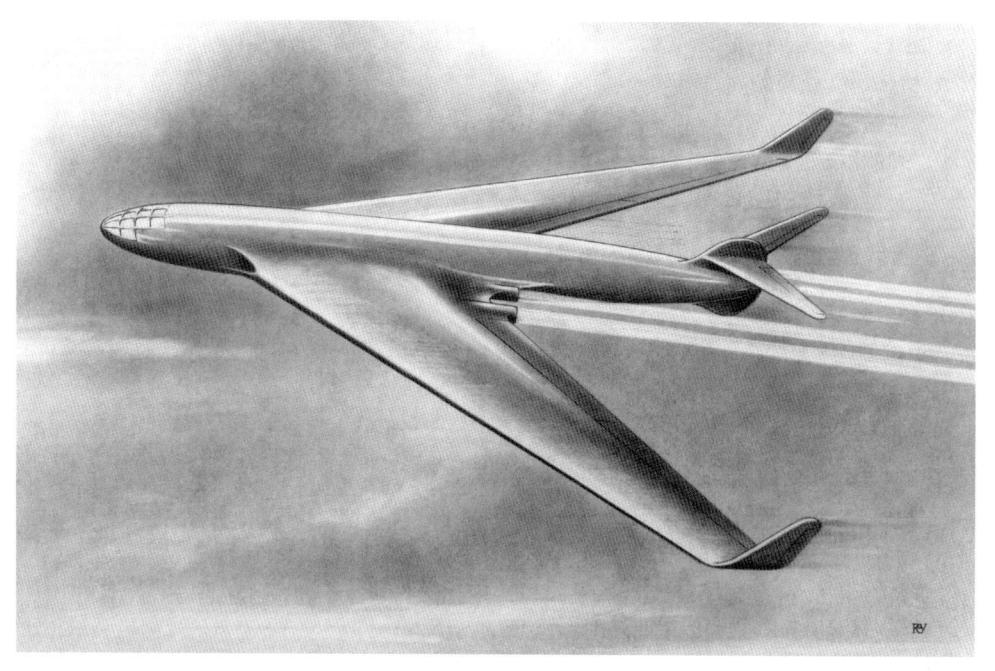

One of Godfrey Lee's early post-war design studies for a high speed unarmed bomber showing the upturned wing tips reminiscent of present-day winglets.

The all-blue HP88 crescent winged research aircraft VX330 appeared too late to influence the design of the Victor. It was lost in an accident in 1951 just a few weeks after its first flight. *(BAE SYSTEMS)*

work to the New Projects Group under the leadership of Charles Joy. Godfrey Lee remained the driving force behind the aerodynamics.

The wing design for the new bomber, now formally designated the HP80, was evolving into something radical for its day to satisfy a number of conflicting requirements. Wing sweep was necessary to obtain high subsonic performance, but swept wings are more prone to tip stall. Straight wings have to be thinner to achieve the high Mach numbers, but thin wings on a large aircraft posed structural problems and could not accommodate the engines and undercarriage. The solution was to design a wing which was highly swept (53 degrees) at the root, allowing a deep section to provide strength and to house the four Armstrong Siddeley Sapphire engines and the undercarriage, and much less swept (35 degrees) and thinner at the tips. An intermediate section of moderate sweep and thickness completed what became known as the 'crescent' wing, because the sweep back decreased in stages towards the tip. The progressive reduction in sweep and thickness on the HP80 also ensured a constant critical Mach number (where local flow reaches sonic speed) across the whole span. Another advantage of the highly swept inboard section of the wing was that it put the main spar well forward in the fuselage, leaving space for a long and unobstructed bomb bay.

The term 'crescent wing' was a reminder of the wing design of Handley Page's early monoplanes. These were also described as crescent-winged, but in their case the crescent was derived by increasing the sweep back towards the tip, and it was also, of course, for totally different aerodynamic reasons.

When the HP80 design was well advanced a small one-third scale research aircraft was built to obtain flight data on the crescent wing and the 'T' tail arrangement. The resulting aircraft, the **HP88**, was a bit of a hybrid. It had a Supermarine Attacker fuselage modified to have Swift-type air intakes and it was built by Blackburn Aircraft. It retained the Rolls-Royce Nene and the tail wheel arrangement of the Attacker. Its first flight took place at Carnaby in Yorkshire on 21 June 1951.

The HP88 was being progressively cleared for speeds up to 550kt when it broke up during a low level run at Stansted on 26 August 1951. Handley Page's test pilot Douglas Broomfield was killed. The official statement at the time said it was undertaking airspeed calibration runs but in fact it was practising a routine for the SBAC Show, which was only a week away. The aircraft was seen to perform a series of violent pitch oscillations before the break-up. The cause was later determined as an inertial coupling in the elevator control circuit between the elevator power unit and a 'g' limiting bob-weight. It was ironical that the bob-weight had been added on the recommendation of the Royal Aircraft Establishment as a safety precaution.

The HP88 had accumulated only fourteen flying hours in its short existence. Its loss made little difference to the HP80 programme, with the prototype already under construction. There had also been changes to the wing planform since the HP88 was designed, with an increase in the chord of the outer section to improve the stalling characteristics. This had been achieved by extending the leading edge forward, effectively moving the outer 'kink' further inboard, making the middle intermediate sweep section much shorter.

The structure of the HP80 made much use of 'sandwich construction' for the outer skin. It comprised a corrugated inner section sandwiched between two aluminium skins. The outer skin was spot welded to the corrugations, giving a very smooth external surface, while the inner skin was attached to the corrugations by hollow rivets. For the wing skins the corrugations would lie spanwise and the whole skin assembly was capable of taking much of the end load arising from bending. It had a great advantage over the conventional skin/stringer construction because it did not buckle under load and so would not give rise to local waviness. This was a very important consideration for the HP80's aerodynamics in order to maintain the critical Mach number across the whole span. Godfrey Lee was always proud of the fact that the pressure distribution had been calculated for every square inch of the HP80's external surface to ensure that the specified cruising performance was met.

The rear fuselage incorporated a pair of powerful airbrakes, one each side, which could swing outwards to a maximum of about sixty degrees. The top and bottom edges of these brakes were fitted with strakes which greatly increased the drag force when open, but caused negligible drag when closed because they lay parallel to the local air flow. The upper strake was larger than the lower one to ensure that there was no longitudinal trim change as the brakes were opened or closed. They were to become popular with the pilots because they could be used on the approach to landing as if they were a fast reacting and precise throttle.

The all-silver prototype, WB771, was completed at Cricklewood by May 1952. As Radlett's runway was being extended to cater for flight testing the new bomber, the decision was taken to transport it to Boscombe Down for the initial flights. This

The first three of seventy-five Canberra B.2s built by Handley Page in the early 1950s pictured outside the Colney Street works. The nearest is WJ566, with WJ565 and WJ564 beyond.

The first Victor prototype WB771 at Boscombe Down around the time of its first flight in December 1952. The wing leading edge flaps are in the lowered position. It is in its original all-silver colour scheme but the fuselage was later repainted black with a red stripe. That scheme was also applied initially to the second prototype, before it was repainted blue!

called for a bit of subterfuge because the very existence of the aircraft was still a secret. The fuselage was therefore mounted on a bus axle and towed as an articulated trailer, covered by a frame and white sheet material. On the side of the sheeting was a bogus ship's name 'GELEYPANDHY SOUTHAMPTON'. An observant spy might have solved the anagram, despite a spelling mistake!

Sixty men from Park Street, led by chief engineer MacRostie, were detailed to Boscombe Down to reassemble the prototype, hoping that it could be flown in time to appear at that year's Farnborough air show. However, a problem with the centre of gravity meant that a major provision for ballast had to be made within the nose radar compartment (this was resolved on production aircraft by lengthening the nose by forty-two inches). There was also a problem with the elevator powered flying controls which had to be resolved. A further blow was struck by a tragic accident. A sudden hydraulic fire in the rear compartment of the fuselage damaged the aircraft and resulted in the death of electrician Eddie Eyles.

By December 1952 WB771 was finally ready. Hazel, who already had experience of the HP80's engines from flying the Sapphire-Hastings and a Sapphire-Canberra, completed the taxiing trials but bad weather caused a delay to the start of flight trials. The skies eventually cleared on Christmas Eve so Hazel, accompanied by Ian Bennett as observer, took the HP80, shortly to be named the **Victor**, into the air for its first flight which went well and lasted twenty minutes. Hazel reported afterwards that he did not have to raise the nose just prior to touching down because the aircraft automatically pitched up and carried out a smooth landing – a characteristic that had been predicted by the design team.

Much comment was made in the press at the time on the Victor's ability to 'land itself'. It came about because of the combination of the high mounted tailplane and the swept wing which, when near the ground, provided just the required amount of pitch-up at the right moment. However, this was not seriously seen as an advantage, and anyway the effect was to be lost in later developments when the tailplane was lowered and the all-up weight was increased.

Handley Page had wanted to call the HP80 'Harpoon' to preserve their alliterative tradition of starting their aircraft names with the letter 'H'. They were overruled by the Air Ministry who imposed the name Victor in keeping with the names of the other two medium bombers then going into production, the Vulcan and the Valiant. The squadrons of these V-Bombers were to be known collectively as the 'V-Force.' One person likely to have been pleased with the HP80's name was Gustav Victor Lachmann!

On WB771's fourth flight at Boscombe Down, the first on which the undercarriage had been retracted, the landing resulted in all sixteen main wheel tyres bursting. It was explained at the time time as being due to 'the parking brake being inadvertently applied because of an interlock fault'. When Hazel reported this back to Cricklewood, HP's first reaction was 'Have you got shares in Dunlop Hazel?' Each main undercarriage leg on the Victor had four wheels, each fitted with two tyres. It was always a delight to watch the whole unit fold up and squeeze itself into what seemed an impossibly small space in the wing.

On 24 February 1953 the Victor came back home to Radlett which now had its newly extended runway available. Test flying continued apace, often with two or more flights in a day. In April Hazel had to carry out a difficult landing when the port undercarriage bogie oscillated violently and jammed over-centre in the vertical position so that only the two rear wheels were available. Large oleo-pneumatic dampers (dashpots) were subsequently fitted to the bogies to prevent the oscillations. They also gave the characteristic tilt to the bogie when it was off the ground, making the rear wheels touch first.

The Victor's first official public appearance was at the Queen's Coronation Review fly-past at Odiham on 15 July 1953. For the SBAC show at Farnborough in September the Victor received a new colour scheme, said to have been chosen by Sir Frederick. It retained the silver wings and tail but the fuselage was painted black with a red cheat line from nose to tail.

In October 1953 WB771 was flown to over 50,000ft and by February 1954 it had flown at Mach numbers above 0.9. In July it commenced airspeed position error flight trials at Cranfield. On 14 July Hazelden had to go to Woodley for a special demonstration of the Marathon so that day's flying passed to the recently arrived assistant test pilot, Ronald 'Taffy' Ecclestone. He had completed several runs at increasing speeds at low level when the tailplane suddenly detached and the Victor dived into the ground, with no chance of any of the crew escaping. Also on board were the chief flight observer Ian Bennett and the other crew members Albert Cook and Bruce Heithersay.

The primary cause of the accident was flutter – a violent oscillation of the tailplane/fin assembly which quickly led to the failure of the three bolts holding the tailplane to the top of the fin. As a result of the accident the fin design was modified to increase the stiffness and the number of tailplane attachment bolts was increased from three to four. On production aircraft the fin was reduced in height by fifteen inches. Godfrey Lee was to admit in later years that it had been a mistake to give dihedral to the Victor tailplane because it directly contributed to the accident by producing a yaw/roll coupling. The dihedral had been added in the middle of the design process when it was found that more fin area was required.

Fortunately for the trials programme the second prototype WB775 was almost complete. It first flew on 11 September 1954, again in the black and silver colour scheme and it appeared at the Farnborough air show. Development continued satisfactorily and it included flight trials to confirm the effectiveness of the solution to the tail flutter problem. Most of this flutter work was done by Flt Lt J.W. Allam and flight observers Bob Williams and Geoff Wass, later joined by another newly-recruited pilot, Jock Still. John Allam had joined Handley Page from the RAF in 1954 and over the coming years was to play a major role in Victor development flying.

The speed in the flutter tests was increased in increments one flight at a time as the crew used control inputs to try to excite the early stages of flutter. An oscilloscope was used in the cockpit to observe the damping characteristics. Asnalysis of records also took place in between each flight. Flutter testing was to continue until May 1958 using an early production aircraft, XA918, up to Mach numbers above 0.9, or 435kt at 18,500ft. Full flutter clearance was satisfactorily achieved.

Also included in the trials work by Handley Page was the dropping of bombs from WB775, with John Allam doing the flying. Until February 1955 the bomb doors had not been opened in flight and considerable buffeting had been expected, but to everyone's surprise it turned out to be of fairly low amplitude. The effect of dropping 1,000lb bombs individually could not be felt and the bombs fell away cleanly. Later a dummy '10,000lb store', representing Britain's atomic bomb, was dropped in the English Channel. That one could be felt leaving!

The bomb bay on the Victor was huge in comparison with those of the Valiant and Vulcan. The maximum conventional internal load for a Victor comprised thirty-five 1,000lb bombs. The maximum for the other two V-Bombers was twenty-one. The Victor bomb bay could have held forty-eight but this was deemed not to be operationally necessary as the range would have been too limited in those days, before in-flight refuelling was available. If a Handley Page proposal for underwing bomb carriers had been accepted the total number of 1,000lb bombs could have been increased to seventy-six! As Hazel once jokingly put it 'You'd have just enough fuel to take off from London, bomb Manchester, and get home again!' Nevertheless, the 'mere' thirty-five bombs would have made the Victor a potent weapon on shorter range operations. The first Victor to make a simultaneous drop of thirty-five 1,000lb bombs was XA921 in June 1959.

In 1955 WB775 was repainted in an overall cerulean blue finish. It appeared at that year's Farnborough show in the blue paint scheme and retained it until the end of its flying days in 1959. It was known among Park Street staff as *Bluebird*, recalling the name given to HP's Type A monoplane of 1910.

At 2.20 p.m. on Thursday 14 July 1960 an otherwise peaceful afternoon at Hatfield was interrupted by a thunderous roar as Victor B.1 XA930 got rapidly airborne with assistance from two de Havilland Spectre boost rockets. XA930 had also been the first Victor to fly with the underwing fuel tanks and the nose-mounted flight refuelling probe.

To keep the production lines operating in the period between the Hastings/Hermes and the Victor, Handley Page were fortunate to receive an order for 150 Canberra B.2 bombers to supplement the production of the parent company, English Electric. Shorts and Avro also received similar orders, sparked off by the tensions at the time of the Korean War. The order was later reduced to seventy-five to avoid compromising Victor production but it provided a useful and lucrative way of keeping the workshops busy. They were all built between 1952 and 1955 and several were still serving into the 1990s, after conversion to target tugs and radar trainers. Canberra production by Handley Page represented a reversal of roles from the Second World War, when English Electric had built Hampdens and Halifaxes.

The first pre-production Victor XA917 was taken on its maiden flight on 1 February 1956 by John Allam. XA917 achieved lasting fame on 1 June 1957 when it became the largest aircraft up to that time to achieve supersonic flight. John Allam and the crew were engaged in longitudinal trim investigations up to Mach 0.985, requiring a dive of about fifteen degrees, when for a moment the Mach meter reading was inadvertently allowed to reach 1.01. There was no indication of this happening other than the meter reading. A sonic boom was heard over a large area of the south Midlands. Having achieved this the crew decided to do it once more and this time aim a bang at Radlett, not an easy task in a shallow dive at high altitude, but it was confirmed as being heard in nearby Watford by none less than chief designer Charles Joy. Another achievement on this flight was that of flight observer Paul Langston, who was credited with being the first person to fly faster than sound backwards! Other Victors also went supersonic, both Mark 1s and Mark 2s, but there was no more publicity about it.

The second pre-production Victor B.1 XA918 was used in 1962 for trials of the Red Neck sideways-looking radar reconnaissance pods. They were over 40ft in length but the system did not go into service. The pods also simulated the carriage of two Skybolt ballistic missiles. The photographer clearly kept his presence of mind.

The first few Victors off the production line were mainly employed as development aircraft. The earliest aircraft to eventually reach the bomber squadrons was XA926, although prior to that XA923, 924 and 925 did serve for a while at Wyton with the Radar Reconnaissance Flight, equipped with Yellow Aster radar.

The first official delivery of a Victor bomber to the RAF took place on 28 November 1957 when XA931 was delivered to No.232 Operational Conversion Unit at Gaydon to begin the conversion of RAF crews to the Victor. On 15 April 1958 XA927 became the first Victor to be delivered to the newly re-formed 10 Squadron at Cottesmore. Victors then began to form part of Britain's nuclear deterrent force, alongside the Vulcan and Valiant. The next squadron to receive the Victor B.1 was No.15, also at Cottesmore.

A total of fifty Victor B.1s was built, the first twenty-five carrying the serial number XA917 to XA941. The final twenty-five had serial numbers commencing XH and this batch was subsequently modified with electronic countermeasures (ECM) equipment. They were then designated B.1A and were distinguishable from the B.1 by the shape of the tail cone which was more rounded on the B.1A, whereas that of the B.1 came almost to a point. Two more squadrons received Victor B.1s and B.1As, the Honington based 55 and 57 Squadrons.

Other modifications to the Victor were the addition of a nose-mounted refuelling probe and under-wing drop tanks. These installations were first flown on B.1 XA930 on 27 August 1958. It appeared with these new additions at that year's SBAC Show where it also made a name for itself by performing barrel rolls and half loops with a roll off the top. The latter manoeuvre was explained as being part of the Low Altitude Bombing System (LABS), whereby a nuclear weapon was released during a steep climb so as to follow a high ballistic trajectory to the target. This would allow the attacking aircraft time to make a quick change of direction before the nuclear explosion. On the other hand the public demonstration might have been more about showing that anything the Vulcan could do, the Victor could do too! Whatever the reason it made a marvellous spectacle seeing those great white aircraft inverted at 7,000ft as they reached the top of a loop.

XA930 was involved in another spectacular demonstration a couple of years later when it was used to test the installation of boost rockets under the wings. The rockets were intended to assist take-off at high weights at hot and high airfields, after which they would be jettisoned and parachuted back to the ground. Although tested, the system was never used in service, mainly because the much more powerful Victor B.2 had no need for such a performance boost.

When the Victor B.1 development was well under way it was becoming clear that an enhanced performance would eventually be required to increase operational altitude

RATO, or Rocket Assisted Take-Off

On 11 July 1960 Victor B.1 XA930 was flown from Radlett to nearby Hatfield to be fitted with two de Havilland Spectre rockets for a demonstration of the benefits of RATO. Ground runs were carried out prior to the flight test with flight test engineer Alan Vincent on board who described the noise of the rockets as being like thousands of rivet guns all hammering the fuselage at once.

On the big day of the flight test, Thursday 14 July, Alan Vincent's place was taken by fellow engineer Mike Wilson, who described the event as follows:

'It was a gloomy day, with 8/8 stratus at about 2,000ft. We lined up, Spud Murphy opened up the Sapphires, held on to the brakes until they slipped and away we went. When the RATO button was pressed there seemed to be a long pause, probably about a second in retrospect. Then there was a most terrible noise that Alan certainly hadn't overstated. The aircraft lifted off very quickly and we held a steep angle. The Spectres cut out in about sixty seconds, by which time we were at cloudbase. The RATO units were not jettisonable on this flight.

There followed a Murphy-style very low beat-up along Hatfield's runway, which allegedly made the official photographer fling himself full length and shake his fist on recovery. We landed back at Radlett after ten minutes in the air. It was all very spectacular. The photograph looks stunning, with the Victor well nose-up on unstick and diamond shock patterns from the Spectre units bending parallel to the runway after striking it – and melting the tar! A large white aircraft under a dark sky with flames pouring out of it – Gotterdammerung indeed. And the noise! Actually the occasion must have been more of a spectacle for the onlookers than it was for the crew.'

as well as to improve runway performance at high weights. The Sapphire engines of the Mark 1 Victor had been gradually developed to give 11,000lb of thrust, but they were becoming old technology. A study of the available options led to the choice of four Rolls-Royce Conway engines, which were then developing over 17,000lb of thrust. These were new-technology bypass turbojets, forerunners of the present day turbofans, and considerably larger than the Sapphires. The wing root sections had to be made deeper to accommodate them and the intake area increased to handle the much larger air flow. And so the Victor B.2 was born. Apart from the increase in power the wing span was increased from 110 to 120ft by extending both the tips and the roots. Maximum take-off weight increased from the B.1's 170,000lb to 223,000lb.

The Victor B.2 also introduced much improved systems. The B.1 already had more advanced systems than the other V-Bombers, but the Mk.2 went a stage further. An AC electrical system was introduced, as was an Artouste auxiliary power unit (APU) in the starboard wing root. To provide emergency electrical power there were also ram-air turbines fed by pop-up air scoops on top of the rear fuselage.

The prototype, XH668, was first taken into the air by John Allam from Radlett on 20 February 1959 and by August it had accumulated 100 hours of flying. On 20 August it was flying from Boscombe Down with an A&AEE crew plus Handley Page's chief flight test observer Bob Williams to investigate wing buffet up to Mach 0.94. While at high altitude off the South Wales coast it disappeared from radar screens and evidence from the crew of a ship suggested that it had crashed at high speed into the sea. None of the crew escaped. A prolonged salvage operation recovered over two-thirds of the wreckage. The conclusion from the investigation was that the pitot head on the starboard wing tip had become detached due to its retaining collet working loose. Since the Mach trimmer derived its information from this pitot the result would be an immediate demand for nose down pitch and a lowering of the leading edge flaps on the wings. If the aircraft had been doing Mach 0.94 at the time the conclusion was that the crew would have had great difficulty recovering from the situation. A modification was put in hand to provide a more positive locking of the collet.

The conclusion of the accident investigation has always been seen as unsatisfactory by many people. John Allam, with all his experience of the Victor's handling characteristics, believes the situation should have been recoverable without any excessive control forces. He had experienced an unexpected Mach trim runaway in XH668 at 52,000ft and described it as a non-event, because the resulting elevator movement was so slow that he had ample time to react. There were some other facts which came out of the enquiry:

(a) The engines went back to Rolls-Royce where it was determined that they were at maximum continuous power when the aircraft hit the sea.
(b) The air brakes remained closed.
(c) It was calculated that the aircraft was supersonic down to 8,000ft (local fishermen heard sonic booms at the time).
(d) There were no distress calls.

Victor B.1A XH648 puts on a demonstration of its conventional bombing capability with a simultaneous drop of thirty-five 1,000lb bombs at a bombing range in Malaysia. This was part of the propaganda war during the Indonesian confrontation of 1963/64. XH648 was later converted to a two-point tanker and is now preserved at Duxford.

Why would two pilots let all this happen without reducing power, without opening the air brakes or making any emergency call? Were they conscious?

To further deepen the mystery an unnamed member of the audience at a Royal Aeronautical Society lecture on the Victor in the early 1990s stood up and told the speaker and audience during question time that he knew the real reason for the accident and that he was sworn to secrecy over it! So perhaps there wasn't a technical reason after all, and there is still a quarter of the aircraft on the sea bed. Will we ever know?

After the loss of XH668 there was concern at the Royal Aircraft Establishment regarding the operation of the Victor B.2 in the high speed buffet boundary regime being explored at the time of the accident. Further flight trials, this time with Handley Page pilots, were therefore conducted from August 1960, using the third B.2, XH670. The aircraft was modified for two pilot operation so that no rear crew members had to be carried. This entailed fitting a special instrument panel in the second pilot's position to enable him to perform the duties of the Air Electronics Officer (AEO). Harry Rayner undertook an AEO's course and flew in this dual role throughout the trials. The first pilot was either John Allam or Peter Baker.

Such was RAE's concern that they insisted on having a chase aircraft in attendance to observe the Victor's behaviour during the trials, which required turns of up to 2g at Mach 0.95 and 55,000 feet. John Allam suggested that the only aircraft capable of

135

The first Victor B.2 XH668 seen parked up against the test house at Park Street during systems tests prior to its first flight in February 1959. In the foreground is the first pre-production Victor B.1 XA917, still in its original all-silver colour scheme which it retained until written-off after a landing mishap at Radlett in 1961. Its nose later served as the RAF's Victor crew escape trainer for many years. It carried a plaque to commemorate its supersonic flight in 1957.

staying with the Victor B.2 would be another Victor B.2! RAE were not amused and arranged for a Gloster Javelin to do the task. The only problem with the Javelin was that it ran out of puff at about 48,000 feet and its endurance when it reached that altitude was limited, whereas the Victor could stay on condition for up to two hours. The solution was to use a relay of three Javelins, with the Victor only allowed to perform the manoeuvres in sight of a Javelin, albeit from 7,000 feet below. The relay system worked well, the trials were completed and faith in the Victor B.2 was fully restored.

Two squadrons were to receive the Victor B.2. They were Nos 139 and 100, both based at Wittering, and they were formed on 1 February and 1 May 1962 respectively. Also based at Wittering was the Victor Training Flight, formed from part of 232 Operational Conversion Unit. Initially the B.2s, like the B.1s still with the front line squadrons, were armed with free-fall weapons, either conventional or nuclear.

By 1964 the B.1 force had been withdrawn, but the B.2s were being upgraded in a retrofit programme which had begun in 1962 to convert the aircraft as a carrier for the Blue Steel rocket-powered stand-off missile armed with a nuclear warhead. The missile had a range of up to 200 miles and was partly enclosed within the bomb bay. This required the replacement of the normal bomb doors by snug fitting fairings. After the missile had been released smaller doors closed to fill the gap. The trials work with the Blue Steel weapon was carried out using three Victors, XH674, XH675 and XL161, much of the work being done over the Woomera range in Australia. After incorporation of the retrofit modifications the B.2s became known within Handley Page as B.2Rs. The first example to be delivered to Wittering was XL511 in July 1963.

Another modification carried out during the retrofit programme was the replacement of the hydraulically operated wing leading edge flaps by a fixed droop. This had originally been tested on the second prototype WB775 in 1959 and later became standard on the B.1A. The first Mark 2 so equipped was XL159 which, sad to say, was lost in a tragic accident on 23 March 1962 during a flight from Radlett to investigate stall approaches at the aft centre of gravity limit. Spud Murphy was flying, accompanied by an A&AEE pilot, Flt Lt John Waterton, and three Handley Page flight observers, John Tank, Peter Elwood and Mike Evans. On the final test the aircraft entered a stable stall followed by a flat spin. At 10,000ft Murphy ordered the three rear crew members to bale out and John Tank managed to get to the door. The two pilots 'banged out' but the two remaining observers failed to leave the aircraft before it crashed on to a farmhouse at Stubton, near Newark. Two women in the house also died. Spud Murphy was injured during the ejection but returned to flying duties a few months later. The accident was not connected with the fixed droop leading edges. The stable stall condition also claimed a number of other British 'T-tailed' aircraft during the 1950s and 1960s – the Javelin, BAC One-Eleven and Trident.

The crash renewed the debate over the provision of ejection seats for the rear crew members, but this would have required major structural changes to the cockpit roof and did not meet official approval. However, Handley Page developed the so-called 'swivel-seat' which was easily turned towards the door. It also incorporated an inflatable cushion fed by compressed air which lifted the occupant up from the seat to help overcome G-forces. These seats were adopted for the Victor and were also ordered for the other V-Bombers.

Victor B.2 XL164 was used for the trial installation of the retrofit modifications associated with the Blue Steel stand-off weapon. It is seen here at Park Street in June 1963 and shows the chaff dispenser pods on each wing and the fixed droop on the leading edge of the outer wing sections. The ram air turbine scoops are in the raised position on the rear fuselage. In the left background can be seen the partly dismantled remains of XA917.

With the Blue Steel weapon semi-buried in the bomb bay, Victor B.2R XL189 makes a slow fly past with undercarriage down, flaps at take-off setting and airbrakes extended.

Another external change which began to appear on the B.2 was the fitting of wing-mounted chaff dispensers. Chaff, or window, was a cloud of foil strips ejected for radar countermeasures purposes. The original chaff dispenser, or 'window box', was in the lower front fuselage but another location had to be sought and the design team came up with the idea of pods extending aft from the wing trailing edge. The purpose of the pods is often wrongly portrayed as being an application of the area rule for transonic drag reduction, but in truth there was probably nowhere else to put them. Godfrey Lee always maintained that with all the effort put into blending the wings into the fuselage and analysing the pressure distributions, no area rule add-ons were necessary. However the pod installation was achieved with a barely measurable drag increase.

In the early 1960s there were plans to give the Victor and Vulcan an autoland capability for all-weather operations. The system to be used was a combination of the standard Instrument Landing System and a mile-long 'leader cable' buried in the ground below the final approach. It worked very well with the Victor and the trials were speedily completed by John Allam, with considerable help from Alf Camp, an RAF pilot who had done much of the earlier autoland work with a Comet at RAE Bedford and who came to join Handley Page as a test pilot. Approximately two hundred automatic landings were successfully demonstrated. The only unsuccessful sortie occurred when a landing had to be abandoned because of a test instrumentation problem. Although about five military aerodromes had been equipped with leader cables the system was suddenly cancelled, to the dismay of all those at Handley Page who had striven to perfect it on the Victor.

The Victor was the only one of the three V-Bombers which did not drop bombs in anger. Valiants went into action against Egyptian airfields during the brief Suez campaign in 1956, and Vulcans raided Port Stanley airfield during the Falklands War in 1982. The nearest that Victors came to being used as bombers was probably during the Indonesian confrontation in 1963/64. The newly independent Malaysia was under threat from its belligerent neighbour and detachments from the Mark I Victor squadrons were rotated out to Singapore. From there they would have attacked Indonesian airfields if Malaysia had been attacked. As a reminder of the Victor's conventional bombing capability, B.1A XH648 was posed for a photograph while carrying out a simultaneous drop of thirty-five 1,000lb bombs. The presence of the Victors was probably instrumental in preventing the confrontation developing into a conflict.

Following the shooting down of Gary Powers' U-2 reconnaissance aircraft over the USSR in 1960 the future of the high altitude bomber began to look uncertain. This led to a decision to switch the V-Bomber force to low altitude operations in order to stay below the Soviet radar. The overall white anti-flash paint scheme of the bombers therefore changed, with the upper surfaces receiving a grey/green camouflage finish. Low altitude training operations, sometimes at indicated airspeeds of over 400kt, were very punishing for the Victor's structure, which had been designed for a nominal 4,000 hours in the smooth upper atmosphere. A full-scale fatigue test specimen was put into operation in the test house at Park Street to keep ahead of the fleet in simulated flying hours. A number of strengthening modifications were incorporated into the Victor's wing as a result.

The B.2 squadrons remained home-based, maintaining the deterrent. At least two aircraft would be fully fuelled and armed on 'Quick Reaction Alert', or QRA, waiting for the order to scramble. The Victors would have been on their way to their targets within fifteen minutes of the order being given. Victor B.2s would continue in the deterrent role until 1968, when the task of deterrence passed from the RAF to the Royal Navy. The RAF had been due to receive the American Skybolt air-launched ballistic missile to equip both the Victor and the Vulcan, but the Americans cancelled the development of the missile in 1962. In the Nassau Agreement of December 1962 Prime Minister Harold Macmillan and President John F. Kennedy agreed on a deal to supply the Navy with the Polaris submarine-launched missile.

Nine Mark 2 Victors were converted to the strategic reconnaissance version known as the B(SR).2, often abbreviated to just SR.2. These served with 543 Squadron at Wyton from 1966 until 1974. They were equipped for radar mapping and also carried a large camera crate and extra fuel tanks in the bomb bay. As a measure of its capability in the radar mapping role, one Victor SR.2 could record the position of every ship in the Mediterranean Sea in a single sortie.

In 1969 the *Daily Mail* organised a transatlantic race to commemorate the fiftieth anniversary of the first crossing by Alcock and Brown in 1919. The timing of the crossing started when one crew member left the top of the Empire State Building in New York and finished when a crew member reached the top of the GPO Tower in London, so a bit of motor cycling and running was involved as well. Among the RAF entrants were two of 543 Squadron's Victor SR.2s, XL161 and XM717. They were finished in a new high-gloss polyurethane camouflage paint and achieved impressive times. For the 3,450 statute mile journey the best time by the Victor team was XL161's five hours, forty-nine minutes, twenty-eight seconds. They did not win the race because the flight-refuelled Royal Navy Phantoms had a definite speed advantage, but at least they were refuelled by Victors! The best Phantom time was four hours, forty-six minutes, fifty-seven seconds.

From the late 1950s up until 1964 the in-flight refuelling capability of the RAF was provided by the Vickers Valiant squadrons. The Valiants had been modified to have the option of carrying a Flight Refuelling hose-drum unit (HDU) in the bomb bay. This could deploy a hose and drogue to refuel another aircraft.

It had been decided in 1962 that many of the Mark 1 Victors would be converted to tankers once they were retired from the bomber force. The second pre-production and trials Victor B.1, XA918, was converted as a prototype three-point tanker. It had the HDU and extra fuel tanks in the bomb bay and in addition it had two under-wing refuelling pods (Flight Refuelling Type FR20B). The wing pods were for refuelling fighter aircraft, two at a time if required, and the HDU, with its higher flow rate, was for use by larger aircraft. XA918 made its first flight in this configuration on 8 July 1964. Other B.1s and B.1As were to follow but an unexpected fatigue problem with the Valiants led to their rapid withdrawal from service, leaving the RAF with no tankers.

As a stop-gap measure six B.1As were converted to two-point tankers, having just the wing pods. These were to receive the RAF designation B.1A(K2P) and retained a bombing capability. The first example, XH620, made its first flight on 15 April 1965. The first production three-point tanker was B.1 XA937 which first flew on 2 November 1965 and became designated K.1. Similarly the conversions from B.1As were known as K.1As. Although they could have been converted back to the bombing role if circumstances required it, this was never done. Three squadrons were to be equipped with Mark 1 tankers, Nos 55, 57 and 214, all based at Marham in Norfolk.

The Mark 1 tanker force, comprising six two-point and twenty-four three-point aircraft, served the RAF well in many overseas deployments, for example ferrying fighters out to the Middle and Far East. They represented a big improvement over the Valiant which was only a single-point tanker and could only dispense half the fuel that the Victor could. The last of the Mark 1 tankers was withdrawn in 1977, but by then the much higher performance Victor K.2 was in service.

When the Victor B.2 bomber squadrons stood down in 1968 the aircraft were flown back to Radlett for storage pending a contract for converting them to tankers. Handley Page had a very neat proposal for the Victor K.2, as it would be called. It would have the same three-point arrangement as the K.1. It would also retain the underwing tanks of the B.2, although they would no longer be jettisonable (the K.1 had been too weight limited to make use of them). The main external innovation was to have been the introduction of 350 gallon wing tip tanks. These would have served the dual purpose of providing more fuel capacity and also some relief from in-flight bending forces, so conserving the wing fatigue life. The disadvantage of tip tanks on a large wing span is that they can produce large downward bending loads on the ground, for example when taxiing on bumpy surfaces. This had been the subject of some investigation at Radlett where taxiing trials were performed with XA918 with large sections of steel girder clamped to its wing tips to simulate the tanks.

The actual award of the K.2 contract was slow in coming and when Handley Page went into receivership in August 1969 all seemed to be lost. The rescue bid by the American K.R. Cravens Corporation at the end of the year (albeit with the Jetstream mainly in mind) appeared to have Ministry of Defence approval for work to continue on the Victor. Yet again however, no contract seemed to be forthcoming. At the end of February 1970 the American backers withdrew support for the company and Handley Page effectively ceased to exist. Within a few weeks the contract for K.2 conversions was awarded to the old Avro factory at Woodford, by then part of Hawker Siddeley Aviation. Some Handley Page staff were retained at Radlett on the Hawker Siddeley payroll to prepare the Victors for ferry flights. Other former members of staff were offered permanent jobs at Woodford to assist with the design and proving work.

The ferrying task was completed on 10 July 1970 when XL190 made the last take-off by a Victor from Radlett. John Allam was the pilot, accompanied by flight test engineer Ray Funnell and one of the Woodford pilots. A farewell beat-up rounded off the occasion.

Initially twenty-eight were to be converted, mostly from B.2Rs but including some SR.2s. The order was later reduced to twenty-four. The K.2 which emerged from Woodford was not as Handley Page had designed it. Gone were the tip tanks and instead, to keep down the wing bending loads, the span was reduced by 3ft, combined with a slight up-rigging of the ailerons. There was also a change to the elevator gearing. These measures combined to have an adverse effect on the handling and performance of the K.2 in comparison with the B.2. For example the K.2 lacked the high altitude performance of the B.2, and the centre of gravity range was more restricted. The aircraft also became prone to pilot-induced oscillations in pitch.

Unlike the K.1, there was no bombing capability retained with the K.2. All equipment associated with bombing was removed, including openable bomb doors. The first example to fly was XL231, which first took to the air on 1 March 1972. The first to go into service was XL233 which joined 232 OCU on 8 May 1974. Eventually two squadrons were equipped, the Marham-based Nos 55 and 57. Much of the service life of the K.2 was very routine and unsung, continuing the tasks formerly carried out by the K.1s, such as overseas deployments and keeping the RAF's air defence fighters on station way out over the North Sea.

Two major events were to prove the worth of the Victor tanker fleet in times of crisis. The first was the Falklands War in 1982, when up to sixteen Victors were based on Ascension Island to support, among others, Nimrod reconnaissance aircraft and the lone Vulcans carrying out the bombing raids on Port Stanley airfield. These bombing operations required a large number of Victors to get the Vulcan to its target and back. Victors had to refuel Victors to ensure the Vulcan could get a top-up over 2,000 miles from Ascension.

Before the arrival of the Nimrods a Victor made one of the longest reconnaissance flights in history when it carried out a radar reconnaissance around the island of South Georgia to assess whether any Argentinian ships were in the area. The flight lasted fourteen hours forty-five minutes and covered a distance of 6,500 miles, with flight refuelling support from other Victor tankers. Throughout the whole campaign the reliability of the Victors was remarkable. No missions had to be cancelled due to aircraft unserviceability.

Although they did an excellent job in the Falklands War it was achieved at some cost in terms of fatigue life. In the two months of the conflict the Victors accumulated 3,000 flying hours. Some rationalisation of the fleet had to be carried out in

A Victor K.2 tanker shows how the underwing tanks, chaff dispensers and flight refuelling pods all conspire to break up the lines of the crescent wing. The Flight Refuelling hose-drum unit is in the retracted position below the fuselage, at the rear of the former bomb bay.

1986 with some of the high time aircraft being withdrawn. No.57 Squadron and 232 OCU were disbanded, leaving 55 Squadron with ten aircraft and another five kept in reserve. By this time the tankers had relinquished the grey/green camouflage dating from their low-level bomber days. From 1983 they were being repainted in an overall 'hemp' scheme, sometimes referred to as 'café-au-lait'. The scheme was designed to reduce the visibility of the aircraft on the ground.

Just when the squadron thought it might stay with the relatively gentle peacetime routines until the Victor's retirement, the Gulf War erupted in 1991 and the Victors were in demand for yet more intensive tanking operations to support the coalition forces attacking Iraq. Once again the Victors carried out their task with complete reliability, operating from the desert heat of Saudi Arabia.

Their long service had to come to an end eventually as the fatigue lives were approaching the limits and the decision had been made to replace the Victors with converted VC-10s and TriStars. On 15 October 1993 No.55 Squadron was disbanded and the Victor was formally retired from the RAF inventory, almost forty-two years after the first flight of the prototype. Some are preserved. XL 231 is now privately owned by André Tempest and maintained with the able assistance of Roger Brooks. It can be seen at Elvington alongside the Yorkshire Air Museum collection and still wears its Gulf War artwork on the nose – a Second World War-style scantily clad lady named 'Lusty Lindy'. The aircraft is taxiable and on display days may be seen making fast runs along the runway. XM715 is also preserved in taxiable condition at Bruntingthorpe. XH673 serves as a 'gate guardian' at RAF Marham, and B.1A(K2P) XH648 is displayed at Duxford, the only Mark 1 still in existence. The nose section of XM717 can be seen in the RAF Museum at Hendon.

The very last Victor, and V-Bomber, to fly was XH672 which made its final flight on 30 November 1993 from Marham to Shawbury, after which it was dismantled and taken by road to the Royal Air Force Museum, Cosford, where it is now on display. Among the crew members for that last flight was John Allam, who had made the first flight of the Mark 2 Victor on 20 February 1959 and whose total experience of Victor test flying went back as far as 1954.

Despite all the technical and political challenges the Victor had to overcome, it emerged as a remarkable success story for Handley Page. With thirty-six years of service, much longer than any of the other V-Bombers, it also represented a good return of investment for the Nation.

So, was there anything to chose between the Victor and the Vulcan? Both have their protagonists, but in popular writings the Vulcan seems to be the favourite. Comments gleaned over the years from RAF personnel with experience of both types suggest that the Victor was preferred for flying fast, whereas the Vulcan, with its lower wing loading, had the edge when it came to low speed flying. The latter, if true, was certainly exploited at air shows, where the Vulcan performed low and slow manoeuvres in front of the crowds. However, John Allam insists that the Victor could perform all the low speed manoeuvres at least as well as the Vulcan. He has quoted a former chief test pilot of Rolls-Royce who occasionally flew in Victors during the Conway engine development programme, and also flew the Vulcans which were used by Rolls-Royce as engine test beds. On one occasion he was flying with John Allam and they were returning to Radlett in poor weather conditions which required some rather sharp manoeuvres under low cloud in the final stages to position for landing. He said afterwards that he was very impressed with the Victor's handling in the circuit and that those manoeuvres could not have been performed in a Vulcan. Other senior test pilots with experience of both the Victor K.2 and the Vulcan B.2 have stated privately that they thought the Victor was the better. Had they experienced the Victor in its B.2 form they would have been even more impressed.

The Victor B.2 had a higher service ceiling and a longer range than the Vulcan B.2. The Victor B.1 on the other hand was somewhat under powered in comparison with the Vulcan B.1, which had Bristol Olympus engines of 13,500lb thrust each. The Victor flew faster than sound on several occasions, whereas the Vulcan would have struggled beyond Mach 0.93. The Victor could also carry a far larger bomb

An artist's impression of the HP111, a 1958 proposal for a military transport derivative of the Victor B.2 with a pressurised cabin capable of holding 200 troops on two decks. The upper deck floor could be lowered to allow the carriage of bulky cargo. Despite the Air Staff's preference for the HP111, the order went to the Short Belfast.

load. The Vulcan probably owed its popular appeal to its looks, reminiscent of a huge menacing bat or a giant ray. The big delta certainly made an impression on the beholder and devotees loved the howl, the thunder and the smoke of those Olympuses.

In the final analysis both the Victor and the Vulcan performed the tasks that were required of them, and performed them well, for much longer than their designers could have envisaged in the 1940s. We should be proud of them both.

Several transport derivatives of the Victor were proposed during the 1950s, both military and civil. The **HP97** was an airliner originally publicised in 1953 and revived again in 1957. It had a twin deck 'double bubble' fuselage with interconnecting spiral staircases and would have carried 172 passengers. Attempts to interest BOAC were not successful.

In 1958 a military transport version of the Victor B.2 with a circular section fuselage, the **HP111**, was selected by the Air Staff to meet a long range strategic transport need. It would have carried 200 troops or twenty-four tons of cargo for 3,300 nautical miles, while also having the ability to land on 1,000 yard grass strips. However it was vetoed from an RAF order in favour of the Short Belfast, which had less load capacity and was about 200mph slower. But the Belfast was built in Northern Ireland where there was high unemployment, and the decision was announced about two weeks before a general election. This was another of the political decisions which contributed to the premature demise of Handley Page.

Victor Production List

WB771 and WB775	Prototypes
XA917 to XA941	First batch of 25 B.1s
XH587 to XH594 XH613 to XH621 XH645 to XH651 XH667	Second batch of 25 B.1s All converted to B.1A except XH617 (lost in accident)
XH668 to XH675 XL158 to XL165 XL188 to XL193 XL230 to XL233 XL511 to XL513 XM714 to XM718	Total of 34 B.2s Numerous conversions to B.2R, SR.2 and K.2

Grand total: 84 plus 2 prototypes.

Two men who played a large part in the success of the Victor. On the left is Chief Test Pilot John Allam, and on the right is Godfrey Lee who was at the heart of the design process which started in 1945. The picture was taken at Marham in 1984 during celebrations marking the 75th anniversary of the formation of Handley Page Ltd.

Chapter 10

Handley Page (Reading) Ltd

In November 1947 Miles Aircraft Ltd at Woodley, near Reading in Berkshire, went into receivership. During the Second World War they were the suppliers of training aircraft for the Royal Air Force, aircraft such as the Magister and Master. With the ending of the war there appeared to be a good civil market for their light aircraft, and they were also producing the Aerovan short range utility aircraft.

Of particular significance, as far as the Ministry of Supply were concerned, was the Miles M60 **Marathon**, the company's first all-metal design. This small four-engined airliner could carry up to twenty-two passengers and had been ordered into production for use on internal air services and for BOAC's overseas subsidiaries. There was much financial and political investment in the Marathon and therefore the Government were anxious to salvage the company.

Ideas for a rescue plan were circulated around the rest of the aircraft industry without much success at first. Sir Frederick Handley Page finally made an offer which was gladly accepted by the Ministry of Supply, on the condition that no design staff were diverted from the Victor project. On the other side of the bargain HP received an assurance that the order for Marathons would be honoured. The takeover was formally completed on 21 June 1948 and a party of top Handley Page

The first production Marathon I, G-ALUB *Rob Roy* of BEA, who used it briefly on their Scottish Highlands and Islands services in 1951. It later served with the RAF as XA249, the first of twenty-eight Marathon T.11 navigation trainers. It was retired in 1959.

The sole example of the Marathon II, G-AHXU, powered by Armstrong Siddeley Mamba turboprop engines performs a low fly past at Woodley. It was later re-engined with two Alvis Leonides Major radial engines as a flying test-bed for the engines initially used in the Herald.

people toured the offices and factory that day. When they got to the Buying Office the occupants appeared to have fled, taking their desks and files with them, leaving only a dozen or so telephones on the floor. HP remarked, perhaps a little cynically, that he supposed the 'phones were still needed to answer Miles' angry creditors!

Until the name Handley Page (Reading) Ltd could be registered, the new firm traded briefly as Handley Page Transport Ltd, which had been a dormant company since 1924. It was resurrected as an expedient and renamed later.

The prototype Marathon, G-AGPD, had flown for the first time on 19 May 1946 and a second, G-AILH, first flew on 27 February 1947. An event which hastened the demise of Miles was the loss of the first aircraft in a fatal accident just weeks before the Handley Page take-over. A third aircraft was under construction at the time. This was the M69 Marathon II, G-AHXU, which was powered by two Armstrong Siddeley Mamba turboprops in place of the four de Havilland Gipsy Queens of the Marathon I. It first flew on 23 July 1949, but this version did not go into production.

The Handley Page (Reading) design team, under chief designer Edwin Gray, had to re-appraise the structural design of the Marathon. As originally designed it was not suitable for building in quantity so they introduced modifications to facilitate production and to take advantage of the split construction techniques which were the standard practice at Cricklewood and Radlett.

The first production Marathon I was G-ALUB and on 14 January 1950 it left for a prolonged world sales tour, reaching as far as Australia and New Zealand. It was flown by Woodley's chief test pilot, Hugh Kendall, and Gp Capt. A.F. 'Bush'

Bandidt. Bandidt had been an Air Ministry resident technical officer at Woodley during the war years and was appointed sales manager of Handley Page (Reading) Ltd. He had been raised in Queensland and had a good knowledge of the needs of Australian civil aviation.

When all its sales tours were over G-ALUB was delivered to British European Airways in May 1951 as the first of an order for twenty-five aircraft. The order was reduced to seven when the airline found that their old de Havilland Rapides were more economical and versatile on the remote 'Highlands and Islands' routes. In the event none went into full service with BEA and six were transferred to West African Airways with whom they served from 1952 until 1954. BEA had also refused the Mamba-powered Marathon II, mainly on the grounds of its high cabin noise level. Other civil operators of the Marathon included Union of Burma Airways, Derby Aviation and Far East Airlines of Japan. One even saw service in Jordan as King Hussein's personal transport.

When it appeared that large orders for the Marathon were not forthcoming, the Government agreed that twenty-eight should be adapted as navigation trainers. These were delivered to the RAF as Marathon T.11s. Offering a roomy fuselage and a range of 1,100 miles, they served well in this role until replaced by Vickers Varsities in 1959. A few returned to civil operations but all Marathons appear to have been scrapped by 1962. Handley Page's total production of the Marathon was forty aircraft. In addition there were the two prototypes and the one Marathon II produced by Miles – forty-three aircraft in all.

A former acquaintance of the author who had flown in Marathons in West Africa once referred to them as a strange design because the outward opening cabin door could not be opened if the flaps were down. This would hardly meet present day emergency exit criteria!

Handley Page aircraft produced at Woodley were given a new series of type numbers with the prefix HPR, so the Marathon I became the HPR1. The sole Marathon II was later re-engined with Alvis Leonides Major radial engines, which were to power the Herald airliner prototypes in 1955. In this form it was designated HPR5.

With Marathon production under way, the Reading team turned their attention to a requirement for an RAF trainer to succeed the Percival Prentice. The specification called for a two-seat fully aerobatic cabin monoplane with a robust structure. The major components had to be easily replaceable, a requirement which would be met by Handley Page's split construction method. The 480hp Armstrong Siddeley Cheetah engine was chosen because it met the requirement for 800 hours between overhauls. The resulting aircraft, the first new design from Handley Page (Reading) Ltd, was designated **HPR2**.

The first of two prototypes, serial number WE496, made its first flight on 24 April 1950 with Douglas Broomfield at the controls. As soon as it left the ground the cockpit canopy flew off, fortunately without causing any further damage to the structure or controls. Broomfield managed to complete a low circuit and land safely.

The aircraft was quickly repaired with improvements to the canopy attachments. Later the canopy was redesigned with a cleaner shape which created less turbulence

The second prototype of the HPR2 basic trainer built to meet an RAF requirement. WE505 first flew with a Leonides engine but is seen here after being fitted with a Cheetah 18.

as well as giving the aircraft more aesthetic appeal. The fin was made taller and more triangular in shape. Automatic slats were also fitted to the outer wings and the aircraft was delivered to RAE Farnborough for spinning trials. Meanwhile the second prototype, WE505, was being completed with the Leonides engine and with the original fin shape. It appeared in the SBAC flying display at Farnborough in September 1950. The Leonides was soon replaced by a Cheetah because the former still had to be approved by RAF Training Command.

During its Service evaluation the HPR2 was in competition with the Percival Provost. Criticism of the Handley Page machine's control forces and other handling characteristics led A&AEE to recommend the Leonides-powered Provost for the production order. The HPR2s were returned to Woodley and probably did not fly again because the Ministry of Supply requested the return of the Cheetah engines.

The possibility of a lucrative market for a DC-3 replacement was taxing the minds of the aircraft makers in the early 1950s. Many major airlines were still using the venerable Douglas military transport-turned-airliner, as were many minor operators who wanted something simple, cheap and easy to maintain.

Handley Page's contender for the market began as a private venture at Woodley in 1952 under Eddie Gray. Information from Bush Bandidt arising from his extensive world tours with the Marathon had built up a picture of the requirements for this elusive DC-3 replacement. It led to a proposal for a forty-seat airliner with four piston engines. At that time many operators, especially the smaller ones, were wary of committing themselves to turboprop powered aircraft. Servicing organisations, particularly in more remote areas, were geared up to piston engines which were of trusted reliability. Furthermore, the safety advantage of four engines was being offered.

Sir Frederick had been expressing some concerns in the course of the new airliner design and he wanted George Volkert to give a second opinion. Volkert had been living in peaceful retirement in Bristol since 1948 and had had enough of the business. He was reluctant to become involved again. HP sent his assistant Gordon Roxburgh to visit him at home to try to persuade him to return. This was successfully accomplished and Volkert returned on a part time basis as assistant chief designer. Gray, who did not have the best of relationships with Sir Frederick, was eventually moved to other projects and his place as chief designer was taken by the former assistant chief designer, John Allan.

What finally emerged was the **HPR3 Herald**, with four Alvis Leonides Major engines of 870hp each. This engine was a two row, fourteen cylinder version of the earlier Leonides and had been flight tested in the Marathon II. The prototype Herald, G-AODE, was completed at Woodley by August 1955 and then dismantled for transport to Radlett. There it was quickly reassembled and was flown for the first time by Hazelden on 25 August 1955. By this time there were already twenty-nine provisional orders on the books, the first having come from Queensland Airlines of Australia, in whose colours the prototype was painted.

The Herald in its original form with four Leonides Major engines. This is the second prototype G-AODF taking off from the grass runway at Alderney in the Channel Islands during a demonstration for Jersey Airlines in October 1956. Both prototypes were later re-engined with two Rolls-Royce Dart turboprops. *(Via R. Burridge)*

Fire in the Air

On 30 August 1958 the prototype Dart-Herald was on its way to the SBAC show at Farnborough. On board were chief test pilot Hedley Hazelden, observer Ray Wood and seven others, including Hazel's wife. A rendezvous had been arranged with Victor B.1 XA930 for some formation photographs to be taken from the RAE's Hastings, WD480. After the photographs had been taken the Herald was at 6,000ft over Godalming in Surrey when there was a loud bang from the starboard engine, which immediately caught fire. Hazel shut off the fuel, feathered the propeller and operated the fire extinguishers but the fire continued to rage. An immediate forced landing was the only option.

Aileron control was becoming difficult and much vibration was coming through the structure. Then the burning engine became completely detached and the aircraft started a rapid roll to the right but fortunately responded to aileron control and resumed a level descent. There was an increasing pitching motion because the outer half of the starboard tailplane had broken away due to the fire. As he approached the chosen field Hazel realised there was a tall tree on the approach and an item of farm machinery at the optimum touchdown point. To add to the difficulties there were high-voltage electrical cables crossing the field further on. He cleared the tree and the other obstacle, made a firm wheels-up landing at 130kt, slid under the cables, which removed the tip of the fin, and slewed to a halt but not before striking a previously unseen tree stump which tore a hole in the front fuselage. The occupants all made a rapid exit through this hole and got clear while the Herald burned.

Initial reports of the accident back at Cricklewood suggested that there had been fatalities, but Hazel recalled how he was touched by HP's words on the phone soon afterwards. 'Hazel', he said, 'we can build another aeroplane, I'm just glad no one got hurt'.

The whole episode had lasted about five minutes and there were certainly moments when Hazel, not to mention the others on board, thought 'This is it!' For his superb airmanship and cool presence of mind Hazel was awarded (for the second time) a Queen's Commendation for Valuable Services in the Air. Sir Frederick later showed his appreciation by making a special presentation of a gold watch.

The incident had originated from a failed hollow gear shaft in the engine's auxiliary drive which prevented oil reaching the turbine bearings, leading to failure of a turbine disc. A large part of the disc went out through the engine casing, severing an engine mounting strut and a fuel line, causing the engine compartment to be flooded with fuel before the fuel cock was closed. Rolls-Royce had already commenced a modification programme to improve the suspect shaft, but this particular engine was still awaiting modification. It is a tribute to the Herald's multiple-load path, fail-safe wing design that the structure withstood the fire for so long.

Barely had the flight development programme begun when it was becoming apparent that the choice of piston engines was a mistake. The Vickers Viscount was by then in service with British European Airways and its Rolls-Royce Dart engines were establishing for themselves a reputation for reliability, which was constantly improving. Furthermore, the Fokker F-27 Friendship, powered by two Darts and of similar size to the Herald, had made its first flight only three months after the Herald and it was winning orders. Although the Leonides Major was also developing into a

The second prototype Herald after conversion to Dart engines. Its fuselage was later lengthened to serve as a prototype for the Series 200.

reliable engine the operators were becoming increasingly turboprop oriented and in May 1957 Sir Frederick took the decision that the Herald should be converted to two Darts. A second Leonides Major powered prototype had made its first flight on 14 August 1956 and this too was reworked to the twin Dart configuration. The first prototype, G-AODE, re-emerged as the **HPR7 Dart-Herald** and Hazelden took it on its first flight on 11 March 1958. Although it was at first formally marketed as the Dart-Herald, it was still popularly known simply as the Herald.

The change to the twin turboprop power was not that straightforward because the propeller diameter had to increase from 11ft to 12ft 6in. In order to maintain a satisfactory fuselage/propeller clearance the engine centreline was moved 21 inches outboard, which also allowed a straight run for the Dart's jet pipe. However, the undercarriage remained in its original position which, together with the inboard intakes for the air conditioning and oil coolers, bestowed upon the Herald the characteristic asymmetry of its engine nacelles.

The performance and handling with the Darts were soon confirmed as much improved over the original piston-engined Herald. It was hoped that a quick certification programme could be accomplished to enable lost orders to be regained and surpassed. But then fate struck a cruel blow when G-AODE was lost following an engine disintegration while on its way to the SBAC show at Farnborough in 1958, thus depriving the sales team of a much needed opportunity to show the new Herald to the world's airlines.

Fortunately the conversion of the second prototype, G-AODF, was already well advanced and it made its first flight on 17 December 1958. Also, to speed up development and marketing, the first production aircraft, G-APWA, was given extra priority over the following production aircraft and it took to the air on 30 October 1959. It was designated a Series 100 and could carry up to forty-four passengers. Sir Frederick's own persistence with the Ministry of Civil Aviation resulted in their ordering three Heralds for use by British European Airways on the Highlands and Islands routes. These Heralds were also Series 100s and were registered G-APWB, C and D.

Meanwhile G-APWA and G-AODF were embarking on some gruelling world sales tours. These culminated in a 19,000 mile tour of South America by 'WA early in 1962 in the company of Prince Philip, who personally logged 99 hours at the controls of this aircraft out of the total of 127 hours for the whole tour. G-APWC was also on this tour. Both aircraft performed excellently, there being only one technical delay caused by a minor electrical fault which was quickly fixed. It was most fortuitous for Handley Page to have the Royal patronage and much useful publicity was generated by it.

Following on from the first four Series 100 Heralds came the Series 200, which was to be the main production variant. An extra 42in were added to the fuselage length which allowed the maximum passenger capacity to increase from forty-four to fifty. The second prototype, G-AODF, was first modified to this standard after which it was re-registered G-ARTC.

The first customer to receive the Series 200 was Jersey Airlines, who ordered six, G-APWE being the first. Other orders followed, but generally only in ones and twos to customers like Derby Airways (later British Midland), Maritime Central Airways of

Herald Series 100 G-APWC commences rotation on the snow covered grass at Woodley aerodrome on its delivery flight to BEA in January 1962.

The thirty-third Herald to be built, and the twenty-third Series 200, was D-BEBE of Bavaria Flug-Gesellschaft. This is a pre-delivery 'beat-up' at Radlett in 1965. It was still flying with Channel Express into the 1990s.

Canada (later absorbed into Eastern Provincial Airways), Itavia (Italy), Globe Air (Switzerland), Arkia (Israel), Royal Jordanian Airlines, Bavaria Flug-Gesellschaft (Germany), Sadia (Brazil) and Far East Air Transport (Taiwan). The Herald showed that it was capable of a high utilisation rate with an excellent serviceability record. One incident which made the headlines happened to a Globe Air Herald which was transporting a number of animals when a lion was found to be loose in the cabin (there were no human passengers). The crew were thankful that their cockpit door was shut!

The Woodley factory and aerodrome closed in 1963 and Handley Page (Reading) Ltd was absorbed into the parent company. All Herald work was transferred to Radlett and Cricklewood. In 1965 the Cricklewood factory was closed and all Handley Page's activities were then concentrated at Radlett.

Production seemed to have settled to a steady, if slow rate when two tragedies occurred in quick succession. CF-NAF of Eastern Provincial Airways crashed on 17 March 1965 after breaking up at 11,000ft above Nova Scotia, killing the three crew and five passengers. Less than three weeks later, on 5 April, JY-ACQ of the Jordanian Airline ALIA crashed in similar circumstances near Damascus. There were strong indications that both accidents were the result of explosive decompression following a failure of the lower fuselage skin. The cause was corrosion brought about by an accumulation of 'bilge fluid' – water containing a strong concentration of spillage from the toilets and galley. All in-service aircraft were immediately subjected to inspection of the 'bottom boat' section of the fuselage and a cabin pressure limitation was imposed. In the end the solution was to return all Heralds to Radlett for re-skinning of the bottom fuselage, with riveted stringers replacing the original spot welded stringers. An epoxy based anti-corrosion paint was applied internally.

The 'bilge' problem had come at a crucial time in the Herald sales effort, when there were hopes of sales of uprated Series 700s to Brazil and other customers. As things turned out the sales did not materialise and the Series 700 was not built. Series 200 production came to an end in 1968 after the thirty-sixth aircraft.

In 1963 and 1964 the Royal Malaysian Air Force took delivery of eight special Heralds, designated Series 400s. They were derived from the Series 200 but had a strengthened floor for carrying military cargo and they were able to accommodate fifty troops. Four of these aircraft also had an inward opening rear door which was openable in flight as a parachute exit. On 2 November 1964 one of the RMAF Heralds was sent on a leaflet dropping mission over neighbouring Indonesia during the confrontation of the early 1960s. In a pre-dawn operation, escorted by RAF fighters, the Herald overflew many of the Indonesian forward bases and dropped two-and-a-half million propaganda leaflets with a message for any potential invader.

In the late 1970s most of the Series 400s returned to the United Kingdom to be sold to commercial operators. The very last Herald in service was G-BEYF of Channel Express, which had originally been FM1022 of the RMAF. It made the last flight by a Herald on 9 April 1999 when it flew into Bournemouth from Guernsey.

A number of derivations of the Herald had been proposed over the years, but none were to see the light of day. One of these was the **HPR8** car ferry project which

An impression of the HPR8 car-ferry project for Silver City Airways. Cars are shown being loaded side-by-side in the wide fuselage.

originated in 1959 to meet a requirement of Silver City Airways for their cross-Channel service. It was to have been a larger aircraft than the Herald, with the wing span increased from 95ft to 120ft. It had a wide oval section fuselage which sat low on the ground to ease loading of cars through the front clamshell doors. Silver City's order went to a cheaper rival bid from Sir Freddie Laker's Aviation Traders Ltd who offered the Carvair conversion of the Douglas DC-4. This too had front clamshell doors but needed specialised lifting equipment to raise the cars to floor level.

Another proposal was the **Jet-Herald**, designed to compete with the Fokker F.28. It had a reduced span version of the Herald wing and a longer fuselage, designed to hold seventy passengers. The engines were to be Rolls-Royce Spey Juniors housed in nacelles under the wings, with the engines themselves at the rear end of the nacelles, aft of the wing trailing edge.

In 1960 there was an Air Staff requirement for a replacement for the Vickers Valetta tactical medium transport. Handley Page tendered the **HP124** which was a Herald with uprated Darts and a swept up rear fuselage to enable vehicles and cargo to be loaded directly via the built-in ramp doors. These rear doors would also provide the parachute exit. The HP124 was in competition with the Avro Andover,

A model of the HP124 which the RAF wanted as a tactical transport. The government refused to place the order because Handley Page had not joined one of the two large aircraft manufacturing groups. A fuselage mock-up was built at Cricklewood to demonstrate the loading of military vehicles. In a separate demonstration it also accommodated Sir Frederick's Rolls-Royce!

a low wing design based on the Avro 748 airliner, the Herald's other rival in the civilian world. The Andover required the development of a 'kneeling' undercarriage to bring the rear fuselage down to an acceptable loading height, something quite unnecessary with the HP124 with its fuselage floor close to ground level.

The Herald had performed well in comparative trials with the 748 and the Air Staff wanted the HP124, but again politics intervened and the RAF were told they would have to accept the Andover. The Ministry of Aviation would only place contracts with the two big rationalised groups, Hawker Siddeley and the British Aircraft Corporation. Although Sir Frederick had been agreeable in principle to a merger, the price per share which was offered by Hawker Siddeley fell far short of his expectations for the value of his company. No other suitable deal appeared to be in prospect and HP, who was in declining health throughout the competition, died on 21 April 1962, perhaps finally broken by this blow to his company. There is no doubt that the HP124, with 3,000ehp Dart R.Da.12 engines would have given the RAF the rugged, high performance aeroplane it needed at the time. It was denied this on purely political principles.

Why did the Herald not achieve the same commercial success as its rivals? There is no simple answer. It was certainly late coming into the twin turboprop market, giving Fokker a head start. Each of the three aircraft had their own merits. The Herald was the best from the pure handling point of view – more fun to fly, but it is not the pilots who buy the aeroplanes, it is the hard businessmen running the airlines. They want good performance, economics and ease of operation. Pilots were also critical of the Herald cockpit for its ergonomics and lack of space. They like somewhere to stow their big flight cases and other paraphernalia.

The Herald had a wider (and therefore heavier) fuselage, which allowed greater elbow room for the passengers, but the hard businessmen in charge were happy to cram passengers into any space, and most of these passengers would not complain about such conditions for short haul flights.

The Fokker was the fastest of the three, although it did have some handling vices. The 748 was said to be the best to operate. Airlines like quick turn rounds so, for example, an aircraft which can be simply and quickly refuelled has a great advantage.

So there is no one simple reason why the Herald did not make the big time sales – forty-eight production aircraft in all – and the DC-3, which they all set out to replace, will probably still be flying in many parts of the world when all the remaining F-27s and 748s have been retired. The old Douglas airliners had one big advantage at the height of the sales battles, they were 'two-a-penny' with over 10,000 having been built as military transports during the Second World War.

A number of Heralds are preserved in the UK. One of them has literally gone home to roost, at its Woodley birthplace. G-APWA, the first production machine, is now with the Museum of Berkshire Aviation, on the boundary of the former aerodrome. It is fully restored and in the markings of BEA. This aircraft logged more than 25,000 flying hours in a career lasting over thirty years.

Chapter 11

Research and Some 'Paper Projects'

Throughout its existence Sir Frederick Handley Page's company had a reputation for innovation and research. The big bombers of the First World War were the first really successful large aircraft. By the sheer size of their structures they were bold advances in their day and they firmly established Handley Page as a major force in aircraft design and manufacture. They enabled Britain's armed forces to develop the concept of strategic bombing. They also ushered in mass civil air travel following the Armistice when the bombers proved to be readily convertible for passenger carrying prior to Handley Page's own purpose-built airliners going into service.

The aerodynamic research which began in 1919 and led to the 'Handley Page slot' has been covered in Chapter 4. The slot was adopted worldwide and is still in evidence today, both as a wing leading edge device and in the form of slotted flaps. By ensuring safe, controlled flight at low speeds it saved many lives in the earlier days of flying. For the modern airliner it contributes to lower landing speeds.

During the late 1930s, Handley Page's research department under Gus Lachmann began studies of tailless aircraft designs as a possible answer to the need for heavy rearward firing defensive armament on bombers. A cannon-armed turret to match the firepower of the new generation of fighters would be too heavy to mount at the rear of a conventional aircraft design because it would shift the centre of gravity too far aft. The tailless layout offered the opportunity of fitting such a turret because it could be mounted far closer to the centre of gravity.

Handley Page built the small scale HP75, later to be named **Manx**, to investigate the stability and control of a suitable tailless design. At the start of hostilities in 1939 Lachmann, who was still a German citizen, was detained under emergency legislation and sent to Canada. Appeals from the likes of Lord Brabazon eventually secured his return in 1943, but he had to spend the remainder of the war on the Isle of Man, where he was at least more accessible to his research department colleagues. The name Manx for the tailless aircraft therefore had another significance, although the name had first been used by Jim Cordes in his test reports back in 1940.

The Manx was built largely of wood and, due to the run-down of the woodworking skills at Handley Page during the 1930s, the building of the aircraft was subcontracted to the glider and light aircraft makers Dart Aircraft at Dunstable. It was a twin-engined monoplane powered by de Havilland Gipsy Major engines driving pusher propellers. At first it had a fixed undercarriage but the main wheels were later made retractable. A short, elliptical section fuselage housed the pilot and a rearward facing observer and it had a fixed fin at the rear. Fins and rudders were also fitted to

The HP75 Manx at Park Street in October 1945 showing its enlarged elevons at the wing tips. The fuselage tail cone hinged upwards to allow the observer to enter and exit and was jettisonable in an emergency.

the tips of the swept back outer sections of the wings. It was painted with dark green/dark earth camouflage on the top surfaces and the lower surfaces were yellow.

Taxiing trials began in 1940 with Jim Cordes and Ginger Wright on board. These tests showed that improvements to the controls and undercarriage would be required. However, work on the Manx was to be shelved for a couple of years because the Halifax had priority. When work resumed in 1942 Handley Page's research engineer Godfrey Lee was assigned the task of getting the HP75 airborne. He would always insist, even in his later years, that it was never officially called the Manx. He continued to refer to it as 'H-O-two-twenty-two', from the class B registration which it carried – H0222.

Lee suggested increasing the size of the elevons (combined ailerons and elevators) to overcome the original reluctance to get into the air, and sure enough a successful first flight took place on 12 September 1942 with J.F. Marsh at the controls (Cordes had left the company in 1941). The nose undercarriage leg broke on landing and during the repairs the main gear was made retractable. It was ready for flight again on 14 December but in a tragic accident the fitter who had attended to the engine starting and removing the chocks made his exit rearwards, straight into a propeller and was killed. After repairs and further modifications the Manx eventually flew again on 11 June 1943 with Handley Page's new chief test pilot, Flt Lt James R. Talbot. This flight was marred by the canopy flying off after ten minutes. The aircraft eventually flew quite nicely, demonstrating a top speed of 142 mph and a ceiling of over 10,000ft.

The Manx went on to complete about eighteen hours of flying by 1946 when it was found to have serious fatigue cracking in the elevon attachment brackets brought about by torsional vibration in the long drive shafts of the pusher propellers. The aircraft was then grounded and languished at Park Street until scrapped in 1952.

There had been plans from the outset to test a so-called 'rider-plane' on the Manx. This was a patented idea of Lachmann's and comprised a freely pivoting foreplane controlled by rear mounted servo tabs. Although one was eventually built by Percival Aircraft it did not arrive until mid-1945 and was never fitted. A larger transport derivative of the Manx with a span of 72ft and also known as the HP75, was proposed but not built. In appearance it would have been reminiscent of the modern Beech Starship, but with a fatter fuselage. The importance of the Manx was in the more advanced ideas it germinated in the immediate post-war period, after Godfrey Lee's visit to Germany, ideas which gradually evolved into the Victor. The cannon-armed bomber idea was not pursued any further.

Beginning around 1950 Handley Page devoted many years of research into boundary layer control (BLC). This was to remain one of the major areas of interest of the research department under Gus Lachmann and his deputy Brian Edwards. It promised a means of obtaining significant reductions in drag by maintaining smooth, or laminar flow over the aircraft surfaces, especially the wings. The 'boundary layer', a very thin region of air close to the surface, starts off at the leading edge as laminar, but almost immediately this smooth, orderly flow breaks down into eddies and becomes 'turbulent'. This causes a relatively high skin friction drag. When the majority of this turbulent layer is removed by sucking it into the wing through a porous surface, or through closely positioned narrow slits or holes in the surface, the smooth, low drag laminar layer is re-established. If this can be done across the whole surface, a very low drag results.

The air removed is at low pressure and has to be pumped up to be ejected back into the airstream. This requires some power to be expended and consequently some

The Vampire WP250 used by Handley Page for their early laminar flow flight testing using the suction glove on the port wing. The glove on the starboard wing was for aerodynamic balance purposes.

Research and Some Paper Projects

The College of Aeronautics' Lancaster PA474 fitted with a test wing section on top of the fuselage for laminar flow tests. This Lancaster now flies with the RAF's Battle of Britain Memorial Flight.

fuel has to be used. Also, the double skin of the suction surfaces, ducting, pumps, metering valves etc, all have a cost in weight and money, but overall a significant saving in operating costs was shown in all the studies conducted. Concentrated efforts were therefore made to solve the associated engineering problems.

Wind tunnel testing on models built by Handley Page to Lachmann's design was carried out by the National Physical Laboratory and also at the RAE tunnels at Farnborough and Bedford. The results were promising so the next stage was to start flight testing. A special glove incorporating spanwise porous strips was fitted over part of the port wing of a de Havilland Vampire NF10 night fighter, WP250, in 1953. A dummy glove was fitted to the starboard wing to maintain symmetry. It took a while to achieve successful results, partly because the Vampire's limited size meant that some of the fuel tank space had to be used to accommodate equipment. This resulted in limited endurance, particularly for the high altitude tests. There were also some problems associated with wing flexure distorting the glove surface. This was resolved by replacing the original glove with one having spanwise bands of holes. Eventually the trials were successfully completed and proved the feasibility of a BLC system.

It was a few years before further flight trials were conducted. A Lancaster, PA474, operated by the College of Aeronautics at Cranfield was made available during 1962 to 1965. A specially designed swept wing section incorporating spanwise slits was mounted on top of the fuselage, rather like a shark's fin. The flight tests demonstrated that laminar flow could be established and that the expected low values of drag were obtained. One unexpected spin-off from the Lancaster trial was that it kept this aircraft flying much longer than any other Lancaster in the country, long enough to attract the attention of the RAF's Battle of Britain Memorial Flight. The fact that the old Avro rival has been a popular air show performer since 1970 must be largely credited to Handley Page!

The HP113 long range business jet project was designed for a full payload range of 5,300 nautical miles making use of boundary layer control.

The HP117 was a large all-wing airliner project designed around boundary layer control under the leadership of Godfrey Lee. It was proposed in several versions. This is a military derivative with missile carrying capability and differs from the civil versions in having a short, rear loading fuselage projecting behind the wing

Dr Gustav Lachmann's final design study before his retirement in 1965 was the HP135 military transport which would have employed boundary layer control to achieve its design range of 7,300 nautical miles.

Meanwhile design studies had been covering a wide variety of applications for BLC, from small business jets to large transports. The **HP113** proposed in 1957 was a long range executive jet of 71ft wing span designed to carry eight to twelve passengers at 530mph over a range of 5,300 miles. Two rear mounted Bristol Orpheus engines were to provide the power. Despite enthusiasm in some quarters no orders were received and the HP113 was not built.

Also on the executive jet theme was the **HP130**. This 1963 design was a modified HS125 with larger wings equipped for BLC. This came close to being built, although the Ministry of Aviation contract would have required it to be manufactured by Hawker Siddeley Aviation at Hatfield, another of the penalties arising from Handley Page's failure to join one of the large groups.

In 1959 Godfrey Lee again became involved in an all-wing design with the **HP117**, a large transatlantic airliner holding up to 300 passengers. The flying wing idea was specially attractive for a BLC project because there was obviously no fuselage and no conventional tail surfaces. This made it easier to apply BLC to the whole exterior of the aircraft. In its final proposed version the HP117 would have had a span of 148ft, a weight of 330,000lb and a range with fuel reserves of over 5,000 miles. Unfortunately no contract was forthcoming and the HP117 remains as another tantalising 'might-have-been' among Handley Page's unbuilt projects.

The last project worked on by Lachmann before he retired in 1965 was the **HP135** military transport. It was designed to carry a payload of 100,000lb at Mach

0.875 over a range of 7,300 miles. It had a large circular section fuselage with a high-mounted swept wing of 205ft span. Suction for the wing was to be provided by turbines mounted in pods under each wing. The four bypass jet engines were mounted around the rear fuselage and these would also have provided suction for the high mounted tailplane. A model was exhibited at the Paris Air Show in 1965, but the HP135 was to remain another unbuilt project.

Would laminar flow have worked in the real commercial world? The system certainly promised greater aerodynamic efficiency, but at the expense of manufacturing complexity and operational difficulties. For example a Boeing 747 size of aircraft would require up to eight miles of suction slits of three to four thousandths of an inch in width plus 125,000 throttling orifices, not to mention all the associated ducting and the pump installations. In service the aircraft would have to be kept very clean because even a minor surface blemish can re-introduce turbulence in its wake. One common problem with all aircraft is the accumulation of flies on the leading edges during flight at lower levels. During an approach to landing this is not such a problem because a slight loss of efficiency can be tolerated for a short period and the aircraft can be cleaned after landing. It is a different matter after take-off when the aircraft has several hours of cruise ahead of it and requires the maximum efficiency. Two solutions were proposed. The first involved a thin film of plastic material covering the leading edge which would be cut and jettisoned after the initial climb. This would not have been very popular with the residents near airports! The other and probably more practical solution was the spraying of a water and detergent mixture from nozzles in the leading edge.

From time to time other companies, such as Northrop in the USA, have experimented with laminar flow, but to date it seems no nearer to becoming a commercial reality and remains a kind of aeronautical holy grail. When Gustav Lachmann retired

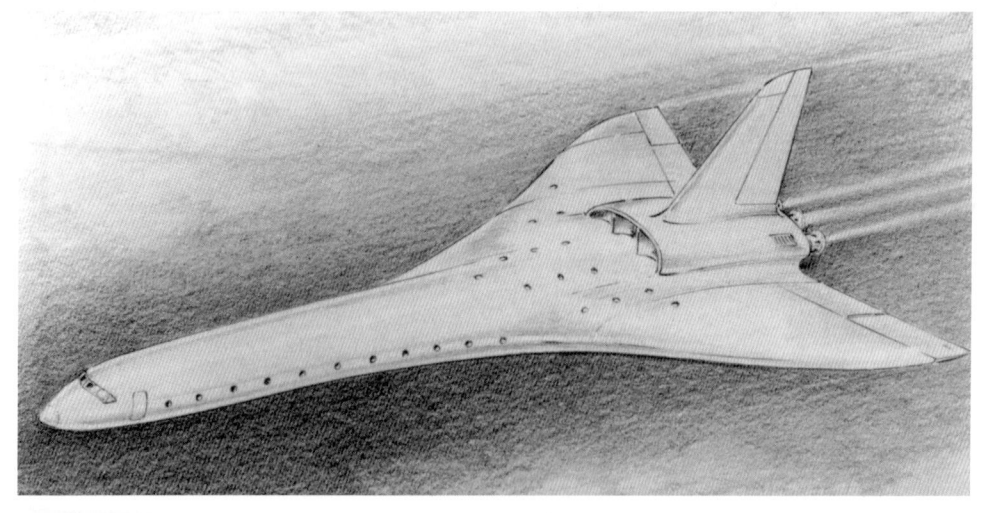

The HP134 Ogee Aerobus of 1965 was a projected short range subsonic airliner with passenger accommodation in the wings as well as the fuselage.

in 1965 he proposed to continue studies but he died the following year and Handley Page's research into the subject faded away.

Another area of design study undertaken by Handley Page in the early 1960s was in the field of large, cheap to operate short range airliners for domestic markets. The work was commissioned by a Government funded working party under the chairmanship of the RAE director, M.J. Lighthill. The first of these was another all-wing 100 passenger aircraft, the **HP126 Aerobus**. It had a thick wing section of 78ft span and with an outer section having greater sweep than the inner section. The other, equally radical design was the 154 passenger **HP134 Ogee Aerobus**, so called because of the wing's ogival delta planform. Godfrey Lee described it as a 'chubby Concorde' because of its thick wing and bulbous forward fuselage. Both these designs had passenger accommodation within the wings. Design studies were also commissioned from Bristol Aircraft and Hawker Siddeley Aviation, but none were built.

In 1952 Operational Requirement 324 was issued for a long range subsonic bomber to act as a carrier for a stand-off missile. Handley Page tendered the **HP99**, nicknamed *Daisy Cutter* by the design staff because much of its mission would have been at low level. It was a crescent-winged aircraft of 75ft span and powered by Armstrong Siddeley Sapphire engines. To give a reasonable airfield performance it would have taken off with a light fuel load followed by in-flight refuelling to fill the tanks. The prospect of an overweight emergency landing was considered an acceptable risk at the time. Other companies also submitted designs but the whole project was cancelled in 1954.

At about the same time Handley Page were embarking on research into a supersonic reconnaissance bomber. This was the **HP100** which had a seventy degree swept delta wing with a delta foreplane. Twelve small diameter Rolls-Royce turbojets would have been mounted under the wings. A Concorde-style drooping nose was planned. The cruising speed was Mach 2.5 with a dash capability of Mach 3. The more conservative submission by Avro, the Type 730, was chosen for further development. However, the whole requirement was cancelled in 1957 with the Duncan Sandys Defence White Paper which famously declared that there would be no more manned combat aircraft for the RAF. The only design of this nature which came to fruition was the North American XB-70 Valkyrie in 1964. Two prototypes were flown but by then even the Mach 3 high altitude bomber was seen as too vulnerable to missile defences.

The HP100 signalled the beginning of a long programme of supersonic research at Handley Page. In 1956 the Supersonic Transport Aircraft Committee was formed at Farnborough to co-ordinate research in the United Kingdom. As a result Handley Page carried out design studies for a number of supersonic airliners. Of particular interest was the **HP109**, a Mach 1.8 transatlantic airliner with an ogival wing. A similar concept which originated at the Bristol Aeroplane Co. eventually saw the light of day as the Concorde.

Another interesting supersonic airliner project was the **HP128**, studies for which began in 1962. It was intended for short ranges, up to 500 miles, cruising at Mach 1.15 but without creating an audible sonic boom on the ground. It featured forty-

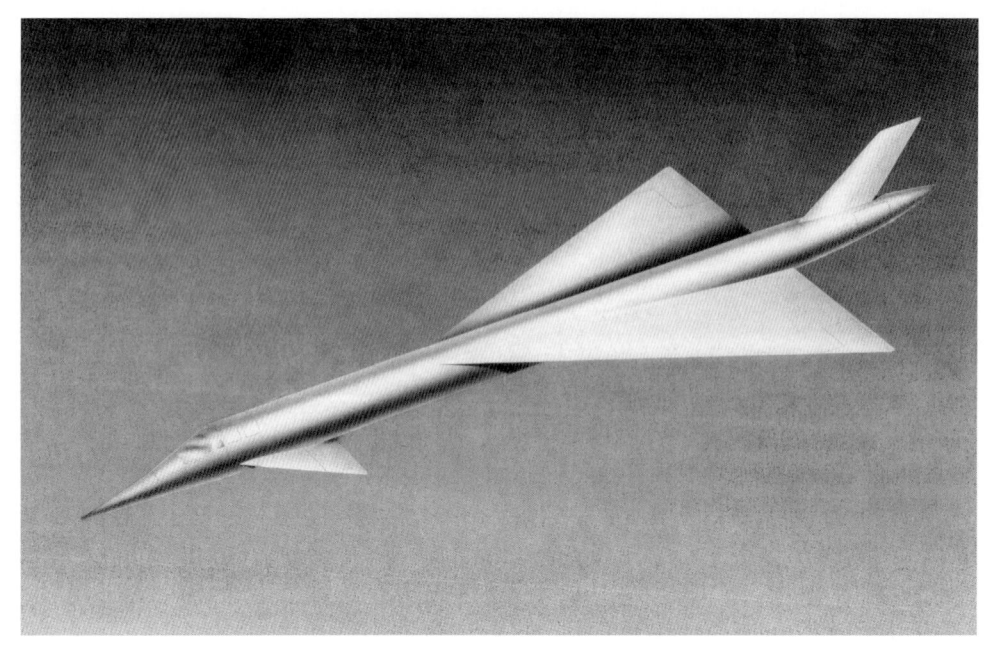

The HP100 was designed in the 1950s for speeds up to Mach 3 at high altitude. However the Soviet Union's anti-aircraft missile defences were to render such aircraft too vulnerable.

The 'slewed wing' airliner proposal by Godfrey Lee in 1961. A swivelling crew cabin, fin and engines enabled the wing angle relative to the air flow to be adjusted throughout the speed range up to Mach 2.

five degree swept wings and tail surfaces and had rear mounted turbojet engines. Analysis of its operating costs eventually showed it to be less economical than the subsonic airliners then coming into service.

Perhaps the most unusual of all the supersonic projects of the time was Godfrey Lee's 1961 proposal for a 'slewed', or 'yawed' wing airliner. It was not allocated an HP type number. It was an all-wing aircraft designed to cruise at Mach 2 and was inspired by earlier research in Germany and the USA. The wing would be angled at about twenty-five degrees for take-off and landing, whilst for supersonic cruising flight the engines and the wing tip-mounted crew cabin and fin would be changed in angle relative to the wing so that the wing was angled to the air flow at about seventy-two degrees.

The great advantage of the slewed wing over the conventional variable geometry arrangement, for example that used on the Tornado or the US B-1 bomber, is that it does not require a massive hinge to transmit the wing bending loads. The hinges required to yaw the engines, the crew cabin and the fin could be comparatively small and light. However, like other all-wing designs it would have to be very large to have sufficient depth within the wing for passenger accommodation. Godfrey Lee remained an enthusiast for this concept. Even in the 1990s his lectures would include standing on the table and launching a small balsa wood model of a slewed wing!

Although Bristol were rewarded with the Concorde project, Handley Page made a very significant contribution to its development with the **HP115** research aircraft. Carrying the serial number XP841, it first flew on 17 August 1961 and until its retirement in 1974 it carried out a large programme of research into the low speed handling of the slender delta wing, an area of concern during the initial design stages of the Concorde. It was an all-metal aircraft but its wing leading edges were made of plywood to facilitate any changes of geometry that might have been required. It had a length of 45ft and its seventy-five degree swept delta wing had a span of 20ft. Full span elevons were fitted at the wing trailing edge and power came from a Bristol Siddeley Viper engine mounted on top of the rear fuselage. Most of its flying in the early years was carried out at Bedford by RAE test pilot Sqn Ldr Jack Henderson.

The slender delta configuration relies on fully separated leading edge vortex flow to give high lift at low speeds and high angles of attack. Despite some early predictions that the aircraft might be difficult to fly, the HP115 turned out to be just the opposite, with pilots finding it simple and pleasant to fly – and it was occasionally barrel-rolled! It went on to achieve over 500 hours of flight testing.

The position of the air intake might have caused a problem with a more conventional design at high angles of attack. With a slender delta, however, as the angle of attack increases the separation vortices from the leading edges grow in size and strength and introduce an increasing volume of air over the central part of the wing. The efficiency of the HP115 intake therefore increased with angle of attack.

The aircraft appeared at several SBAC shows and Jack Henderson was able to demonstrate its controllability at low level, including the 'Dutch roll' condition. It did much investigation of this yaw/roll oscillation which is a typical occurrence with slender delta wings at high angles of attack. It can define a minimum speed limitation rather than the stall. The roll oscillation on the HP115 had an amplitude of about thirty degrees each way and did not seem to cause any danger. It could be quickly checked by the use of aileron or by lowering the nose.

The main reasons for caution in flying the HP115 arose from the low thrust of the Viper engine. It would not have been sufficient for recovery from some high drag conditions, leading to a rapid descent. Fortunately there were no such occurrences and the aircraft can now be seen on display alongside the British Concorde prototype at the Fleet Air Arm Museum at Yeovilton. Perhaps this is a well earned retirement for a most successful research aircraft which went on to explore flight regimes well beyond the original design flight envelope.

Beginning in the late 1950s there began a number of design studies under a contract from The Fighting Vehicle Research and Development Establishment at Chobham. These were for so-called '**Flying Jeeps**' which were basically scout cars equipped with lift engines to enable them to cross natural obstacles without long detours. One version even had short folding wings. They were allocated numbers HP112, 118 and 120 but they never reached the prototype stage. One mock-up was built in a remote workshop at Cricklewood, arousing the curiosity of many a snooping apprentice!

A chapter on research at Handley Page cannot leave out a reference to some of the company's excellent research and test facilities. A first class low speed wind tunnel on the main Colney Street site at Radlett aerodrome, designed by Bob Hounsfield, was commissioned in 1938 and remained in service until the company folded in 1970. It had a working section of about 7ft by 5ft and could produce a maximum air speed of

The Bedford Incident

On Friday 20 November 1964 the HP115 was engaged in a series of touch-and-go landings to investigate ground cushion effects for Concorde-type aircraft. The pilot was Sqn Ldr J.M. (Jack) Henderson, RAF, seconded to Aero Flight, RAE Bedford. He had also been the project pilot for the aircraft during its Handley Page trials.

Just after lift-off on one of these rollers he felt a sharp jolt through the airframe and thought that perhaps a brake had seized. After flying past the control tower they reported that the port main undercarriage leg was cocked to the left almost at right angles.

It so happened that a Varsity aircraft was in the Bedford circuit at the time so it was requested to fly behind the HP115. The pilots confirmed the problem, saying that the whole wheel appeared to be hanging on only by the brake pipes. They then quickly moved to one side in case it came off!

Though told an ejection was justified, Jack Henderson, confident in the precise handling of the aircraft and in his own ability, elected to attempt a landing after a trial 'brush' with the runway. He brought off the landing brilliantly, finishing up on the grass beside the runway with little damage to the aircraft and no personal injury. His courageous behaviour earned him a Commendation for Valuable Service in the Air, and in everyone's opinion it was well deserved.

Jack was taken ill some years later and was invalided out of the RAF. He died in 1990 after some years of ill health, borne with the same courage that he had shown in the 'Bedford Incident'. (A.H. Fraser-Mitchell)

Research and Some Paper Projects

The HP115 slender delta research aircraft was originally proposed as a glider, but this was soon realised to be an impractical proposition. A Bristol Siddeley Viper of 1,900lb thrust was mounted on top of the rear fuselage and the aircraft was destined to provide invaluable data on the low speed handling of this type of aircraft. This had a direct input into the design of the Concorde.

over 200ft/sec. After the firm's closure the tunnel was transported to Glasgow University where it remains in service.

In a separate post-war building on the remote northern boundary of the airfield was the company's high speed wind tunnel. It operated by means of the induced flow from three Rolls-Royce Nene turbojet engines and could produce speeds in the working section up to Mach 1 – in fact it was found that only two of the Nenes were necessary to establish sonic flow. Hounsfield and his team did much excellent work with these tunnels, including some pioneering flutter testing with a flexible model of the Victor and also with a Concorde-like slender wing design.

At the Park Street end of the aerodrome was the Test House, a large hangar where all the structural and systems tests were conducted and where flight test instrumentation was developed. During the development of the Victor, a number of full scale systems test rigs were constructed. These included a three-axis tilting fuel rig to determine all aspects of fuel system performance under normal and failure conditions. There was also a flying control rig built for the prototype and later upgraded to Victor B.1 and B.2 standards. Other large scale rigs were constructed to develop and prove the air conditioning, electrical generation and other systems. During the latter part of the 1960s there were two complete Victor airframes undergoing continuous fatigue testing, a Mark 1 and a Mark 2. These had to keep ahead of the hours being accumulated by Victors in service to confirm their continued structural integrity. The Test House was run by Ken Pratt who became Handley Page's chief engineer after the retirement of William MacRostie in 1958.

Chapter 12

The 1960s – A Turbulent Decade

The 1960s began with the workshops full. Victors and Heralds were in full production and the immediate future looked secure. However, politics had already shown signs of turning against Handley Page. The loss of the HP111 military transport derivative of the Victor in 1959 and the HP124 Herald military transport in 1961 were particularly severe blows.

Another major trauma for the company and its employees occurred on 21 April 1962 with the death of Sir Frederick Handley Page at the age of seventy-six. He had been in declining health and some believe his demise was hastened by the seemingly cruel way that the Herald contract had been taken away by political intervention because of his failure to merge with one of the 'big two.' He had been in negotiation with both HSA and BAC, maintaining that Handley Page Ltd was worth 42*s* (£2.10) per share. HSA had offered 15*s* (75p) and BAC a far more derisory sum and he would not let it go for so little. He probably also feared that the firm would lose its identity and its work would eventually be distributed around the other members of the big groups, with little in prospect for the loyal workforce of the company he had headed for over fifty years.

At heart HP had no faith in large impersonal organisations. He would quote the parable of the rich man who pulled down his barns to build greater ones only to lose his soul in the process. He believed that the soul of an organisation lay in the creativity of its individuals and that elephantine size led to bureaucratic control.

The man who took over the helm after the death of Sir Frederick was George Clifford Dowsett Russell (no relation to the author) who had been deputy managing director for many years. He had been the company's first technical apprentice in 1919 and played an important part in the development of the slotted wing while on the staff of the wind tunnel department.

In the early 1960s there was still more potential with the Victor. In particular there were the contracts for retrofitting Victor B.2s to carry the Blue Steel stand-off missile, the conversions of many of the B.1s into tankers and other B.2s into the SR.2 strategic reconnaissance variant. The last of the new production Victor B.2s, XM718, was completed in April 1963. Herald orders were still being received in small numbers and were sufficient to keep the production line going slowly until 1968. There was also an on-going refurbishment programme with the Hastings. This involved a thorough strip-down to major sub-assemblies. The HP115 research aircraft, although a great technical success, did not make much money for the company.

When Handley Page began to face the implications of having no more

Handley Page collaborated with Frankenstein Ltd in 1963/1964 to produce this air portable hangar, a large canvas structure suspended from three masts. Inside is a Canberra B(I).8.

Government contracts if they did not join one of the big groups, they began some diversification into other engineering work of a non-aeronautical nature. The work included radar scanners, railway truck bodies, prefabricated plumbing units for houses, brewery equipment and air cushion conveyor systems. The radar scanners were in a range of sizes up to a width of 85ft and these were assembled in the former experimental shop at Cricklewood. Several of these large scanners were delivered to Ministry of Defence sites. The radiators included the normal water filled types for domestic central heating systems and the stand-alone oil filled, thermostatically controlled type. The latter proved very popular with Handley Page employees who got them at a discount price. Indeed, some are still in use in 2003!

The conveyor system made use of air jets inclined at fifteen degrees to the horizontal to create a cushion of air under the object to be moved and also to provide a propulsive force. It was marketed as the Jetstream Airveyor. It exploited an American patent and had a number of advantages over the conventional belt system. The Airveyor could accommodate greater changes of direction in both horizontal and vertical planes and there were no moving parts to wear out.

Another diversification was the development of an air portable hangar in collaboration with Frankenstein Ltd, a company with long experience in developing large fabric structures. A number were produced for the RAF. It could be erected on any reasonably level surface and was intended for forward operational areas, primarily for aircraft maintenance. The Tent, as it was often referred to, was large enough to accommodate a Herald, or two Canberras, or seven Buccaneers, or even eighteen Gnats! It was basically triangular in plan view and the three sides were all openable to a width of 83ft.

With the prospect of a decreasing volume of overall production, the operation of three major sites was unsustainable by the mid-sixties. Reading was closed in 1963,

One example of Handley Page's ventures into the non-aeronautical commercial world was the Jetstream Airveyor, which conveyed articles on a cushion of air. Apart from the pumps which supplied the air, there were no moving parts in the system.

followed by Cricklewood in 1965. All activities were then concentrated at Radlett, with new office accommodation being provided at Park Street for the design staff. Later, increased production facilities were also introduced at the Colney Street end of the airfield.

There remained a feeling within the company that the general engineering jobs were all very well but they ought to be getting on with what they were best at – designing and manufacturing aeroplanes! A decision was made in 1965 to make a big commitment to the building of a new aeroplane of a size commensurate with the manufacturing and financial capacity of the company. This was to become the **HP137 Jetstream**, which was aimed mainly at the US market, both as an executive aircraft and as a commuter airliner.

The Jetstream had its origins in discussions between Handley Page, HSA Hatfield and Jack Riley in 1964 when there emerged a possibility that Handley Page might design a pressurised version of the Dove with turboprop engines. Riley was an American who had been specialising in converting existing designs to improve performance. Among his previous projects had been Lycoming powered versions of the Dove and Heron. The idea of the pressurised Dove was soon abandoned in favour of a larger, all-new turboprop powered aeroplane for which Riley suggested the name Jetstream.

It was intended as a small aeroplane offering, as far as possible, big aeroplane comfort. In its airliner configuration it would have three-abreast seating for eighteen passengers, and a recessed aisle giving 6ft of headroom (marred only by having to step over the main spar at one point). This amount of headroom was unique at the time for an aircraft of its size and gave rise to one of Handley Page's advertisements which had the headline 'Toulouse Lautrec is alive and well and designing commuter aircraft for our competitors'.

As a business aircraft it would offer the standard of comfort and the range/payload performance of the current executive jets, but with a lower purchase price, lower operating costs, plus a better airfield performance. On the minus side was the lower cruising speed and also the higher cabin noise of a propeller driven aircraft. It soon became apparent that there was indeed considerable market interest in just such an aircraft.

The Jetstream was fairly conventional in shape, but nevertheless attractive. It had a low wing layout with a span of 52ft and a length of 47ft, small by the contemporary standards of Handley Page aeroplanes. Double-slotted trailing edge flaps were provided. The fin was swept back forty-five degrees to increase the moment arm of the elevator and rudder. It also gave the Jetstream more visual appeal. The long nose forward of the pressure bulkhead housed electrical and avionics equipment. Large elliptical windows provided a good view for the passengers. The engines were initially to be Turboméca Astazou XIVs of 840hp but the prototype had to carry out its first few flights with lower powered Astazou XIIs of 690hp until the XIVs became available.

With many advance orders from distributors in the USA and the UK, the Jetstream prototype G-ATXH was taken aloft on its first flight on 18 August 1967 by chief test pilot John Allam accompanied by Harry Rayner and John Coller. The event was watched by several hundred Radlett employees. Just prior to landing one hour and fifty minutes later they treated the 'neighbours', Hawker Siddeley at Hatfield (formerly de Havilland), to a fly past. The pilot's verdict on the Jetstream? 'A delight to fly'.

This first flight had its minor drama when one of the brake pressure indicators was found to be reading about one third full scale when it should have been reading zero. Operating the toe brakes had no effect, so when it came to the landing Allam was ready with reverse thrust on the opposite side which kept the landing run straight. The aircraft was stopped and shut down on the runway where the ground crew soon diagnosed the problem as a snagged cable in the nose wheel bay, which was quickly fixed. The crew, who had not left the aircraft, then started up and taxied in. The only other snag on the first flight was the extremely light rudder force which was later fixed by a rudder trailing edge strip.

Fin mounted vortex generators were later added to cure a breakaway around the base of the fin where the fuselage curved down rather sharply. There was also a small fairing added on the front of the fin at the tailplane junction to alleviate a breakaway at large sideslip angles.

Initial trials were aimed at certification to the US Federal Aviation Regulations (FAR) Part 23 and the UK British Civil Airworthiness Requirements (BCAR) Section K. These allowed single pilot operation with an AUW limitation of 12,500lb. Structural provision was made in the design for eventual certification for two pilot operation at a weight of 14,000lb under the more stringent FAR Part 25 and BCAR Section D.

The third prototype Jetstream G-ATXJ over Lake Victoria in June 1969 during tropical trials while based at Entebbe in Uganda. The aircraft is in its Mark 1 form with Astazou XIV engines. (A.J. Dowsett)

An intensive flight development programme lay ahead for the Jetstream and to help expedite it G-ATXH was based at Pau in south-west France from December 1967 until March 1968. This was to take advantage of the more clement winter weather and also for the benefits of being close to the engine manufacturer, Turboméca, who had their flight test centre at Pau. The third Jetstream, G-ATXJ, joined 'XH in January. The second prototype, G-ATXI, had not flown by this time because it was being used at Park Street for resonance testing to ascertain vibration modes as part of the flutter investigation programme. The fourth aircraft, G-ATXK, was completed fully furnished as a demonstrator. It first flew on 8 April 1968 and made the Jetstream's public debut at the Hanover Show in May. It then set off on an intensive series of tours around Europe and North America, where it was based at St Louis.

To cope with the anticipated volume of production new purpose-built assembly buildings were erected at Colney Street where the aircraft would move through in the manner of a car assembly line. From there they were to be towed across to the original main assembly hall for final fitting out and preparation for flight.

The development flying encountered some unexpected problems. In particular the stalling characteristics were the subject of some prolonged investigation. The natural stall warning was inadequate and the eventual solution was the fitting of a stick shaker to give warning of an approach to the stall. To complement the shaker there was also a stick pusher as a last resort if the pilot failed to lower the nose.

The weight of the first Jetstreams was some 600lb above the specification figure. This had to be reduced to allow adequate provision for payload within the 12,500lb

AUW limit and resulted in production delays. There were also some performance deficiencies arising from lower than expected engine power and also from higher than expected drag from the wing root and the engine nacelles. All the aforementioned difficulties were combining to delay certification. This would in turn delay the deliveries to customers and increase the overall development costs. With competition from the Beech 99 commuter airliner and more business aircraft coming into the market place this was something Handley Page could ill afford.

Meanwhile Handley Page had put in a bid for a United States Air Force requirement for a light transport and casualty evacuation aircraft, in competition with several other aircraft manufacturers. As a result they were awarded a contract for a trial batch of eleven Jetstreams which were to be powered by American Garrett AiResearch TPE-331 turboprop engines. It would be certificated to FAR Part 25 at a weight of 14,500lb. In USAF service it would be known as the C-10A. The existing passenger door would be supplemented by an extra side opening one to give double the width for loading freight or stretcher cases. The success of this trial batch would almost guarantee an order for several hundred C-10As. At Handley Page this version was designated the Jetstream 3M.

To speed development of the 3M the sixth Jetstream airframe was diverted from its original purpose as a structural test specimen and completed with Garrett engines as G-AWBR. Its first flight was on 21 November 1968. Its early flying was carried out in the yellow primer finish, but it was eventually given an authentic USAF silver and white colour scheme. The second prototype, G-ATXI, also had its Astazous replaced by Garretts to join G-AWBR in the 3M certification work.

A view looking north-west over Radlett aerodrome in 1968. It shows the new buildings being erected at Colney Street for the Jetstream production line. The perimeter track which crosses the main runway threshold leads to the Park Street buildings in the distance.

To further assist with the general production effort some major sub-contracts were negotiated. Scottish Aviation at Prestwick were to build the wings. The Canadian company Northwest Industries at Edmonton in Alberta would build the tail units. A new Handley Page factory was set up at Cumnock in Ayrshire to house a modern machine shop.

The first production aircraft, G-AWSE, made its first flight on 22 October 1968. It went into service with Cal-State Air Lines in the USA in July 1969. Orders for the civil Jetstream were being received but not yet in the numbers to justify the early optimism. The nine month slippage in the production schedule had increased the company's financial commitment to the project to over £10 million.

To try to recover from the effect of the slippage it was planned to increase the production rate to fourteen aircraft a month by the end of 1969, but meanwhile the cash flow situation was becoming serious. Much now depended on the USAF contract and also for the contract to convert Victor B.2s into tankers, which was believed to be imminent.

Plans were also well in hand for the fitting of the Astazou XVI engine to restore the payload/range deficiencies of the Mark 1. The resulting new versions would be known as the Jetstream Series 200 with a maximum AUW of 12,500lb and the Series 300 with the AUW increased to 14,000lb. The new models would require yet more development time and money and the crunch came in August 1969 when the suppliers and major creditors decided enough was enough. The life saving Victor contract did not arrive and on 8 August the Handley Page Board asked Barclays Bank to appoint a receiver. Mr Kenneth R. Cork of Cork Gully & Co. Ltd was duly appointed.

The Jetstream production line in the new 'B1 Building' at Colney Street when production was being geared up to produce fourteen aircraft a month.

The 1960s – A Turbulent Decade

G-AWBR was completed as the Garrett-engined prototype for the USAF C-10A light transport. Among other modifications was an extended tail cone housing a jettisonable crash position indicator.

There were serious attempts to keep the company running, for example by trying to expedite RAF interest in the Jetstream as a multi-engine pilot trainer. The big breakthrough came when the International Jetstream Corporation (originally the Riley Jetstream Corporation set up by Jack Riley), with the backing of its parent company, K.R. Cravens Corporation, and financial backing from the Mercantile Trust Co. of St Louis, agreed to form a new company. It would be known as Handley Page Aircraft Ltd and would continue to fund Jetstream development. Optimism received a further boost when the Ministry of Defence agreed that the new company would be acceptable for military work.

Work on the Series 200 continued, with G-ATXH and G-ATXJ being re-engined with Astazou XVIs. The first of the initial batch of eleven C-10As was nearing its first flight in October 1969 when the USAF order was cancelled. The aircraft was just overcoming its early weight and performance shortcomings, but delivery was behind schedule and also the US Government would not deal with a company that had been through a liquidation. A tremendous amount of precious resources had been invested in the 3M in the hope of securing the big order. Although it was a serious loss there was still the prospect of the Victor contract and on 31 December 1969 the assets of Handley Page Ltd were transferred to the new company. All seemed well.

Another Jetstream, G-AXFV, was re-engined with the Astazou XVI to act as the Series 200 demonstrator. G-ATXH embarked on a programme of intensive engine development flying with Rolls-Royce at Filton. G-ATXJ continued with certification flying and in early February began overseas trials, beginning with temperate performance measurements at Akrotiri in Cyprus and continuing with tropical trials at Fort Lamy in Chad. Mark 1s were still being ferried across the Atlantic for completion and the Mark 1 demonstrator G-AXEK was engaged in a sales tour of Australia.

On 27 February 1970 there came the shock announcement from the Cravens Corporation that no more cash was available. It may have been a coincidence but the organisation's president, Kenneth R. Cravens, had just died. Whatever the reason, the backers had pulled the plug. At this point the Government could have thrown the last remaining lifeline, the Victor contract, but it failed to do so. Handley Page Aircraft Ltd, only two months into its existence, was bankrupt. A few weeks later Hawker Siddeley Aviation at Woodford received the contract to convert the Victors.

The demise of the company might have spelt the end for the Jetstream. Fortunately a few enterprising people had other ideas. Capt. Bill Bright and his company Terravia had been contracted by Handley Page to ferry Jetstreams to customers and completion centres. Following the collapse he expressed an interest in buying up the whole Jetstream project and enlisted some former senior members of the Handley Page staff to assist with its continuation. Peter Cronbach became Technical Director, while John Allam looked after the test flying. One of the aims was to complete the unfinished certification of the Jetstream Series 200 at 12,500lb. They were soon joined by other prominent ex-Handley Page people including Ray Gould, Doug Casley and George Benbow. Operating as Jetstream Aircraft Ltd they became a CAA approved organisation. Later, Frank Tyson joined the company. He had been in charge of structural design at Handley Page.

The company had bought three completed Mark 1 aircraft which were ferried to Sywell, plus several lorry loads of parts and eleven engineless airframes which were taken to Sywell by road. The three airworthy aircraft were sold including one to Zaire and another to Air Wasteels in France, after obtaining French certification.

A certification programme for the Series 200 was agreed with the CAA using G-AXFV. This was formerly Handley Page's Series 200 demonstrator and had been bought by the College of Aeronautics at Cranfield. Arrangements were made to borrow it for the flight trials. Temperate trials were flown at Cranfield, followed by tropical trials at Tehran and Dubai, enabling all the flight manual performance figures to be verified. This latter task was completed with the help of Handley Page's former chief aerodynamicist Harry Fraser-Mitchell, working in his spare time. CAA certification was obtained and Jetstream Aircraft Ltd exhibited at the Paris Air Show in 1972.

Proposals were again put to the RAF to try to revive their interest in the Jetstream. Peter Cronbach produced a revised design for the interior plus additional 'eyebrow' windows for the cockpit. John Allam flew the aircraft in a head-to-head competition for the RAF order with the Rockwell Commander, which the Jetstream won. At about this time Bill Bright sold his interest in the aircraft and control of the project passed to Scottish Aviation. The Jetstream went into service in the training role with the RAF as the T.1 and the Royal Navy as the T.2, both basically similar to the civil Series 200. The Navy aircraft had thimble radomes on the nose for weather and terrain-mapping radar. Many of the RAF and Royal Navy Jetstreams are still there in 2002. They maintain the long-established tradition that the RAF has never been without a Handley Page aeroplane since its formation in April 1918. That this is still so is due in no small part to the efforts of a few Handley Page people in the aftermath

The Jetstream Series 200 G-AXFV was used by Jetstream Aircraft Ltd after the collapse of Handley Page to complete the certification of this more powerful version. This picture was taken during John Allam's demonstration at the Rolls-Royce Open Day at Leavesden on 30 June 1973. *(via P.L. Cronbach)*

of the company's collapse. Peter Cronbach and John Allam, who formed a new company known as Aeronautical Development Associates, continued working on Jetstreams and upgraded eleven Mark 1 aircraft in the USA to obtain better performance at hot airfields.

Scottish Aviation Ltd, which in 1978 became British Aerospace Scottish Division, put new life into the Jetstream in 1980 by installing Garrett engines and making systems improvements to produce the Jetstream 31. These were the engines that had been intended for the USAF C-10A back in the Handley Page days, although the new installation was different because the engine was upside down, which eased some of the production difficulties which had been experienced by Handley Page. This new Jetstream went on to be a very successful design with a total of 382 sold in the form of the Jetstream 31 and the Super 31 (later known as the Jetstream 32).

The final part of the story was the Jetstream 41, a stretched version with uprated (1,650hp) TPE331-14 engines and a twenty-nine-seat cabin achieved by increasing the fuselage length by 16ft. The wing span was increased to 60ft. It first flew in 1992 and 100 had been sold when production ended in 1997.

Could Handley Page have survived if the Victor contract had been awarded? One can only speculate on the medium term prospects. The Jetstream in its Series 200 form would probably have achieved steady sales. Beyond that it would all depend on derivatives of the basic design, such as the Jetstream 31 and 41 models developed later by British Aerospace at Prestwick. It would have been a big challenge for a small company to keep ahead of the competition, but one that all concerned would gladly have accepted.

★ ★ ★ ★

A British Aerospace Jetstream 32 over Sydney Harbour. This one is equipped with an external baggage pannier under the fuselage. *(BAE SYSTEMS)*

What of the man who started it all? Within his company Sir Frederick Handley Page inspired tremendous loyalty and esprit de corps founded upon respect, upon affection and upon admiration for his ability. His style of management was not remote. Until the 1940s he made regular tours of inspection around the drawing office and, accompanied by the chief designer and chief draughtsman, visited every drawing board down to that of the most junior draughtsman. His concern with detail sometimes exasperated his subordinates, although they sometimes had to admit that his intervention had improved matters. He disliked ostentation, and his office at Cricklewood was of modest proportions. HP could be tough and outspoken, but he reserved his severest strictures for those departments of Government responsible for the award of contracts whose parsimony and bureaucratic procedures he believed to be detrimental to the progress of British aviation in general, and of his company in particular.

He was big, both physically and mentally. Typical of the strong, HP could also be gentle and kind. Many employees could testify to the acts of kindness paid out of his own money when they or their relations were ill or in trouble. And it embarrassed him very much to receive in return the merest word of thanks. He had been brought up on Christian principles as a member of the Plymouth Brethren, but his kindness was neither the soft nor easy going kind. He would never have created his company nor nurtured it through the lean years between the wars had it been so. He had a caustic wit which could humiliate the recipient. He would only use surnames for his staff, whatever their level. The only exception was chief test pilot Hazelden, who was known to all, even HP, as 'Hazel'.

The 1960s – A Turbulent Decade

HP had a finger in nearly every aeronautical pie. For the Royal Aeronautical Society he had a deep and lasting affection ever since he had played a leading role in its reform in the years before the First World War. He contributed numerous papers to the RAeS on technical subjects including the Wilbur Wright Lecture in 1928 and the Louis Blériot Lecture in 1950. He was RAeS President from 1945 to 1947. He was appointed by the Government to chair a sub-committee to look into the question of regulating air safety. He advocated the establishment of a body which would be representative of all aviation interests, but independent of any Government department. He was a founder member of the Air Registration Board (ARB), as this body subsequently became known, and a Vice-Chairman from 1937 to 1958. The ARB eventually became the Civil Aviation Authority. He helped to found the Society of British Aircraft Constructors (as the SBAC was then known) in 1916, was twice its Chairman, and its first President in 1938-39, and was Treasurer from 1943 until his death. He was a Vice-President of the Royal Aero Club and a President of the Chartered Institute of Transport.

Outside aviation Sir Frederick's interests were many and varied. His successor G.C.D. Russell wrote of HP in the 1966 Centenary issue of the Royal Aeronautical Society Journal – 'But so fine was his intellect, so great was his energy and so immense was his zest for life that he also had time for much else: for his family; for theology; for philosophy; for technical education; for architecture; for his daily crossword; for such diverse reading as the Bible (from cover to cover) and the lascivious footnotes of Gibbons' Decline and Fall of the Roman Empire; for golf; for his accordion; for prehistoric paintings in Brittany caves; for the paper, handprinting and bindings of fine books; for his farm's management; for good food and wine of which he was a connoisseur whose palate he would not ruin by smoking; for both witty and profound conversation; and for hilarious after dinner speeches.' To that could be added his ability to entertain with a pack of cards in some postprandial prestidigitation.

The final version of the Jetstream is the British Aerospace Jetstream 41 which is a larger and virtually new aircraft. It first flew in 1992 and has a capacity for twenty-nine passengers. *(BAE SYSTEMS)*

181

His qualities were much in demand in public life. In 1943-44 he was Master of the Worshipful Company of Coachmakers and Coach Harnessmakers, and in 1956 he was appointed Her Majesty's Lieutenant for the County of Middlesex.

Throughout his life HP took a deep and positive interest in technical education. His company was one of the first in the aircraft industry to establish technical apprenticeships with day release, and he was a member of the SBAC committee which in 1938 developed an industry-wide apprenticeship scheme.

He became a member of Council of the City and Guilds of London Institute in 1944 and was Chairman of Council from 1950 until his death. He was instrumental in persuading industry to take a greater interest in the Institute as well as supporting it financially, and during his time as Chairman the Institute's activities grew enormously. He was also a Governor of the Imperial College of Science and Technology, and, from 1953 to 1962, Chairman of the Board of Governors of the College of Aeronautics at Cranfield. Thus, his appointments spanned the whole range of technical education from craft to post-graduateship.

Whilst Chairman of the College of Aeronautics he recognised that to become financially viable the College would have to broaden its scope and embrace other disciplines. It was during his Chairmanship that the School of Production Engineering was established – the first step along the road that was to lead to the Cranfield Institute of Technology and then Cranfield University.

Although Sir Frederick believed that a technical education was a sound basis for life in a modern society, he was well aware of the limitations inherent in a narrow vocational training. He lost no opportunity to impress upon his younger audiences

Frederick Handley Page on a family winter sports holiday at Pontresina in Switzerland during the Christmas holiday of 1937. (*Via Mrs M. Varnill*)

Three Victor K.2s fly over the disbandment parade of 55 Squadron at Marham on 15 October 1993. This marked the end of almost thirty-six years of service which started when the first Victor B.1 was delivered to 232 OCU in November 1957. *(G. Burling)*

the importance of broadening their horizons by participation in intellectual pursuits, emphasising his argument by apt quotations from the classics.

Though circumstances of history decreed that HP's name should be associated with large warplanes, his lifelong ambition was the achievement of safe, economical and comfortable air transportation. He looked forward to the day when air travel would be cheap enough for the ordinary family to enjoy holidays in the warmth and sun of the Mediterranean. He strongly supported his company's research into laminar flow wings carried out under the direction of his long time friend Dr Gustav Lachmann, which aimed to achieve greater operating economy through reduction in drag and lower fuel consumption.

Lord Brabazon of Tara, a fellow aviation pioneer, was one of the speakers at the company's fiftieth anniversary dinner in June 1959. He said of Sir Frederick 'He has helped with his genius, his personality and his inspiring ability. I can say with all sincerity that the whole movement, starting fifty years ago, would have been a good deal poorer without him for he always was and is a very great man'.

★ ★ ★ ★

What were you doing on the day Handley Page collapsed?

Handley Page went into receivership for the final time on Friday 27 February 1970. The full impact of this was not felt by most employees until the Monday morning of 2 March, a day when events moved with dramatic and, for some, traumatic speed. The accounts below give some feeling of what it was like to be there.

2 March 1970 – As Seen by Dereck Couzens

As a production worker having already survived the practically seamless transition from Handley Page Ltd to Handley Page Aircraft Ltd, like many others, I was confident that the company would survive. After all, how could a firm such as HP's not survive? At that time, apart from three years in the RAF I had spent all of my twenty-four-year working life at HP's. No, it would go on forever. Naiveté, or wishful thinking, omitted the positive factor that had kept the old firm alive – the late Sir Frederick with his unstinting efforts, authoritative presence and his hands at the controls. I chose to ignore the incumbent American business men and an unforgiving Government.

Having worked overtime on a Jetstream at the weekend, I was only moderately surprised to see the lights blazing in the administration offices as I drove past Colney Street late on Sunday night. It was probably just another meeting with the American bosses planning their next move. Nothing could have prepared me for that dreadful Monday morning.

As usual, I arrived early but unusually I was almost instantly ushered into the office of the Prior-to-Flight Foreman, Bill Mason. Soon all the other chargehands were in the office. A sombre Bill Mason pointed to some neat piles of papers on a table and said simply, 'Hand these to your chaps. The company is finished. Those of you in this room will be retained by HSA (Hawker Siddeley Aviation) who will be represented on site later today. The Victors are to be flown to Woodford'. The papers comprised a typed sheet and some official forms. The typed sheet read:

> *To the employees of Handley Page Aircraft Ltd.*
>
> *It is with deep personal regret that I have to announce the closure of Handley Page Aircraft Ltd. I wish to express my sincere appreciation for the loyal support and hard work that you have given me during my brief stay at Handley Page. May I wish you every possible success in the future.*
> *Sincerely yours,*
>
> *J.W. Rizika*
> *Deputy Chairman and Chief Executive Officer*
>
> *P.S. The Department of Employment and Productivity have asked me to inform you that in order to avoid delay and inconvenience special arrangements are being made to enable you to register for employment and to claim unemployment benefit.*

There followed an alphanumeric listing indicating when and where one should attend to claim any benefit. My mind was in turmoil…mortgage, my family, another job, the future… it was difficult to assimilate the overall situation. Inwardly dazed and confused, I like to think that I appeared outwardly normal as I handed out the forms to be read and filled in by a workforce that were mostly initially shocked, then incensed or, in many cases, extremely emotional. Most were men whose family had worked at 'Pages' for decades and it was their second home. Before them was a hangar full of Jetstreams awaiting delivery and outside there was a fleet of Victors awaiting conversion – it just did not make sense that the firm was no more. The recriminations were to come later. Right now was almost indescribable abject misery for a total workforce so abruptly and harshly dismissed.

After a while, the handful of supervisors who were to be retained were instructed to ensure that everyone else was to leave the premises by ten o'clock. I was posted at one of the main exits, with the duty of attempting to retrieve as many Handley Page tools as possible from the workers as they left the main hangar. I collected far more abuse than tools. In the hangar some fitters were actually attempting to finish off the jobs that they had been working on. They had to be gently persuaded to give up their tasks and leave.

Many unashamed tears were shed that day by many men that I had once been privileged to work alongside. They cried not only for themselves, but also for Sir Fred and the principles that he stood for.

Charlie Read was now the Works Superintendent. The last time that I had worked for him was at Cricklewood in 1947, but at least he was a familiar figure to whom most could relate. Later he sent me some specific tasks. The rest of that day was spent

The memorial which now stands at the former entrance to Radlett aerodrome at Colney Street. It was unveiled there in 1990 and was a joint effort by the Handley Page Association and St Steven Parish Council. (A.H. Fraser-Mitchell)

on a miscellany of activities such as trying to identify the owners of the many apparently abandoned tool boxes left on the benches, getting ready to bring into the hangar the first of the Victors and preparing to inhibit the engines of the finished Jetstreams. Generally, everyone tried to be busy while we waited for a proper definition of the job ahead. It was obvious that some of those dismissed would need to be recalled to meet the proposed timescales. We felt in some kind of limbo, a vacuum that separated us from the reality.

What followed in the ensuing days, weeks and months is another story. The spirit of those that achieved the task of moving the Victors to HSA Woodford was pure Handley Page. Everything else, such as the clearing of offices and equipment (accomplished by the same team), the intrusion of auctioneers, scrap dealers and certain condescending HSA directors was eminently unpleasant to the faithful.

The Design Office Perspective - As Seen by Harry Fraser-Mitchell

At 10.30 a.m. Brian Edwards had just convened a meeting of executives in the Design Department – I represented Aerodynamics – called to discuss a new and improved pay structure. He had asked his secretary not to disturb us, so was a bit put out when she came in and told him he was urgently wanted in Godfrey Lee's office. He went out and returned ten minutes later, white as a sheet, to tell us to return to our departments and inform our staffs the terrible news – 'Collect your personal equipment only and be out of the premises by 12.30.' In fact this was soon modified by the arrival of the technical director of HSA who said we would all be retained (and paid) for differing periods of time while finishing work for the Ministry of Aviation. This work was principally the design of the tip tanks for the Victor Mk.2 tanker.

Following this we were to complete the annotation and packaging of our past military work, which was to be sent to Woodford, with explanatory notes as necessary. Only work for the MoA was authorised. Jetstream and all civil work was prohibited. The Victor fatigue test was to be continued to support the tanker conversion work which, we were told, would be going to HSA. This testing was dependent on the test frame and associated equipment being bought at the auction being planned to dispose of all equipment!

It was a sad time for us to see everything slowly being taken away, and staff leaving. There were several medical problems. Bob Hounsfield was told by the Receiver's representative that all his cherished wooden wind tunnel models of earlier aircraft going back to the First World War would be burnt. He went home and suffered a major heart attack from which he died a few days later.

We were told that the majority of us would be offered a job in an HSA company, though its suitability and status was not guaranteed. Personally, after interviews at Manchester, Hatfield and Kingston, I went to the latter, which was formerly Hawker Aircraft. I was soon to take charge of aerodynamics on the Hawk, and later became Chief Airframe Engineer, retiring in 1988.

Many other staff members joined HSA, some to work on the Victor at Woodford, some to Hatfield and other sites. I believe most were highly thought of, and many received rapid advancement.

An Outside Trials Team Perspective – By the Author

I was a member of the team accompanying the third prototype Jetstream G-ATXJ in February 1970 on what was scheduled to be a three-month series of tropical trials at various locations. It was my job to look after the flight test instrumentation. We had completed two weeks of temperate performance work at RAF Akrotiri in Cyprus and had moved on to Fort Lamy in Chad where the hot trials were taking place. After nearly two weeks there we were at the end of another day's work in the desert heat and the team had gathered in the hotel bar for some welcome refreshment. This was Friday 27 February 1970. Spud Murphy, the company's deputy chief test pilot and our team leader, had stopped at the hotel reception and came to join us in the bar, holding a brief telex message from Radlett. It read something like 'Receiver appointed. Suspend operations. Stand by for return home signal'.

I suppose there was a feeling of shock, but it didn't really show on anyone. After all we had been through it all just six months before.

There was little one could do for a day or two apart from packing all the equipment aboard the Jetstream and Handley Page's Dakota G-ATBE, the trials support aircraft, while the aircraft insurance situation was sorted out. When the clearance was received the long flight home commenced. I was fortunate enough to travel in the Jetstream. The majority of the team had to endure a slow and bumpy ride over the desert in the Dakota, in the capable hands of Neil Williams and John Tank, until the smoother air of the temperate regions was reached. The Jetstream could fly above all that.

We made night stops at Akrotiri and Rome. At the latter the misery was compounded by the news that the newly delivered Jetstream D-INAH of Bavaria Flug-Gesellschaft had crashed with the loss of all on board, including the company's managing director Max Schwabe and members of his family. It was caused by an engine turbine disc failure.

On the final day we made a detour to Pau to drop off the Turboméca representative, Gilbert Pottier. On what was destined to be G-ATXJ's last ever flight, Spud took off from Pau, bound for Luton. Just after take-off, I unstrapped in order to move to a convenient window on the other side to get a final photograph of Pau, the scene of earlier trials. As soon as I was on my feet Spud threw 'XJ into a steep 180 degree turn to the right, flew low past the airport buildings and then pulled up into a climbing barrel roll, with me still standing in the aisle. Quite a farewell gesture to our friends at Pau!

Just under three hours later we landed at Luton, disembarked and cleared the formalities. Waiting for us at the exit was chief flight test engineer John Coller with a handful of brown envelopes, one of which was for me. My time with Handley Page had come to an end.

Appendix A

Handley Page Aircraft Designs

HP No.	Name or Description	Date	Engine(s)	Span ft/in	Length ft/in	No Built	Chapter
1	Type A Bluebird	1910	Advance	32.6	20.6	1	2
2	Type B	1909	Green			1	2
3	Type C	1910	Alvaston/Isaacson	30.0	21.0	1	2
4	Type D	1911	Green/Isaacson	32.0	22.0	1	2
5	Type E Yellow Peril	1911	Gnome	42.6	28.2	1	2
6	Type F	1912	Gnome	43.6	30.2	1	2
7	Type G	1913	Anzani	40.0	25.1	1	2
–	Type K	1914	Anzani	30.0	20.6	–	2
8	Type L	1914	Canton-Unné	60.0	41.0	1	2
9	Type M	1914	Salmson	70.0	37.6	–	–
10	Type N	1914	Gnome	32.6	24.0	–	–
11	O/100	1915	Rolls-Royce Eagle	100.0	62.10	46	3
12	O/400	1918	Rolls-Royce Eagle	100.0	62.10	500+	3
13	Type P triplane	1916	Sunbeam Cossack			–	–
14	Type R	1917	Hispano Suiza	36.0	25.6	3	3
15	V/1500	1918	Rolls-Royce Eagle	126.0	64.0	40?	3
16	W/400 (conversion)	1919	Rolls-Royce Eagle	85.0	63.0	1	5
17	Slotted DH9	1920	Siddeley Puma	45.9	30.1	1	4
18	W.8	1919	Napier Lion	75.0	60.3	1	5
18	W.8a (slotted wing)	1920	Bristol Jupiter	75.0	60.1	–	5
18	W.8b	1922	Rolls-Royce Eagle	75.0	60.1	7	5
19	Hanley	1922	Napier Lion	46.0	33.4	3	4
20	X4B (slotted wing)	1921	Liberty	47.6	30.0	1	4
21	Type S	1923	Bentley	29.3	21.5	2	6
22	Sayers-HP No.25	1923	ABC	36.6	21.0	1	5
23	Sayers-HP	1923	Blackburne	20.0	17.0	1	5
24	W.8d Hyderabad	1923	Napier Lion	75.0	59.2	46	6
25	Hendon	1924	Napier Lion	46.0	34.6	6	4
26	W.8e, W.8f	1924	Siddeley Puma, Eagle	75.0	60.2	14	5
27	W.9a Hampstead	1925	Bristol Jupiter	79.0	60.4	1	5
28	Handcross	1924	Rolls-Royce Condor	60.0	40.0	3	6
30	W.10	1926	Napier Lion	75.0	59.4	4	5
31	Harrow	1926	Napier Lion	46.0	34.10	2	4

Appendices

32	Hamlet	1926	Lucifer/A.S. Lynx	52.0	34.10	1	5
33	Hinaidi I	1927	Bristol Jupiter	75.0	59.3	7	6
34	Hare	1928	Bristol Jupiter	50.0	32.2	1	6
35	Clive I & II	1928	Bristol Jupiter	75.0	59.2	3	6
36	Hinaidi II	1931	Bristol Jupiter	75.0	59.3	34	6
38	Heyford prototype	1930	Rolls-Royce Kestrel	75.0	58.0	1	6
39	Gugnunc	1929	A.S. Mongoose	40.0	25.9	1	4
42	Hannibal class	1930	Bristol Jupiter	130.0	92.2	4	5
43	Bomber transport	1932	Bristol Pegasus	114.0	75.9	1	6
44	Hinaidi III	1929	A.S. Jaguar	75.0	59.3	–	–
45	Heracles class	1931	Bristol Jupiter	130.0	92.2	4	5
46	Torpedo bomber	1932	Rolls-Royce Buzzard	50.0	39.5	1	6
47	General purpose aircraft	1933	Bristol Pegasus	58.0	37.7	1	6
50	Heyford I, IA, II & III	1933	Rolls-Royce Kestrel	75.0	58.0	124	6
51	Bomber transport	1935	A.S. Tiger	90.0	78.4	1	6
52	Hampden	1936	Bristol Pegasus	69.2	53.7	1431	7
52	Hereford	1937	Napier Dagger	69.2	53.7	150	7
53	Hampden second prototype	1937	Pegasus, then Dagger	69.2	53.7	1	7
54	Harrow	1936	Bristol Pegasus	88.5	82.0	100	7
55	Bomber project	1935	Hercules or Merlin	95.0	65.3	–	7
56	Bomber project	1937	Rolls-Royce Vulture	88.0	66.6	–	7
57	Halifax I & prototypes	1939	Rolls-Royce Merlin	98.10	70.1	86	7
59	Halifax II	1941	Rolls-Royce Merlin	98.10	70.1	1977	7
60	Halifax IV	1943	Rolls-Royce Merlin	104.2	71.7	–	7
61	Halifax III	1943	Bristol Hercules	98.10	71.7	2091	7
61	Halifax VI	1944	Bristol Hercules	104.2	71.7	468	7
61	Halifax VII	1944	Bristol Hercules	104.2	71.7	407	7
62	Hampden II (conversion)	1944	Wright Cyclone	69.2	53.7	1	7
63	Halifax V	1942	Rolls-Royce Merlin	98.10	70.1	904	7
64	Transport project	1943	Bristol Hercules			–	8
65	Halifax project (new wing)	1943	Bristol Hercules	113.0	71.7	–	–
66	Halifax project (new wing)	1943	Bristol Hercules	113.0	71.7	–	–
67	Hastings	1946	Bristol Hercules	113.0	82.8	152	8
68	Hermes I	1945	Bristol Hercules	113.0	81.10	1	8
70	Halifax VIII	1945	Bristol Hercules	104.2	73.7	100	7, 8
70	Halton (conversions)	1946	Bristol Hercules	104.2	73.7	12	8
71	Halifax IX	1945	Bristol Hercules	104.2	71.7	145	7

Total Halifax production (all models) 6176 plus 2 prototypes

74	Hermes II	1947	Bristol Hercules	113.0	92.2	1	8
75	Manx	1940	D.H. Gipsy Major	39.10	18.3	1	11
79	Hermes III	1947	Bristol Theseus	113.0	92.2	-	8
80	Victor Mk.1 & Prototypes	1952	A.S. Sapphire	110.0	114.11	52	9
80	Victor Mk.2	1959	Rolls-Royce Conway	120.0	114.11	34	9
81	Hermes IV	1948	Bristol Hercules	113.0	96.10	25	8
82	Hermes V	1949	Bristol Theseus	113.0	96.10	2	8
88	Crescent wing research aircraft	1951	Roll-Royce Nene	40.0	40.0	1	9
94	Hastings 4 (VIP)	1951	Bristol Hercules	113.0	82.8	4	8
95	Hastings 3 (RNZAF)	1952	Bristol Hercules	113.0	82.8	4	8
97	Victor airliner derivative	1953	A.S. Sapphire	126.0	126.3	-	9
99	'Daisy Cutter' bomber	1953	A.S. Sapphire	75.0		-	11
100	Supersonic bomber	1954	Rolls-Royce RB121	59.4	185.0	-	11
109	Supersonic airliner	1958	Not known	107.9	172.6	-	11
111	Victor transport derivative	1958	Rolls-Royce Conway	130.0	137.8	-	9
112	Flying jeep	1958	Rolls-Royce RB108			-	11
113	Laminar flow executive jet	1958	Bristol Orpheus	71.3	71.6	-	11
115	Slender Delta Research a/c	1961	Bristol Siddeley Viper	20.0	45.0	1	11
117	Laminar flow airliner project	1960	Rolls-Royce Spey	125.0	101.0	-	11
118	Flying jeep	1960	Rolls-Royce RB162			-	11
120	Flying jeep	1960	R-R RB172 & 175	27.0	24.8	-	11
124	Herald tactical transport	1960	Rolls-Royce Dart	94.9		-	10
-	Slewed wing airliner	1960	Not known	270 max	320 max	-	11
126	Aerobus	1965	Not known	78.0	72.6	-	11
127	Jet-Herald	1962	Rolls-Royce Spey Jnr	80.0	106.0	-	10
128	Supersonic airliner project	1962	Not known	67.6	156.0	-	11
130	Laminar flow HS125 project	1963	A.S. Viper			-	11
134	Ogee Aerobus	1965	Not known	55.0	95.0	-	11
135	Laminar flow transport project	1965	Not known	205.0		-	11
137	Jetstream	1967	Turboméca Astazou	52.0	47.1	50+*	12
HPR1	Marathon I & T.11	1946	D.H. Gipsy Queen	65.0	52.3	42	10
HPR2	Basic trainer	1950	A.S. Cheetah	37.0	29.11	2	10

HPR3	Herald	1955	Alvis Leonides Major	94.9	70.3	2	10
HPR5	Marathon II (final version)	1955	Alvis Leonides Major	65.0	52.3	1	10
HPR7	Dart-Herald (Series 200)	1958	Rolls-Royce Dart	94.9	75.6	48	10
HPR8	Car ferry project	1959	Rolls-Royce Dart	120.0	82.2	-	10

* 77 construction numbers allocated by Handley Page, including 15 for USAF, but not all completed.

The Handley Page numbering system originated in the mid-1920s. Earlier aircraft were allocated their HP Nos retrospectively.

Appendix B

Sir Frederick Handley Page –
(15 November 1885-21 April 1962)
Honours & Achievements

Founded Handley Page Ltd 1909.

CBE 1918.

Married Una Helen Thynne (1891-1957) 1918.
Three daughters: Helen Anne Niney Page (1919-2001)
Phillish Elizabeth Page (1921-1987)
Patricia Mary Handley Page (1923-1992)

Knighthood 1942.

HM Deputy Lieutenant of the County of Middlesex 1953 to 1956.

HM Lieutenant of the County of Middlesex 1956 to 1960.

City & Guilds of London Institute – Fellow.

Vice-President and Chairman of Council 1950 to 1962.

College of Aeronautics, Cranfield. Chairman of Board of Governors 1953 to 1962.

Harrow East Conservative Association – President 1946 to 1962.

Imperial College of Science and Technology – Member of the Governing Body. Fellowship in 1951.

Institute of the Aerospace Sciences, USA. Hon. Fellowship in 1944.

Institute of Transport – Hon. Member. President 1945 to 1946.

Manchester College of Science and Technology – Associate.

Birmingham College of Advanced Technology – Hon. Associate.

Royal Aero Club – Vice-President and Hon. Member.

Royal Institute of British Architects – Hon. Associate.

Royal Society of Arts.

Wissenschaftliche Gesellschaft für Luftfahrt (Scientific Society for Aviation).

Worshipful Company of Coachmakers and Coach Harnessmakers – Master 1943 to 1944.